Books in the AMERICAN CLASSICS™ Series

Child Life in Colonial Days
by Alice Morse Earle

Home Life in Colonial Days
by Alice Morse Earle

As We Were: Life in America 1814
by Gaillard Hunt

American Utopias
by Charles Nordhoff

Forthcoming:

Amasa Delano: Voyages and Travels
edited by Eleanor Roosevelt Seagraves

Child Life in
Colonial Days

John Quincy

AMERICAN CLASSICS™

Child Life in Colonial Days

Written by

ALICE MORSE EARLE

Author of *Home Life in Colonial Days*

Introduction by Jack Larkin

Berkshire House Publishers
Stockbridge, Massachusetts

CHILD LIFE IN COLONIAL DAYS
by Alice Morse Earle

First published in 1899
This edition and introduction © 1993 by Berkshire House Publishers

Library of Congress Cataloging-in-Publication Data

Earle, Alice Morse, 1853–1911
Child life in colonial days / Alice Morse Earle
p.   cm. — (American Classics Series)
Originally published: New York: Macmillan, 1899.
ISBN 0-936399-52-x (pbk.)
1. United States — Social life and customs — to 1775.
2. Children — United States.   I. Title.   II. Series: American classics
(Stockbridge, Mass.)
[E162.E13   1993]
973.2 — dc20   93-24347
CIP

Berkshire House Publishers
Box 297, Stockbridge MA 01262
800-321-8526

Printed in the United States of America
10   9   8   7   6   5   4   3

This book has been written
in tender memory
of a dearly loved and loving child

HENRY EARLE, JUNIOR

1880-1892

Contents

List of Illustrations

List of Illustrations

Page

INTRODUCTION

Written in 1899, Alice Morse Earle's *Child Life in Colonial Days* was part of an immense upsurge of interest in early American life that marked the last decades of the 19th century. Powerful tides of change — urbanization, industrialization, immigration — were pulling Americans relentlessly toward the 20th century. One response was an effort to recover the past, marked by a great expansion in the writing of local history, the founding of hundreds of local historical societies, the growth of interest in collecting "relics" and bygones," and the emergence of the historic preservation movement, American folklore studies, graduate training in American history, and the Colonial Revival in domestic architecture. At nearly a hundred years' distance, it is revealing, and slightly odd, for us to read Earle's judgment that an "old, and tired America, after much tumultuous change, was impelled to explore and preserve the historical roots of its national life.

The specific subject of childhood can also be located in time and place. As Earle noted, in the distant American past, "there was none of that exhaustive study of the motives, thoughts and acts of a child which is now rife." The 19th century United States, with its increasing focus on the moral and emotional centrality of motherhood, and its growing concern with theories of education and psychological development, had created an historically unprecedented child-consciousness. And it was to this, as much as to America's general concern with the past, that the book owed its existence. Without it, neither the concept of "Child Life" as a meaningful subject nor a significant readership would have been possible.

Today, Alice Morse Earle can be seen as one of the pioneers in writing integrated social and material history, especially of American subjects. Taking the everyday and domestic as a realm set off to her gender, she devoted exemplary scholarship to it while producing works of popular appeal. All of the subjects taken up in *Child Life* are of great interest today to students of material life, social history, and folkways. Earle's work takes both objects and the documents of ordinary existence very seriously indeed and provides a still-powerful sense of the material density of the life of the past. Earle clearly combined the instincts of a final social historian and a first-rate curator. She interprets the objects of childhood in a context of use and meaning, and makes striking use of artifacts, particularly portraits, as historical evidence. In a real sense she was the founder of current scholarship in American material culture studies.

Child Life was a work of generalization and popularization, but one written from a deep knowledge of primary sources — from diaries and letters to samplers and hornbooks. These materials are now the concern of many scholars, who see them as the archive for social history. She knew these collections better than anyone else, and used them with great authority. But virtually none of America's emerging group of professionally trained historians thought much of them at the time; they considered them trivial and insubstantial. Earle's vindication as a serious scholar came only recently, as the study of these taken-for-granted aspects of past existence has gained some intellectual respectability.

The book's lack of footnotes and lists of sources, natural in a popular work, proves intensely frustrating to the late-20th-century historical who would like to know precisely what she read, what she saw, what she transcribed and took notes on in the course of her extensive researches — sometimes, certainly, in private collections that no longer exist today.

We can put this book in the context of its time, but is it still worth reading today? The answer is yes. With all its anecdotalism and occasional coyness, Earle's work has a wide imaginative span and a documentary richness that can still command our attention.

Earle did not approach her study of the past with reverence, but with an enormous curiosity. Rather than searching for moral connections and instructive examples in the past, she often concentrates on what was different, distant, strange. She frequently finds the colonial past a harsh and alien place, and takes pleasure in pointing this out to her readers. This is in part rooted in the later 19th century's confident belief — based on the dominant social science of the time — in the evolutionary progression of mores and morals, as well as health and wealth, from the past to present. Her explanatory categories were, as she noted, those of "comparison and progress." Yet in equally large part this stance is due to the concentrated attention she pays to source or object, her intensely curious gaze.

Earle does not provide a sweeping, integrated interpretation of the rich material she gathered. The time was many generations from being ripe for this. But with considerable power she describes and she evokes. *Child Life* is not an extended argument but a tour of an historical landscape, like a late-19th-century guide book. "Look," she asks, "at this different world our ancestors lived in. Be surprised, or shocked, or amused, but look." For anyone interested in exploring American everyday life *Child Life* still provides us a richly documented and often engrossing place from which to start — or to visit along the way.

Jack Larkin
Old Sturbridge Village
June 1993

Foreword

When we regard the large share which child study has in the interest of the reader and thinker of to-day, it is indeed curious to see how little is told of child life in history. The ancients made no record of the life of young children; classic Rome furnishes no data for child study; the Greeks left no child forms in art. The student of original sources of history learns little about children in his searches; few in number and comparatively meagre in quality are the literary remains that even refer to them.

We know little of the childhood days of our forbears, and have scant opportunity to make comparisons or note progress. The child of colonial days was emphatically " to be seen, not to be heard," — nor was he even to be much in evidence to the eye. He was of as little importance in domestic, social, or ethical relations as his childish successor is of great importance to-day; it was deemed neither courteous, decorous, nor wise to make him appear of value or note in his own eyes or in the eyes of his seniors. Hence there was none of that exhaustive study of the motives, thoughts, and acts of a child which is now rife.

The

The accounts of oldtime child life gathered for this book are wholly unconscious and full of honesty and simplicity, not only from the attitude of the child, but from that of his parents, guardians, and friends. The records have been made from affectionate interest, not from scientific interest; no profound search has been made for motives or significance, but the proof they give of tenderness and affection in the family are beautiful to read and to know.

The quotations from manuscript letters, records, diaries, and accounts which are here given could only have been acquired by precisely the method which has been followed, — a constant and distinct search for many years, combined with an alert watchfulness for items or even hints relating to the subject, during as many years of extended historical reading. Many private collections and many single-treasured relics have been freely offered for use, and nearly all the sentences and pages selected from these sources now appear in print for the first time. The portraits of children form a group as rare as it is beautiful. They are specially valuable as a study of costume. Nearly all of these also are as true emblems of the generous friendship of the present owners as they are of the life of the past. The rich stores of our many historical associations, of the Essex Institute, the American Antiquarian Society, the Long Island Historical Society, the Deer-
field

field Memorial Hall, the Lenox Library, have been generously opened, carefully gleaned, and freely used. The expression of gratitude so often tendered to these helpful kinsfolk and friends and to these bountiful societies and libraries can scarcely be emphasized by any public thanks, yet it would seem that for such assistance thanks could never be offered too frequently, nor too publicly.

Nor have I, in gathering for this, — as for my other books, — failed to exercise what Emerson calls " the catlike love of garrets, presses, and cornchambers, and of the conveniences of long housekeeping." Many long-kept homes have I searched, many an old garret and press has yielded conveniences for this book.

Though this is a record of the life of children in the American colonies, I have freely compared the conditions in this country with similar ones in England at the same date, both for the sake of fuller elucidation, and also to attempt to put on a proper basis the civilization which the colonists left behind them. Many statements of conditions in America do not convey correct ideas of our past comfort and present and liberal progress unless we compare them with facts in English life. We must not overrate seventeenth and eighteenth century life in England, either in private or public. England was not a first-class power among nations till the time of the Treaty of Paris, in 1763. When our
colonies

colonies were settled it was third-rate. Life among the nobility was magnificent, but the life of the peas-antry was wretched, and middle-class social life was very bleak and monotonous in both city and country. From early days life was much better in many ways in America than in England for the family of moderate means, and children shared the benefits of these better conditions. A child's life was more valuable here. The colonial laws plainly show this increased valuation, and the child responded to this regard of him by a growing sense of his own importance, which in time has produced "Young America."

It is my hope that children as well as grown folk will find in these pages much to interest them in the accounts of the life of children of olden times. I have had this end constantly in my mind, though I have made no attempt, nor had I any intent, to write in a style for the perusal of children; for I have not found that intelligent children care much or long for such books, except in the very rare cases of the few great books that have been written for children, and which are loved and read as much by the old as by the young.

As our tired century has grown gray it has developed an interest in things youthful, — in the beginnings of things. Its attitude is akin to that of an old man, still in health and clear-headed, but weary; who has lived through his scores of crowded years of action, toil, and strife,

strife, and seeks in the last days of his life a serene and peaceful harbor, — the companionship of little children. There is something of mystery, too, in " the turn of the century," something which then makes our gaze retrospective and comparative rather than inquisitive into the future.   Hence this year of our Lord MDCCCXCIX has been the allotted day and hour for the writing of this book.   There has been a trend of destiny which has brought not only a book on oldtime child life, and that book at this century end, but has included the fate that it should be written by Alice Morse Earle. Kismet!

Child Life in Colonial Days

Child Life in Colonial Days

CHAPTER I

BABYHOOD

Some things are of that nature as to make
One's fancy chuckle, while his heart doth ache.
— *The Author's Way of Sending Forth His Second Part of the*
Pilgrim. John Bunyan, 1684.

THERE is something inexpressibly sad in the thought of the children who crossed the ocean with the Pilgrims and the fathers of Jamestown, New Amsterdam, and Boston, and the infancy of those born in the first years of colonial life in this strange new world. It was hard for grown folk to live; conditions and surroundings offered even to strong men constant and many obstacles to the continuance of existence; how difficult was it then to rear children !

In the southern colonies the planters found a climate and enforced modes of life widely varying from home life in England ; it took several generations to accustom infants to thrive under those con-

ditions.

ditions.   The first years of life at Plymouth are the
records of a bitter struggle, not for comfort but for
existence.   Scarcely less sad are the pages of Governor Winthrop's journal, which tell of the settlers
of Massachusetts Bay.   On the journey across seas
not a child "had shown fear or dismayedness."
Those brave children were welcomed to the shore
with good cheer, says the old chronicler, Joshua
Scottow; "with external flavor and sweet odor;
fragrant was the land, such was the plenty of sweet
fern, laurel, and other fragrant simples; such was
the scent of our aromatic and balsam-bearing pines,
spruces and larch trees, with our tall cedars."   They
landed on a beautiful day in June, "with a smell on
the shore like the smell of a garden," and these
happy children had gathered sweet wild strawberries
and single wild roses.   It is easy to picture the merry
faces and cheerful laughter.

Scant, alas! were the succeeding days of either
sweetness or light.   The summer wore on in weary
work, in which the children had to join; in constant fears, which the children multiplied and mag-
nified; and winter came, and death.   "There is not
a house where there is not one dead," wrote Dudley.
One little earth-weary traveller, a child whose "family and kindred had dyed so many," was, like the
prophets in the Bible, given exalted vision through
                                                    sorrow,

sorrow, and had "extraordinary evidence concerning the things of another world." Fierce east winds searched the settlers through and through, and frosts and snows chilled them. The dreary ocean, the gloomy forests, were their bounds. Scant was their fare, and mean their roof-trees; yet amid all the want and cold little children were born and welcomed with that ideality of affection which seems as immortal as the souls of the loved ones.

Hunger and privation did not last long in the Massachusetts colony, for it was a rich community — for its day — and soon the various settlements grew in numbers and commerce and wealth, and an exultant note runs through their records. Prosperous peoples will not be morose; thanksgiving proclamations reflect the rosy hues of successful years. Child life was in harmony with its surroundings; it was more cheerful, but there was still fearful menace to the life and health of an infant. From the moment when the baby opened his eyes on the bleak world around him, he had a Spartan struggle for life; half the Puritan children had scarce drawn breath in this vale of tears ere they had to endure an ordeal which might well have given rise to the expression "the survival of the fittest." I say half the babies, presuming that half were born in warm weather, half in cold. All had to be baptized

within

within a few days of birth, and baptized in the meeting-house; fortunate, indeed, was the child of midsummer.   We can imagine the January babe carried
through the narrow streets or lanes to the freezing
meeting-house, which had grown damper and dead-
lier with every wintry blast; there to be christened,
when sometimes the ice had to be broken in
the christening bowl.   On January 22, 1694, Judge
Samuel Sewall, of Boston, records in his diary: —

"A very extraordinary Storm by reason of the falling and
driving of Snow.   Few women could get to Meeting.   A
Child named Alexander was baptized in the afternoon."

The Judge tells of his own children — four days
old — shrinking from the icy water, but crying not.
It was a cold and disheartening reception these children had into the Puritan church; many lingered
but a short time therein.   The mortality among
infants was appallingly great; they died singly, and
in little groups, and in vast companies.   Putrid
fevers, epidemic influenzas, malignant sore throats,
"bladders in the windpipe," raging small pox,
carried off hundreds of the children who survived
baptism.   The laws of sanitation were absolutely
disregarded—because unknown; drainage there was
none — nor deemed necessary; disinfection was
feebly desired — but the scanty sprinkling of vinegar

Edward Winslow

gar was the only expression of that desire; isolation of contagious diseases was proclaimed — but the measures were as futile when the disease was known to be contagious as they were lacking in the diseases which our fathers did not know were communicable. It is appalling to think what must have been the unbounded production and nurture of disease germs; and we can paraphrase with truth the words of Sir Thomas Browne, and say of our grandfathers and their children, "Considering the thousand roads that lead to death, I do thank my God they could die but once."

It is heartrending to read the entries in many an old family Bible — the records of suffering, distress, and blasted hopes. Until this century these sad stories may be found. There lies open before me an old leather-bound Bible with the record of my great-grandfather's family. He had sixteen children. When the first child was a year and a half old the second child was born. The baby was but four days old when the older child died. Five times did that mother's heart bear a similar cruel loss when she had a baby in her arms; therefore when she had been nine years married she had one living child, and five little graves bore record of her sorrow.

In the seventeenth century the science of medicine had not wholly cut asunder from astrology and necromancy;

romancy; and the trusting Christian still believed
in some occult influences, chiefly planetary, which
governed not only his crops but his health and life.
Hence the entries of births in the Bible usually
gave the hour and minute, as well as the day, month,
and year. Thus could be accurately calculated what
favoring or mischief-bearing planets were in ascen-
dency at the time of the child's birth; what influences he would have to encounter in life.

The belief that meteorological and astrological
conditions affected medicines was strong in all minds.
The best physicians gravely noted the condition of
the moon when gathering herbs and simples and
concocting medicines; and certain drugs were held
to be powerless at certain times of the year, owing
to planetary influences. "Sympathetical" medicines were confidingly trusted, and tried to a surprising extent upon children; apparently these were
as beneficial as our modern method of healing by
the insinuation of improved health.

We cannot wonder that children died when we
know the nostrums with which they were dosed.
There were quack medicines which held sway for a
century — among them, a valuable property, *Daffy's
Elixir*. These patented — or rather secret — medicines had a formidable rival in snail-water, which
was used as a tonic and also a lotion. Many of the
                                              ingredients

ingredients and extracts used in domestic medicines were incredibly revolting.

Venice treacle was a nasty and popular compound, traditionally invented by Nero's physician; it was made of vipers, white wine, opium, "spices from both the Indies," licorice, red roses, tops of germander and St.-John's-wort, and some twenty other herbs, juice of rough sloes, mixed with honey "triple the weight of all the dry spices." The recipe is published in dispensatories till within this century. The vipers had to be put, "twelve of 'em," into white wine alone. Mithridate, the ancient cure-all of King Mithridates, was another dose for children. There were forty-five ingredients in this, each prepared and introduced with care. Rubila, made chiefly of antimony and nitre, was beloved of the Winthrops, and frequently dispensed by them — and with benefit.

Children were grievously afflicted with rickets, though curiously enough it was a new disease, not old enough to have received adequate observation in England, wrote Sir Thomas Browne in the latter part of the seventeenth century. Snails furnished many doses for the rickets.

Exact instruction of treatment for the rickets is given in a manuscript letter written to Rev. Joseph Perry of Windsor, Connecticut, in 1769 : —

"Rev'd

" REV'D SIR :

"In ye Rickets the best Corrective I have ever found is a Syrup made of Black Cherrys. Thus. Take of Cherrys (dry'd ones are as good as any) & put them into a vessel with water. Set ye vessel near ye fire and let ye water be Scalding hot. Then take ye Cherrys into a thin Cloth and squeeze them into ye Vessell, & sweeten ye Liquor with Melosses. Give 2 Spoonfuls of this 2 or 3 times in a day. If you Dip your Child, Do it in this manner : viz : naked, in ye morning, head foremost in Cold Water, don't dress it Immediately, but let it be made warm in ye Cradle & sweat at least half an Hour moderately. Do this 3 mornings going & if one or both feet are Cold while other Parts sweat (which is sometimes ye Case) Let a little blood be taken out of ye feet ye 2nd Morning and yt will cause them to sweat afterwards. Before ye dips of ye Child give it some Snakeroot and Saffern Steep'd in Rum & Water, give this Immediately before Diping and after you have dipt ye Child 3 Mornings Give it several times a Day ye following Syrup made of Comfry, Hartshorn, Red Roses, Hog-brake roots, knot-grass, pettymoral roots, sweeten ye Syrup with Melosses. Physicians are generally fearful about diping when ye Fever is hard, but oftentimes all attemps to lower it without diping are vain. Experience has taught me that these fears are groundless, yt many have about diping in Rickety Fevers ; I have found in a multitude of Instances of diping is most effectual means to break a Rickety Fever. These Directions are agreable to what I have practiced for many years."

Among

Among other English notions thrust upon American children was one thus advertised in ante-Revolutionary newspapers : —

"THE FAMOUS ANODYNE NECKLACE
"*price 20 shillings*

"For children's teeth, recommended in England by Dr. Chamberlen, with a remedy to open and ease the foregums of teething children and bring their teeth safely out. Children on the very brink of the Grave and thought past recovery with their teeth, fits, fevers, convulsions, hooping and other violent coughs, gripes, looseness, and all proceeding from their teeth who cannot tell what they suffer nor make known their pains any other way but by crying and moans, have almost miraculously recovered after having worn the famous Anodyne Necklace but one night's time. A mother then would never forgive herself whose child should die for want of so very easy a remedy for its teeth. And what is particularly remarkable of this necklace is, that of those vast numbers who have had this necklace for their children, none have made any complaints but express how glad they have been that their children have worn it whereas if they had not had it, they believed their children would have been in the grave, all means having been used in vain until they had the necklace."

These anodyne necklaces were akin to the medicated belts of our own day, and were worn as children still wear amber beads to avert the croup. Various

Various native berries had restorative and preventive properties when strung as a necklace. Uglier decorations were those recommended by Josselyn to New England parents, strings of fawn's teeth or wolf's fangs, a sure promoter of easy teething. He also

Mayflower Cradle, owned by the Pilgrim William White

advised scratching the child's gums with an osprey bone. Children died, however, in spite of these varied charms and doses, in vast numbers while teething.

There were some feeble expressions of revolt against the horrible doses of the day. In 1647 we hear of the publication of "a Most Desperate Booke

Booke written against taking of Phissick," but it was promptly ordered to be burnt; and the doses were continued until well into this century. The shadow of their power lingers yet in country homes.

Many alluring baits were written back to England by the first emigrants to tempt others to follow to the new world. Among other considerations Gabriel Thomas made this statement: —

" The Christian children born here are generally well-favored and beautiful to behold. I never knew any to come into the world with the least blemish on any part of the body; being in the general observed to be better-natured, milder, and more tender-hearted than those born in England."

John Hammond lavished equal praise on the children in Virginia. It was also asserted that the average number of children in a family was larger, which is always true in a pioneer settlement in a new country. The promise of the Lord is ever fulfilled that he will " make the families of his servants in the wilderness like a flock."

A cheerful home life was insured by these large families when they lived. Sir William Phips was one of twenty-six children, all with the same mother. Green, the Boston printer, had thirty children. Another printer, Benjamin Franklin, was one of a family

family of seventeen. William Rawson had twenty children by one wife. Rev. Cotton Mather tells us : —

" One woman had not less than twenty-two children, and another had no less than twenty-three children by one husband, whereof nineteen lived to man's estate, and a third was mother to seven and twenty children."

He himself had fifteen children, though but two survived him. Other ministers had larger families. Rev. John Sherman, of Watertown, Massachusetts, had twenty-six children by two wives. Rev. Samuel Willard, the first minister of Groton, Massachusetts, had twenty children, and was himself one of seventeen children. It is to the honor of these poorly paid ministers that they brought up these large families well. Rev. Abijah Weld, of Attleboro, Massachusetts, had an annual salary of about two hundred and twenty dollars. He had a small farm and a decent house; he lived in generous hospitality, entertaining many visitors and contributing to the wants of the poor. He had fifteen children and reared a grandchild. In his fifty-five years of service as a minister he was never detained from his duties nor failed to perform them.

Rev. Moses Fiske had sixteen children; he sent three sons to college and married off all his daughters;

ters; his salary was never over ninety pounds, and usually but sixty pounds a year, paid chiefly in corn and wood. One verse of a memorial poem to Mrs. Sarah Thayer reads: —

> " And one thing more remarkable
> Which here I shall record ;
> She'd fourteen children with her
> At the table of her Lord.''

These large families were eagerly welcomed. Children were a blessing. The Danish proverb says, " Children are the poor man's wealth." To the farmer, especially the frontiersman, every child in the home is an extra producer. No town in New England had less land to distribute than Boston, but on all allotments women and children received their full proportion; the early allotments of land in Brookline (then part of Boston) were made by " heads," that is, according to the number of people in the family.

It is an interesting study to trace the underlying reason for naming children many of the curious names which were given to the offspring of the first colonists. Parents searched for names of deep significance, for names appropriate to conditions, for those of profound influence — presumably on the child's life. Glory to God and zealous ambition

for

Townes Cradle

for the child's future were equally influential in deciding selection.

Rev. Richard Buck, one of the early parsons in Virginia, in days of deep depression named his first child Mara. This text indicates the reason for his choice: " Call me Mara for the Almighty hath dealt very bitterly with me. I went out full and the Lord hath brought me home empty." His second child was christened Gershom; for Moses' wife " bare him a son and called his name Gershom, for he said I have been in a strange land." Eber, the Hebrew

Hebrew patriarch, called his son Peleg, "for his days were divided." Mr. Buck celebrated the *Pelegging*, or dividing of Virginia, into legislative districts by naming his third child Peleg. Many names have a pathos and sadness which can be felt down through the centuries. Dame Dinely, widow of a doctor or barber-surgeon who had died in the snow while striving to visit a distant patient, named her poor babe Fathergone. A little Goodman child, born after the death of her father, was sadly but trustingly named Abiel — *God is my father*. Seaborn was the name indicative of the introduction into life of one of my own ancestors.

In the old Ropes Bible in Salem is given the reason for an unusual name which often appears in that family; it is Seeth. One of the family was supposed to be dead, having disappeared. On his sudden reappearance a pious Ropes exclaimed in joy, "The Lord seeth not as man seeth, and my child shall be named Seeth." An early example of the name is Seeth Grafton, who became the wife of Thomas Gardner in 1636.

Judge Sewall named one son Joseph,

"In hopes of the accomplishment of the Prophecy of Ezekiel xxxvii. and such; and not out of respect to any Relation or any other Person except the first Joseph."

Judge

Judge Sewall again made an entry in his diary after a christening.

" I named my little Daughter Sarah.   Mr. Torrey said call her Sarah and make a Madam of her.   I was struggling whether to call her Mehetable or Sarah.   But when I saw Sarah's standing in the Scripture, viz : Peter, Galatians, Hebrews, Romans, I resolv'd on that suddenly."

Abigail, meaning father's joy, was also frequently given, and Hannah, meaning grace ; the history of these two Hebrew women made their names honored of New England Puritans.   Zurishaddai, the Almighty is my rock, was bestowed on more than one boy.   Comfort, Deliverance, Temperance, Peace, Hope, Patience, Charity, Faith, Love, Submit, Endurance, Silence, Joy, Rejoice, Hoped for, and similar names indicative of a trait of character, a virtue, or an aspiration of goodness, were common. The children of Roger Clap were named Experience, Waitstill, Preserved, Hopestill, Wait, Thanks, Desire, Unite, and Supply.   Madam Austin, an early settler of old Narragansett, had sixteen children.   Their names were Parvis, Picus, Piersus, Prisemus, Polybius, Lois, Lettice, Avis, Anstice, Eunice, Mary, John, Elizabeth, Ruth, Freelove. All lived to be threescore and ten, one to be a hundred and two years old.

Edward

Edward Bendall's children were named True-grace, Reform, Hoped for, More mercy, and Restore.   Richard Gridley's offspring were Return, Believe, and Tremble.

With the exception of Puritanical names, double Christian names were very rare until after the Revolution, as may be seen by examining any document with many signatures; such, for instance, as the Declaration of Independence, or the lists of officers and men in the Continental Army.   Return Jonathan Meigs was a notable exception.

There exists in New England a tradition of "groaning-cakes" being made and baked at the birth of a child, to give to visitors.   I have found no record of it.   The Frenchman, Misson, in his *Travels in England*, says, "At the birth of their children they (visitors) drink a glass of wine and eat a bit of a certain cake, which is seldom made but upon these occasions."   Anna Green Winslow, a Boston schoolgirl, tells of making what she calls "a setting up visit" to a relative who had a baby about four weeks old.   She wore her best and most formal attire and says, "It cost me a pistareen to Nurse Eaton for two cakes which I took care to eat before I paid for them."   There certainly was a custom of giving money, clothing, or petty trinkets to the nurse at such visits.   Judge Sewall
frequently

frequently writes of these "vails" which he made at the house of his friends. He writes in one case of brewing "groaning-beer," and in his household were held two New England amphidromia. The midwife, nurses, and all the neighboring women who had helped with work or advice during the early days of the child's life were bidden to a dinner. One Sewall baby was scarcely two weeks old when seventeen women dined at the Judge's house, on boiled pork, beef, and fowls; roast beef and turkey; pies and tarts. At another time "minc'd Pyes and cheese" were added. Judge Winthrop's sister, Madam Downing, furnished sack and claret also. A survival of this custom lasted till this century in the drinking of caudle by the bedside of the mother.

A pincushion was for many years and indeed is still in some parts of New England a highly conventional gift to a mother with a young babe. *Poor Robin's Almanack* for the year 1676 says: —

> " Pincushions and such other knacks
> A childbed woman always lacks."

I have seen in different families five of precisely the same pattern and size, all made about the time of the Revolution. One given to a Boston baby, while his new home was in state of siege, bore the inscription,

inscription, "Welcome little Stranger, tho' the Port is closed." These words were formed by the heads of pins. Another, about five inches long and

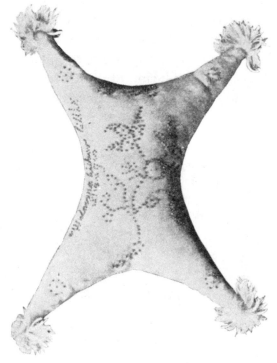

three inches wide, is of green figured silk with a flowered vine stuck in pins and the words, "John Winslow, March, 1783, Welcome, Little Stranger." Anna Green Winslow tells of her aunts making one with "a planthorn of flowers" and the name. I have

have seen one with similar inscription knitted of
fine silk and with the name sewed on in steel beads,
among which pins were stuck in a graceful pattern.

The seventeenth-century baby slept, as his nineteenth-century descendant does, in a cradle.   Nothing could be prettier than the old cradles that have
survived successive years of use with many generations of babies.   In Pilgrim Hall still may be seen
the quaint and finely wrought wicker cradle of Pere-

Indian Cradle

grine White, the first white child born in Plymouth.
This cradle is of Dutch manufacture ; and is one of
the few authentic articles still surviving that came
over on the *Mayflower*.   It was brought over by
William White, whose widow married Governor
Edward Winslow.   A similar wicker cradle may be
seen

seen at the Essex Institute in Salem, together with
a heavy wooden cradle in which many members of
the Townes family of Topsfield, Massachusetts,
were rocked to sleep two centuries ago.   Judge
Sewall bought a wicker cradle for one of his many
children and paid sixteen shillings for it.   A graceful variant of the swinging cradle is shown in the
Indian basket hung at either end from a wooden
standard or frame.   In this strong basket, fashioned
by an Indian mother, many a white child has been
swung and sung to sleep.   A still more picturesque
cradle was made of birch bark, that plentiful
material so widely adaptive to household uses, and
so deftly manipulated and shaped by the patient
squaws.

In these cradles the colonial baby slept, warmly
wrapped in a homespun blanket or pressed quilt.

Poor Robin's Almanack for the year 1676 enumerates among a baby's outfit : —

> " Blanckets of a several scantling
> Therein for to wrap a bantling."

Of these wraps, of the thinner sort, may be named
the thin, close-woven, homespun " flannel sheet,"
spun of the whitest wool into a fine twisted worsted,
and woven with a close sley into an even web as
enduring as the true Oriental cashmere.   The baby's
initials

initials were often marked on these sheets, and fortunate was the child who had the light, warm wrap-

Governor Bradford's Christening Blanket, 1590

pings.   My own children had " flannel sheets" that
had seen a century or more of use with generations
of forbears.

A finer coverlet, one of state, the christening
blanket

blanket, was usually made of silk, richly embroidered, sometimes with a text of Scripture. These were often lace-bordered or edged with a narrow home-woven silk fringe. The christening blanket of Governor Bradford of the Plymouth Colony still exists, whole of fabric and unfaded of dye. It is a rich crimson silk, soft of texture, like a heavy sarcenet silk, and is powdered at regular distances about six inches apart with conventional sprays of flowers embroidered chiefly in pink and yellow, in minute and beautiful cross-stitch. It is distinctly Oriental in appearance, far more so than is indicated by its black and white representation here. Another beautiful silk christening blanket was quilted in an intricate flower pattern in almost imperceptible stitches. These formal wrappings of state were sometimes called bearing-cloths or clothes, and served through many generations. Shakespeare speaks in *Henry VI.* of a child's bearing-cloth.

A go-cart or standing-stool was a favourite instrument to teach a child to walk. A standing-stool a century old in which Newburyport babies stood and toddled is a rather crude frame of wood with a ledge or narrow table for toys. The method of using a go-cart is shown in this old print taken from a child's book called, *Little Prattle over a Book of Prints*, published for sixpence in 1801. In

In the writers of Queen Anne's day frequent references are made to go-carts.

I find strong evidence that Locke's *Thoughts on Education*, published in England in 1690, found

Standing Stool

many readers and ardent followers in the new world. The book is in many old-time library lists in New England, and among the scant volumes of those who had but a single book-shelf or book-box. I have seen abstracts and transpositions of his precepts on the pages of almanacs, the most universally circulated and studied of all eighteenth-century books save the Bible. In contemporary letters evidence is found of the influence of Locke's principles. In the prefaces of Thomas' reprints he is quoted and eulogized. The notions of the English philosopher appealed to American parents because they were, as the author said, " the consideration

consideration not what a physician ought to do with
a sick or crazy child, but what parents without the
help of physic should do for the preservation of an
healthy constitution." Crazy here is used in the
old-time sense of feeble bodily health, not mental.
In these days of hundreds of books on child-study,
education, child-culture, and kindred topics, it is a
distinct pleasure to read Locke's sturdy sentences ;
to see how wise, and kindly, and logical he was in
nearly all his advices, especially on moral or ethical
questions. Even those on physical conditions that
seem laughably obsolete to-day were so in advance
of the general practices of his day that they are
farther removed from the notions of his time than
from those of ours. In judging them let us
remember Dr. Holmes' lines : —

> " Little of all we value here
> Wakes on the morn of its hundredth year
> Without both looking and feeling queer."

Certainly an existence of two centuries may make us
pardon a little queerness in advice.

One of Locke's instructions much thought on in
the years his book was so widely read was the advice
to wash the child's feet daily in cold water, and " to
have his shoes so thin that they might leak and let
in water." Josiah Quincy was the suffering subject
of some of this instruction ; when only three years
old

old he was taken from his warm bed in winter as
well as summer (and this in Eastern Massachusetts),
carried downstairs to a cellar kitchen and dipped
three times in a tub of cold water fresh from the
pump.   He was also brought up with utter indifference to wet feet; he said that in his boyhood
he sat more than half the time with his feet wet and
cold, but with no ill results.

Locke also strongly counselled learning dancing,
swimming, and playing in the open air.   In his diet
"flesh should be forborn as long as the boy is in
coats, or at least till he is two or three years old"; for
breakfast and supper he advises milk, milk-pottage,
water-gruel, flummery, and similar "spoon-meat,"
or brown bread with cheese.   If the boy called for
victuals between meals, he should have dry bread.
His only extra drink should be small-beer, which
should be warm; and seldom he should taste wine
or strong drink.   Locke would not have children
eat melons, peaches, plums, or grapes; while
berries and ripe pears and apples, the latter especially after October, he deems healthful.   The bed
should be hard, of quilts rather than of feathers.
Under these rigid rules were reared many of our
Revolutionary heroes and statesmen.

The adoption of Locke's ideas about the use of
cold water, or indeed of any frequent bathing,
was

De Peyster Twins

was perhaps the most radical innovation in modes
of living. The English never bathed, in our sense
of the word, a complete immersion, nor, I suppose,
did our Puritan, Cavalier, or Quaker ancestors.
Sewall makes not one reference to anything of the
kind, but that is not strange; nor is his omission
any proof, negative or positive, for he refers to no

Go Cart

personal habits, and very shortly and infrequently
to dress. Pepys, the courtier and dandy, tells of
rare monumental occasions when he cleaned himself
— far too rare, we may judge from side-lights thrown
by other of his statements. The *Youth's Behavior*, an old-time book of etiquette, lays down
an assertion that it is a point of wholesomeness to
wash

wash one's face and hands as soon as one is up and dressed, and " to comb one's head in time and season, yet not too curiously." Bathing the person in unaccustomed spots was a ticklish proceeding — a water ordeal, to be gravely considered. Mistress Alice Thornton, a Yorkshire dame, records in her account of her life one occasion when she washed her feet, but she was overbold. " Which my mother did believe it was the cause of that dangerous fitt the next day." In the Verney volumes we find that forlorn Verney boy, poor sickly " Mun," wearing a harness for his crooked back till his shirt was black, when the famous surgeon changed the harness, and Mun his shirt, with no thought on the part of either of a bath being a necessity.

In 1630 a ship was sent from England to Massachusetts which was provisioned for three months. Among the stores for the passengers' use were two casks of Malaga and Canary; twenty gallons of aqua-vitæ; forty-five tuns of beer; and for drinking, washing, cooking, bathing, etc., but six tuns of water. The ships sent out to Georgia by Oglethorpe were so scantily supplied with water that it is positive no fresh water could have been used for bathing even in minute amount. The reputation of hidden malevolence which hung around water as a beverage seems to have extended to its use in any form

form. It was believed to be permeated with minute noxious particles, which in those ante-bacteriological days could not be explained, but which were distinctly appreciated and dreaded.

But these be parlous words. Let us rather show some sympathy for our ancestors. We bathe in well-warmed rooms, often in cold water, but with steaming hot water in ample command at a turn of the hand. Had we to carry all the water for our bathing use from a well whence we laboriously raised it in small amounts, and were we forced to bathe in an icy atmosphere, with cutting draughts striking us on every side, with the basins of water freezing on the hearth in front of a blazing fire, and the juices of the wood freezing at the ends of burning logs, we might not deem our daily bath such an indispensable necessity.

We have heard an advanced thinker like Locke suggest brown bread, cheese, and warm beer as food for young children. What, then, must have been the notions of less thoughtful folk? Doubtless in England such food would have been simple; but in the new world less beer was drank and more milk, which must have proved the salvation of American children. And the plentiful and varied cereal foods, many of them from Indian corn, were a suitable diet for young children. Samp, hominy, suppawn, pone,

pone, succotash, — all Indian foods and cooked in Indian ways, — were found in every home in every colony. Baked beans, another Indian dish, were also good food for children. Native and domestic fruits were plentiful, but, with the exception of apples and pears, were not very attractive. The succession of summer's and autumn's berries must have been eagerly welcomed. They were in the rich and spicy plenty offered by a virgin soil.

A curious, rare, and quaintly named English book is owned by Earl Spencer. Its title runs thus : —

"Dyves Pragmaticus. A booke in English metre of the great marchuant man called Dyves Pragmaticus, very pretye for chyldren to rede, whereby they may be the better and more readyer rede and wryte Wares and Implements in this World contayned. . . . When thou sellest aught unto thy neighbour or byest anything of him deceave not nor oppress him, etc. Imprinted at London in Aldersgate strete by Alexander Lacy dwellynge beside the Wall. The XXV of Aprill, 1563."

It contains a list of sweetmeats for the enticement of children which may be confidently relied on as a full one if we can judge by the exhaustiveness of the lists of other commodities found in the poem : —

"I have Sucket, Surrip, Grene Ginger, and Marmalade,
    Bisket, Cumfet, and Carraways as fine as can be made."

A

A sucket was a dried sweetmeat such as candied orange peel. A caraway was a sweet cake with caraway-seeds.

Apples and caraways were a favorite dish, still served at some of the anniversary feasts of English universities. Comfits were highly flavored, often scented with strong perfumes like musk and bergamot.

Sweetmeats appear to have been plentiful in the colonies from early days. The first native poet of New England wrote complainingly as early as 1675 that —

"From western isles now fruits and delicacies
Do rot maids' teeth and spoil their handsome faces."

Ships in the "Indian trade" brought to the colonies abundance of sugar, molasses, chocolate, ginger, and other dried fruits. These were apparently far more common here than in England; Mr. Ernst says these constant relays of sweets "produced the American sweet-tooth — a wonder." Candied eringo-root, candied lemon-peel, angelica candy, as well as caraway comfits and sugared coriander-seed and dried ginger, were advertised for sale in Boston, and show the taste of the day. In 1731 Widow Bonyet had a notice of her specialties in the *Boston News Letter*. It has quite the modern ring in its meat jellies for the sick, and home-made preserves, jellies,

jellies, and sirups. She also made those ancient sweets, macaroons, marchpanes, and crisp almonds. These latter do not appear to be the glazed and burnt almonds of the confectioner, and may have been salted almonds. The only candy Sewall refers to is sugared almonds. He frequently speaks of gifts of oranges, figs, and " raisins of the sun." Raisins were brought into all the colonial ports in vast amounts, and were until this century regarded by children as a great dainty.

Each large city seems to have had some special confectioner or baker who was renowned for special cakes. Boston had Meer's cakes. New York children probably had the greatest variety of cookies, crullers, and various small cakes, as these were distinctly Dutch, and the Dutch vrouws excelled in cake-making.

Strings of rock-candy came from China, but were rivalled by a distinctly native sweet — maple sugar. Equally American appear to us those Salem sweets, namely, Black Jacks and Salem Gibraltars. Base imitations appeared elsewhere, but never equalled the original delights in Salem. Children who were fortunate enough to live in coast towns reaped the sweet fruits of their fathers' foreign ventures. When a ship came into port with eighty boxes of sugar candy on board and sixty tubs of rock-candy, poor indeed was
the

the child who was not surfeited with sweets.   There
was a sequel, however, to the toothsome feast, a
bitter dessert.   The ship that brought eighty
boxes of sugar candy also fetched
a hundred boxes of rhu-
barb and ten of
senna.

CHAPTER II

Man's earthly Interests are all hooked and buttoned together and held up by Clothes.
— *Sartor Resartus. Thomas Carlyle, 1833.*

O F the dress of infants of colonial times we can judge from the articles of clothing which have been preserved till this day. Perhaps I should say that we can judge of the better garments worn by babies, not their everyday dress; for it is not their simpler attire that has survived, but their christening robes, their finer shirts and petticoats and caps.

Linen formed the chilling substructure of their dress, thin linen, low-necked, short-sleeved shirts; and linen even formed the underwear of infants until the middle of this century. These little linen shirts are daintier than the warmest silk or fine woollen underwear that have succeeded them; they are edged with fine narrow thread lace, hemstitched with tiny rows of stitches, and sometimes embroid-

34

ered

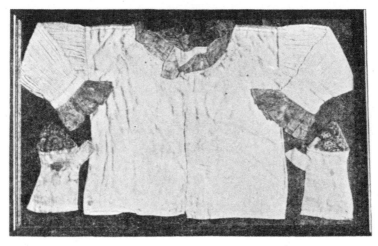

Baptismal Shirt and Mittens of Governor Bradford, 1590

ered by hand. I have seen a little shirt and a cap embroidered with the coat of arms of the Lux and Johnson families and the motto, " God bless the Babe ; " these delicate garments were worn in infancy by the Revolutionary soldier, Governor Johnson of Virginia.

In the Essex Institute in Salem, Massachusetts, are the baptismal shirt and mittens of the Pilgrim Father, William Bradford, second governor of the Plymouth Colony, who was born in 1590. All are of firm, close-woven, homespun linen, but the little mittens have been worn at the ends by the active friction of baby hands, and are patched with colored
" chiney "

" chiney " or calico. A similar colored material frills the sleeves and neck. A pair of baby's mitts of fine lace also may be seen at the Essex Institute. These were wrought in the sixteenth century, and the stitches and work are those of the antique Flanders laces. I have seen many tiny mitts knit of silk and mittens of fine linen, hemstitched, worked in drawn work or embroidered, and edged with thread-lace, and also a few mitts of yellow nankeen which must have proved specially irritating to the tiny little hands that wore them.

I have never seen a woollen petticoat that was worn by an infant of pre-Revolutionary days. It may be argued that woollen garments, being liable to ruin by moths, would naturally not be treasured. This argument scarcely is one of force, because I have been shown infants' cloaks of wool as well as woollen garments for older folk, that have been successfully preserved ; also beautifully embroidered long cloaks of chamois skin. I think infants wore no woollen petticoats ; their shirts, petticoats, and gowns were of linen or some cotton stuff like dimity. Warmth of clothing was given by tiny shawls pinned round the shoulders, and heavier blankets and quilts and shawls in which baby and petticoats were wholly enveloped.

The baby dresses of olden times are either rather shapeless

Robert Gibbs, Four and a Half Years Old, 1670

shapeless sacques drawn in at the neck with narrow cotton ferret or linen bobbin, or little straight-waisted gowns of state. All were exquisitely made by hand, and usually of fine stuff. But the babies in pioneer settlements a century ago had to share in wearing homespun. It is told of one in a log cabin in a New Hampshire clearing that when the grandmother rode out eighty miles on horseback to see her son's first baby, she shed bitter tears at beholding the child, but a few months old, clad in a gray woollen homespun slip with an apron or tier of blue and white checked linen. The mother, a frontier lass, dressed the infant according to the fashions she was accustomed to.

Nothing could show so fully the costume of children in olden times as their portraits, and a series of such portraits of successive dates will be given in these pages. Many of them are asserted to be by the three well-known artists of colonial days, — Blackburn, Smibert, and Copley ; a few are by Peale, Trumbull, and Stuart. I have accepted all family traditions as true, and in many cases believe them to be true, especially since there were few painters of any rank in the community, and no others who could paint portraits such as those which have been preserved. The Gilbert Stuarts and Trumbulls usually have some authentic pedigree. Many of these

these pictures have no artist's signature and are absolutely valueless as works of art, and probably meritless as likenesses; but as records of costume they are always of interest and historical worth.

There is a certain sweetness in some of these old-time portraits; they are stiff and flat, but some of them have a quaintness that reminds me of the angels of the early Florentine painters. They have little grace of figure, but the details of costume make them pleasing even if they are not beautiful.

The first child's portrait in this series is one of extraordinary interest. It is opposite page 4, and has never before been given to the public. It is the reputed miniature of the Pilgrim Father, Governor Edward Winslow, when a boy about six years of age, which would be in 1602; it is the only miniature in existence of any of the Pilgrims at any age. I have, in deference to the wishes of the Rev. Dr. William Copley Winslow of Boston (to whom I am indebted for it), entitled it the reputed miniature of the child Edward Winslow, though the term expresses neither his belief nor mine; and seems scarcely just to a portrait whose claims to authenticity are far more definite than those of many of the family portraits that have descended to us.

The miniature came to Dr. Winslow from Mrs. Hersey of Pembroke, Massachusetts. She died at the

the age of eighty-six. Her grandfather assured her that his father (the famous General John Winslow) received the likeness from his father (the grandson of Edward the Pilgrim), and that it was the Pilgrim's likeness as a child. This — through long-lived Wins-

Infant's Mitts, 16th Century

lows — is a record of few retellings ; and these were told by folk to be trusted. The Winslows were gentlefolk of ample means, such as were likely to have miniatures painted ; and the portrait of Governor Winslow when fifty-six years of age, now in Pilgrim Hall, Plymouth, is the sole one (save this miniature) of any of the Pilgrims. Other strong

strong evidence is the extraordinary resemblance of the child's picture to the "grown-up" portrait, the same brow, contour of face, and other similarity.

There is something in the child's portrait that is singularly suggestive to any one with any historical imagination.   The simplicity of the dress and arrangement of the hair show the influence of Puritanism.   As I look at it I can fancy, yes, I can plainly see, some little English children, twenty years later standing on that crowded historic ship, looking back with childish serenity at the home they were leaving, and then greeting as cheerfully and trustingly the "sad Plymouth" where they disembarked; and the faces that I see have the broad brow, the flowing hair, the bared neck, and simple dress shown in this miniature.

The next portrait, which faces the title page, shows the costume worn in 1690 by a boy a year or two old; it is a charming and quaint picture of the first John Quincy, who was born in 1689, and who when dying, in 1767, gave his name to his great-grandson, John Quincy Adams, who had just been born.   Some have thought the picture that of a sister, Esther Quincy; but to me it has a hard little boy's face, not the features of a delicate girl, and also a boy's hands, and a boy's toy.

Children in America, if gentlefolk, dressed just

as

as children did in England at that date; and boys wore "coats" in England till they were six or seven. One of the most charming of all grandmothers' letters was written by a doting English grandmother to her son, Lord Chief Justice North, telling of the "leaving off of coats" of his motherless little son, Francis Guildford, then six years old. The letter is dated October 10, 1679: —

"DEAR SON:

"You cannot beleeve the great concerne that was in the whole family here last Wednesday, it being the day that the taylor was to helpe to dress little ffrank in his breeches in order to the making an everyday suit by it. Never had any bride that was to be drest upon her weding night more handes about her, some the legs, some the armes, the taylor butt'ning, and others putting on the sword, and so many lookers on that had I not a ffinger amongst I could not have seen him. When he was quite drest he acted his part as well as any of them for he desired he might goe downe to inquire for the little gentleman that was there the day before in a black coat, and speak to the man to tell the gentleman when he came from school that there was a gallant with very fine clothes and a sword to have waited upon him and would come again upon Sunday next. But this was not all, there was great contrivings while he was dressing who should have the first salute; but he sayd if old Joan had been here, she should, but he gave it to me to quiett them all. They were very fitt, everything, and he

looks

looks taller and prettyer than in his coats.   Little Charles
rejoyced as much as he did for he jumpt all the while about
him and took notice of everything.   I went to Bury, and
bot everything for another suitt which will be finisht
on Saturday so the coats are to be quite left off on Sunday.
I consider it is not yett terme time and since you could not
have the pleasure of the first sight, I resolved you should
have a full relation from

> " Yor most affnate Mother
>
> " A North.

When he was drest he asked Buckle whether muffs
were out of fashion because they had not sent him one."

This affectionate letter, written to a great and
busy statesman, the Lord Keeper of the Seals,
shows how pure and delightful domestic life in England could be ; but the writer was not a commonplace woman — she was the mother of fourteen
children, and had had years of experience with a
father-in-law before whom an army of traditional
mothers-in-law would pale.   She lived through this
ordeal and a trying marital experience, and her
children rose up and called her blessed.   Among
her virtues her son Roger dilated at length upon her
delightful letter-writing, her " freedom of style and
matter," and declared that her letters were among
the comforts of her children's lives.

To return to the dress of John Quincy : with the
exception

Jane Bonner, Eight Years Old, 1700

exception of the neck of the body of the frock it is much like the dress of grown women of that day. We have existing portraits of Madam Shimpton and Rebecca Rawson of the same date. In both of these, as in this little boy's portrait, the sleeve is the most noticeable feature, with its single slash, double puff drawn in below the elbow and confined with pretty ribbon knots. This sleeve was known as the virago sleeve, and John Quincy's are darker colored than his frock. All three wear loosely tied rather shapeless hoods, such as are seen on the women in the prints of the coronation procession of King William. The boy has a close cap under his hood. His dress is certainly picturesque and distinctive.

A portrait, facing page 36, of another Massachusetts boy, contemporary with John Quincy, is that of Robert Gibbs, the rich Boston merchant. This is plainly marked as being painted when he was four and a half years old, and with the date 1670. He wears the same stiff cuirass as John Quincy, the same odd truncated shoes of buff leather, and has the same masculine swing of the petticoats. Both figures stand on a checker-board floor, four squares deep, with their toes at the same point on the board. Robert Gibbs wears a more boyish collar, or band, as befits a bigger boy. The sleeves are an important feature of his dress, having a pair of long hanging

hanging sleeves bordered with fur, which do not show in the print in this book, but are plainly visible in the original portrait. Hanging sleeves were so distinctively the dress of a little child that the term had at that time a symbolic significance, implying childishness both of youth and second childhood. Pepys thus figuratively employs the term. Judge Sewall wrote in old age to a brother whose widowed sister he desired to marry : —

"I remember when I was going from school at Newbury to have sometime met your sisters Martha and Mary in Hanging Sleeves, coming home from their school in Chandlers Lane, and have had the pleasure of speaking to them. And I could find it in my heart now to speak to Mrs Martha again, now I myself am reduc'd to Hanging Sleeves."

This roundabout wooing came to naught. The Judge married Widow Mary Gibbs, relict of this very Robert Gibbs whose childish portrait we have here. The artist who painted this picture may have been Tom Child, who is named by Judge Sewall as the portrait-painter of that day.

A demure and quaint portrait, opposite page 42, is that of Jane Bonner. She was born in 1691, the daughter of Captain John Bonner of Boston, and was married in 1710 to John Ellery. She was about

about eight or ten years old when the portrait was painted. Crude as is the painting, it gives evident proof that the lace of the stomacher and sleeve frills is of the nature of what is now called rose point.

In the early settlements of Connecticut, Massachusetts, and Virginia, sumptuary laws were passed to restrain and attempt to prohibit extravagance in dress. The New England magistrates were curiously minute in description of overluxurious attire, and many offenders were tried and fined. But vain daughters and sons " psisted in fflonting," though ministers joined the lawmakers in solemn warnings and reprehensions. Young girls were fined for silk hoods and immoderate great sleeves, and boldly appeared in court in still richer attire. The Dutch never attempted or wished to simplify the dress of either men or women. In New York dress was ample, substantial, varied in texture, and variegated in color. It ever formed a considerable item in personal property. The children of the Dutch settlers had plentiful and warm clothing, and sometimes very rich clothing, as may be seen in the quaint and interesting picture facing page 26, of twin girls, the two daughters of Abraham De Peyster of New York, and his wife, Margaret Van Cortlandt. They are dressed in red velvet trained gowns, but are barefooted. They were born December 3, 1724, and

Eva

Infant's Robe, Cap, and Christening Blanket

Eva died in 1729, a month after the portrait was painted. Catherine was married on her eighteenth birthday to John Livingstone, son of the second lord of the manor. Their son had a daughter Catherine, who became the wife of Don Mariano Velasquez de la Cadenas. To their daughters, Mrs. Azoy and Miss Mariana Velasquez, this interesting portrait now belongs.

The mother of these twins was the daughter of Jacobus Van Cortlandt and Eva De Vries Philipse. The names of Eva and Catherine have ever been given to the little daughters of these allied families, and are borne to-day by many of their descendants.

Another

Another little girl of Dutch blood was Cathalina Post, who married Zegor Van Santvoord. Her portrait was painted in 1750 when she was fourteen years old, and is now owned by Dr. Van Santvoord of Kingston-on-Hudson, New York. A copy of this quaint old picture faces page 204. It is most interesting in costume; the head-gear showing distinct Dutch influence.

There is a suggestion of earrings in this portrait, and Katherine Ten Broeck, another child of Dutch blood, but three years old, wears earrings. The reproduction of her portrait, given opposite page 192, shows these jewels but dimly, but they are visible in the original oil-painting. She was born in Albany in 1715. The portrait is marked Ætat^s Sua, 3 Years, 1719. She was married to John Livingstone, and lived to become a stately old dame, receiving formally on New Year's Day her grandchildren, who always greeted her in Dutch learned for the special occasion.

The devastations of two wars (and in some localities three) — destruction by fire and earthquake — have sadly destroyed the cherished relics of many southern homes. From Mrs. St. Julian Ravenel of Charleston, South Carolina, the delightful biographer of that delightful colonial dame, Eliza Lucas Pinckney, come two portraits of children of the Huguenot settlers. The picture facing page 48 of

Ellinor

Ellinor Cordes of St. John's, Berkeley County, South Carolina, painted about 1740, shows a lovely little child of French features, and French daintiness of dress, albeit a bright yellow brocaded satin would seem rather gorgeous attire for a girl but two years old. Opposite page 50 is a picture of Daniel Ravenel of Wantoot, St. John's, Berkeley County, South Carolina, who was born in 1760, and was about five years old when this portrait was painted; though he still wears what might be termed a frock with petticoats, there is a decided boyishness in the waistcoat with its silver buttons and lace, and the befrogged overcoat with broad cuffs and wrist ruffles, and a turned-over revers, and narrow linen inner collar. It is an exceptionally pleasing boy's dress for a little child.

Two portraits of Flagg children painted, it is said, by Smibert, must be among his latest portraits, for the baby, Polly Flagg, was born in Boston in 1750, and Smibert died in 1751. The portrait facing page 184 shows, as may be seen, a dear little baby not a year old, in baby dress and cap, clasping a toy. It is marked on the back Mrs. Polly Hurd; for the little girl lived to be the wife and widow of Dr. Wilder of Lancaster, Massachusetts, and of Dr. Hurd of Concord, Massachusetts. Of equal interest is the severely beautiful face of James Flagg

Ellinor Cordes, Two Years Old, 1740

Flagg, her brother, shown opposite page 188. He was born in 1739, and was still in " coats " when this portrait was painted. These portraits are owned by Mrs. Albert Thorndike of Boston, Massachusetts, the great-granddaughter of Griselda Apthorpe Flagg, the sister of these two children.

The portrait of Jonathan Mountfort, given opposite page 58, has a special interest to the art student, since it is a specimen of Copley's early work. The boy was born December 6, 1746, and was seven years old when the portrait was painted. He married Mary Bole, a Newfoundland girl, whose father sent her to a school in Halifax, under the charge of Captain Shepherd of Medford, Massachusetts. Finding Halifax in a state of blockade, the captain took the little girl to Boston. He and his wife were childless and became deeply attached to her and finally adopted her. She became engaged to Dr. Mountfort, and went to visit her parents in Ireland, whither they had removed. On her return, bringing with her the gifts, wardrobe, and household furnishings of a bride of that period, she came into Boston harbor only to be wrecked in sight of the town. The ship's mate swam with her to the lighthouse, and the two were the only ones saved. Captain Shepherd gave her a house and fresh outfit, and she married Dr. Mountfort.

fort. They had seven children, but the name of Mountfort is now extinct. Their daughter Elizabeth married Major Thomas Pitts, whose daughter is now Mrs. Farlin of Detroit, Michigan, the present owner of this interesting portrait.

An altogether charming group of children, facing page 54, two sisters and two brothers of Governor Christopher Gore (seventh governor of Massachusetts), was painted about the year 1754, by Copley. The mature little girl of this picture, Frances, married Thomas Crafts, colonel of the regiment of which Paul Revere was lieutenant-colonel in the Revolution. Colonel and Mrs. Crafts were the great-grandparents of the present owners, Miss Julia G. Robins and Miss Susan P. B. Robins. This picture was for a time in the Boston Museum of Art, and on returning it General Loring wrote, "I shall miss the little grown-ups — were there no children in those days?" This look of maturity seems universal to all these portraits. I have photographs of several other groups of children, one of the most charming, that of the Grymes children, now in the Capitol at Richmond, Virginia; but they are all too darkened with age to admit of proper or adequate reproduction, and must be left out of these pages. The baby in the Grymes group is truly a baby, not a " grown-up."

The

Daniel Ravenel, Five Years Old, 1765

Child's Shoes

The handsomest of all the boy-portraits of colonial days is that of Samuel Pemberton, by Blackburn; it is perfect in feature and expression; though he is but twelve years old he wears a wig. It was painted in 1736, and boys of good family then wore costly wigs. Mr. Freeman of Portland, Maine, had in his book of expenses of the year 1750, such items as these : —

" Shaving my three sons at sundry times . £5. 14s.
    Expenses for James' Wig . . . 9.
      "   " Samuel's Wig . . . 9.

The three sons — Samuel, James, and William — were aged eleven, nine, and seven years. The shaving

ing was of their heads. Slaves of fashion were
parents of that day to bedeck their boys with such
rich wigs.

A more exquisite portrait than that of Thomas
Aston Coffin, opposite page 222, can scarcely be
found. It is painted in Copley's best manner
(shown in the highest perfection in the portrait of
his daughter Elizabeth). A light-hued satin petti-
coat-front shows under a rich full-skirted satin over-
dress which brushes the ground. The pretty satin
sleeves have white under-sleeves and wrist ruffles,
but the neck is cut very low and round. The child
holds two pigeons by a leash, and a feathered hat is
by his side. This portrait was much loved by its
late owner, Miss Anne S. Robbins of Boston.

This charming picture of the Pepperell children,
facing page 214, was believed to be by Copley, and
included in Mr. Perkins' list. At present this
authorship is doubted. It is owned by Miss Alice
Longfellow of Cambridge, having been bought by
her father, the poet, from the owner of the Portsmouth Museum, who had in some singular way
acquired it. The children are William, son of the
second Sir William Pepperell, and his sister Elizabeth
Royal Pepperell, who married Rev. Henry Hutton.

A bright-eyed little girl, Mary Lord, has her
portrait, given opposite page 66, hanging in the
rooms

rooms of the Connecticut Historical Society. She was born in 1702, in Hartford, Connecticut, and married, in 1724, Colonel Joseph Pitkin of Hartford. By her side hangs the picture of Colonel Wadsworth and his son, shown opposite page 316. It is the one which the artist Trumbull took to Sir Joshua Reynolds for advice and comment. He was snubbed with the snappish criticism that "the coat looked like bent tin." Other criticism might be made on the anatomical proportions of the subjects.

Copley's genius is shown in the fine portrait of William Verstile, facing page 210, painted in 1769. There is one little glimpse of this boy's boyhood which has so human an element, is so fully in touch with modern life, that I give it. It is from an old letter written by his mother, during a visit in Boston, where possibly this very portrait was painted. It shows the beginning of tastes which found ample scope in his services in the war of the Revolution.

"Boston, June 11, 1766.

"My Dear these leaves me and my friends as I hope they will find you for health. I was obliged to stay a fortnight as I didn't set out till the middle of the week from Weathersfield, was obliged to tarry here a fortnight on account of coming with the Post. We got down safe we got into Boston Wednesday afternoon at four o Clock. The Horse seem'd to enter Boston as free & fresh as when

he

he first set out from home. Mr. Lowder says he is a
prime horse. He wasn't galled or fretted in the least but
would have come right back again. I was a good deal
worried as Billey didn't fill the chaise no more, the horse
might have brought three as well as two & not have felt it.
I have had but very little Comfort since I have bin here on
account of Billey as there's so much powderwork going on
among the Children since the Illumination Billey has bin
very forward of firing iron guns. Since we've bin here its
not only the powder amongst the Children but the wharfes
being so neare he's down there continually. Johnny Bradford & Ned & Dan Warner and Billey was down the
wharfe together when a boy push'd Dan over & lik'd to
bin drown'd & might bin Billey so I can't take much comfort on leaving of him but shall bring him, you needn't be
Concern'd about threes coming up as Mr. Hide tells me
Billey may ride behind him if he's a mind to."

Billey became a portrait painter himself, and got
four guineas apiece for his miniatures. He early
showed artistic predilections, and these tastes were
well supplied. Interspersed with pumps and hose
and hats for Billey are found in his father's purchases
" brass deviders," scales, "books for limning," two
dozen " hair pencils," and " 1 box painter's collurs
on glass," which cost twelve shillings.

I don't know who taught Billey limning. There
was a funny book in circulation among students in
that day. It was written in serious intent, but its
rules

Gore Children, 1754

rules read as though they were dictated by Oliver Herford. It was entitled *Every Young Man's Companion in Drawing*. Here are a few of its instructions to young artists : —

"Make your outlines, which may be mended occasionally.

"From the Elbow to the Root of the Little Finger is Two Noses.

"The Thumb contains a Nose.

"The Inside of Arm to Middle of Arm is Four Noses."

The crowning glory of the Copley portraits is the charming family group opposite page 180, depicting Copley himself, his beautiful wife, his dignified father-in-law, and his lovely children. It is now exhibited in the Boston Museum of Fine Arts. This group seems perfect, and the quaint figure of the child Elizabeth Copley, in the foreground, is worthy the brush of Van Dyck.

Colonel John Lewis, one of the old Virginia gentlemen, had two child wards. As befitted young gentlefolk of that day of opulence and extravagance, they had their dress from England. In 1736, when Robert Carter, the younger child, was about nine years old, suits of fine holland, laced, and of red worsted and of green German serge came across seas for him, with laced hats with loops and buttons. When he was twelve years old part of his

"winter

"winter cloathes" were six pair of shoes and two of pumps, four pair of worked hose and four of thread hose, gloves, hats, and shoe buckles.   His sister Betty had a truly fashionable wardrobe, and the stiff, restrictive dress of the times was indicated by the items of stays, hoops, masks, and fans. When " Miss Custis" was but four years old George Washington ordered for her from England packthread stays, stiffened coats, a large number of gloves and masks.

An order for purchases sent to a London agent by Washington in 1761 contains a full list of garments for both his step-children.   " Miss Custis " was then six years old.   These are some of the items:—

"1 Coat made of Fashionable Silk.
A Fashionable Cap or fillet with Bib apron.
Ruffles and Tuckers, to be laced.
4 Fashionable Dresses made of Long Lawn.
2 Fine Cambrick Frocks.
A Satin Capuchin, hat, and neckatees.
A Persian Quilted Coat.
1 p. Pack Thread Stays.
4 p. Callimanco Shoes.
6 p. Leather Shoes.
2 p. Satin Shoes with flat ties.
6 p. Fine Cotton Stockings.
4 p. White Worsted Stockings.
12 p. Mitts.

6 p. White Kid Gloves.

1 p. Silver Shoe Buckles.

1 p. Neat Sleeve Buttons.

6 Handsome Egrettes Different Sorts.

6 Yards Ribbon for Egrettes.

12 Yards Coarse Green Callimanco."

There is a large-headed portrait of the Custis children which was painted at about this time. A copy of it is shown opposite page 250. While the dress of both children is mature, it is not so elegant as might be expected from the rich garments which were imported for them.

Sir William Pepperell ordered, in 1737, equally costly and formal clothing from England for his little daughter to disport at Piscataquay. Stays and masks are ever on the lists of little gentlewomen. A letter of the day tells of seeing the youthful daughter of Governor Tryon sitting stiffly in a chair, in broad lace collar, with heavy dress, never playing, running, or even walking.

Delicacy of figure and whiteness of complexion were equal fetiches with colonial mammas. Little Dolly Payne, afterward Dolly Madison, wore long gloves, a linen mask, and had a sunbonnet sewed on her head every morning by her devoted mother. Very thin shoes of silk, morocco, or light stuff unfitted little girls for any very active exercise; these

were

were high-heeled.   A tiny pair of shoes for a little
girl of three are shown on page 51.   I have seen
children's stays, made of heavy strips of board and
steel, tightly wrought with heavy buckram or canvas
into an iron frame like an instrument of torture.
These had been worn by a little girl five years old.
Staymakers advertised stays, jumps, gazzets, cos-
trells, and caushets (which were doubtless corsets)
for ladies and children, " to make them appear
strait."   And I have been told of tin corsets for
little girls, but I have never seen any such abomi-
nations.   One pair of stays was labelled as having been worn by a boy when five years old.
There certainly is a suspicious suggestion in some
of these little fellows' portraits of whalebone and
buckram.

In the sprightly descriptions given by Anna Green
Winslow of her own dress we see with much distinct-
ness the little girl of twelve of the year 1771 : —

" I was dress'd in my yellow coat, my black bib &
apron, my pompedore shoes, the cap my aunt Storer sometime since presented me with blue ribbins on it, a very
handsome loket in the shape of a hart, the paste pin my
Hon'd Papa presented me with in my cap, my new cloak
& bonnet on, my pompedore gloves, and I would tell you
they all lik'd my dress very much." . . .   " I was dress'd in
my yellow coat, black bib and apron, black feathers on my
head,

Jonathan Mountfort, Seven Years Old, 1753

head, my paste comb, all my paste, garnet, marquasett, and jet pins, together with my silver plume, — my loket rings, black coller round my neck, black mitts, 2 or 3 yards of blue ribbin, striped tucker & ruffels & my silk shoes compleated my dress."

It would seem somewhat puzzling to fancy how, with a little girl's soft hair, the astonishing and varied head-gear named above could be attached. Little Anna gives a full description of the way her hair was dressed over a high roll, so heavy and hot that it made her head "itch & ach & burn like anything." She tells of the height of her head-gear : —

"When it first came home, Aunt put it on & my new cap on it; she then took up her apron & measur'd me, & from the roots of my hair on my forehead to the top of my notions, I measur'd above an inch longer than I did downwards from the roots of my hair to the end of my chin."

Her picture, shown facing page 164, is taken from a miniature painted when she was a few years older. The roll is more modest in size, and the decorations are fewer in number. Each year the " head-equipage " diminished, till cropped heads were seen, with a shock of tight curls on the forehead — an incredibly disfiguring mode.

In

In the chapter upon the school life of girls a letter is given describing the dress of two young girls who were boarding in Boston while they were being taught. There is no doubt that very rich dress was desired, and possibly required of these young scholar-boarders. The oft-quoted letter in regard to Miss Huntington's wardrobe shows the elegance of dress of those schoolgirls. She had twelve silk gowns; but word was sent home to Norwich that a recently imported rich fabric was most suitable for her rank and station; and in answer to the teacher's request the parents ordered the purchase of this elegant dress.

When cotton fabrics from Oriental countries became everywhere and every time worn, children's dress, as likewise that of grown folk, was much reduced in elegance as it was in warmth. Hoops disappeared and heavy petticoats also; the soft slimsy clinging stuffs, suitable only for summer wear, were not discarded in winter. Boys wore nankeen suits the entire year. Calico and chintz were fashioned into trousers and jackets. A little suit is shown, facing page 60, made of figured calico of high colors, which it is stated was worn in 1784. The labels are very exact and the labellers very cautious of the Deerfield Memorial Hall collection, else I should assign this suit to a ten or even twenty years' later date.

Boy's Suit of Clothing, 1784

date. Children must have suffered sadly with the cold in this age of cotton. Girls' dresses were half low-necked, and were filled in with a thin tucker; separate sleeves were tied in at the arm size, and often long-armed mitts of nankeen or linen took the place of the sleeves.

A family of Cary children had several charming portraits painted in London. Two of them are given opposite pages 240 and 246. They note the transitions of costume which came at the approach of the close of the century. The portrait of the boy is interesting in a special point of costume; it shows the abandonment of the cocked hat and adoption of the simpler modern form of head-covering. The little girl, Margaret, has a most roguish expression, which is suggestive of Sir Joshua Reynolds' *Girl with the Mouse Trap*. The resemblance is even more marked in the portrait of the same child at the age of six, wherein the eyes and half-smile are charmingly engaging; unfortunately the photograph from that portrait is not clear enough for satisfactory reproduction.

A demure little brother and sister were the children of General Stephen Rowe Bradley of Westminster, Vermont, whose portraits face pages 356 and 378. These were painted soon after the Revolution, and show the definite changes in dress which

set

set in with other Republican institutions.   At
this date there began to be worn a special dress
for both boys and girls.   Until then, as soon as a
boy put on breeches he dressed precisely like his
father — in miniature.   By tradition Marie Antoi-
nette was the first who had a special dress made
for her young son.   And sadly was she reviled for
dressing her poor little Dauphin in jacket
and trousers instead of flapped
coat, waistcoat, and
knee-breeches.

CHAPTER III

SCHOOLS AND SCHOOL LIFE

First mark whereof scholes were erected,
And what the founders did intend.
And then doe thou thy study directe
For to obtain unto that end.

Doubtless this was all their meaning,
To have their countrie founded
With all poyntes of honest lernynge
Whereof the public weal had nede.
— *The Last Trumpet.   R. Crowley, 1550.*

NO greater contrast of conditions could exist than between the school life of what we love to call the " good old times," and that of the far better times of to-day.   Poor, small, and uncomfortable schoolhouses, scant furnishings, few and uninteresting books, tiresome and indifferent methods of teaching, great severity of discipline, were the accompaniments of school days until this century.   Yet with all these disadvantages children obtained an education, for an education was warmly desired ; no difficulties could chill that deep-lying longing

longing for learning. " Child," said one noble
New England mother of the olden days, " if God
make thee a good Christian and a good scholar,
'tis all thy mother ever asked for thee."

Not only did parents strive for the education of
their children, but the colonies assisted by commanding the building and maintaining of a school in each
town where there was a sufficient number of families
and scholars. Rhode Island was the only New
England colony that did not compel the building
of schoolhouses and the education of children.

So determined was Massachusetts to have schools
that in 1636, only six years after the settlement of
Boston, the General Court, which was composed of
representatives from every settlement in the Bay
Colony, and which was the same as our House of
Representatives to-day, gave over half the annual
income of the entire colony to establish the school
which two years later became Harvard College.
This event should be remembered ; it is distinguished in history as the first time any body of
people in any country ever gave through its representatives its own money to found a place of
education.

In Virginia schoolhouses were few for over a century. Governor Berkeley, an obstinate and narrow-
minded Englishman, wrote home to England in 1670,
" I

" I thank God there are in Virginia no free schools nor printing, and I hope we shall not have, for learning hath brought disobedience and heresy into the world." Some Virginia gentlemen did not agree with him, however, and gave money to try to establish free schools for poor children. A far greater hindrance to the establishment of schools than the governor's stupid opposition, was the fact that there was no town or village life in Virginia; the houses and plantations were scattered; previous to the year 1700 Jamestown was the only Virginia town, and it was but a petty settlement. Williamsburg was not even laid out; a few seaports had been planned, but had not been built. Hence the children of wealthy planters were taught by private tutors at home, or were sent to school in England.

Occasionally, as years passed on, there might be found in Virginia, the Carolinas, and Georgia, what was called an old-field school, the uniting of a few neighbors to hire a teacher, too often a poor one, like the " hedge-teachers " of Europe, for a short term of teaching, in a shabby building placed on an old exhausted tobacco field.

In one of these old-field schools kept by Hobby — sexton, pedagogue, and " the most conceited man in three parishes "— George Washington obtained most of his education. A daily ride on horseback for a
year

year to a similar school ten miles away, and for
another year a row morning and night even in
roughest weather across the river to a Fredericks-
burg teacher, ended his school career when he was
thirteen ; but he had then made a big pile of neatly
written manuscript school books, which may now
be seen in the Library at Washington ; and he had
acquired a passionate longing to be educated, which
accompanied him through life.

An "advisive narrative" sent from America to
the Bishop of London, toward the end of the
seventeenth century, says : —

" This lack of schools in Virginia is a consequence of
their scattered planting. It renders a very numerous generation of Christian's Children born in Virginia, who naturally are of beautiful and comely Persons, and generally of
more ingenious Spirits than those in England, unservice-
able for any great Employment in Church or State."

This statement was not wholly correct ; for though
Virginians were not usually fitted to be parsons, they
certainly proved suited to state and government.
When the war of the Revolution broke out, the
noblest number of great statesmen, orators, and
generals, who certainly were men of genius if not
of conventional school education, came from the
southern provinces. These brilliant Virginians were
strong

Mary Lord, 1710 *circa*

strong evidence and proof of what the great orator, Patrick Henry, called, in his singular pronunciation, "naiteral pairts"; which he declared was of more account than "all the book-lairnin' on the airth." Different climates and surroundings soon bring out different traits in the same race of people. The warm climate and fruitful soil in the southern colonies developed from English stock an easy-living race who needed the great stimulus and noble excitement of the Revolution to exhibit the highest qualities of brain. The Puritan minister, Cotton Mather, said in 1685, in a sermon before the Governor and Council in Massachusetts, "The Youth in this Country are verie Sharp and early Ripe in their Capacities." Thus speedily had keen New England air and hard New England life developed these characteristic New England traits.

New England at that time was controlled, both in public and private life, by the Puritan ministers, who felt, as one of them said, that "unless school and college flourish, church and state cannot live." The ministers were accredited guardians of the schools; and when Boston chose five school inspectors to visit the Latin School with the ministers, many of the latter were highly incensed, and Increase Mather refused to go with these lay visitors.

By a law of Massachusetts, passed in 1647, it was

was ordered that every town of fifty families should provide a school where children could be taught to read and write; while every town of one hundred householders was required to have a grammar school. In the Connecticut Code of Laws of 1650 were the same orders. These schools were public, but were not free; they were supported at the expense of the parents.

In 1644 the town of Salem ordered " that a note be published the next lecture day, that such as have children to be kept at school, would bring in their names, and what they will give for a whole year; and also that if any poor body hath children or a child to be put to school, and not able to pay for their schooling, that the town will pay it by a rate." Lists of children were made out in towns, and if the parents were well-to-do, they had to pay whether their children attended school or not.

Land was sometimes set aside to support partly the school; it was called the "school-meadows," or "school-fields," and was let out for an income to help to pay the teacher. This was a grant made on the same principle that grants were made to physicians, tanners, and other useful persons, not to establish free education. At a later date lotteries were a favorite method of raising money for schools.

It was not until about the time of the Revolution that

that the modern signification of the word " free " —
a school paid for entirely by general town taxes —
could be applied to the public schools of most
Massachusetts towns, and when the schools of Boston were made free, that community stood alone
for its liberality not only in America, but in the
world.

The pay was given in any of the inconvenient
exchanges which had to pass as money at that time, —
in wampum, beaver skins, Indian corn, wheat, peas,
beans, or any country product known as " truck."
It is told of a Salem school, that one scholar was
always seated at the window to study and also to hail
passers-by, and endeavor to sell to them the accumu-
lation of corn, vegetables, etc., which had been given
in payment to the teacher.

The logs for the great fireplace were furnished by
the parents or guardians of the scholars as a part
of the pay for schooling ; and an important part
it was in the northern colonies, in the bitter winter, in the poorly built schoolhouses. Some schoolmasters, indignant at the carelessness of parents
who failed to send the expected load of wood
early in the winter, banished the unfortunate child
of the tardy parent to the coldest corner of the
schoolroom. The town of Windsor, Connecticut,
voted "that the committee be empowered to exclude
any

any scholar that shall not carry his share of wood for the use of the said school." In 1736 West Hartford ordered every child " barred from the fire" whose parents had not sent wood.

The school laws of the State of Massachusetts, framed in 1789, crystallized all the principles, prac-

" Erudition " Schoolhouse, Bath, Maine, 1797

tice, and hopes that had been developed by a hundred and fifty years of school life. The standard set by these laws was decidedly lower than those of colonial days. Where a permanent English school had been imperative, six months schooling a year might be permitted to take its place ; where every town of a hundred families had had a grammar school in which boys could be fitted for the university, only towns of two hundred families were compelled

compelled to have such schools. Thus the open path to the university was closed in a hundred and twenty Massachusetts towns.

Judge Thomas Holme composed in grammarless rhyme, in 1696, a *True Relation of the Flourishing State of Philadelphia.* In it he says : —

> "Here are schools of divers sorts
> To which our youth daily resorts,
> Good women, who do very well
> Bring little ones to read and spell,
> Which fits them for writing ; and then
> Here's men to bring them to their pen,
> And to instruct and make them quick
> In all sorts of Arithmetick."

These statements were scarcely carried out in fact ; in Pennsylvania educational advantages were few, and among some classes education was sorely hampered. The Quakers did not encourage absolute illiteracy, but they thought knowledge of the "three R's" was enough ; they distinctly disapproved of any extended scholarship, as it fostered undue pride and provoked idleness. The Germans were worse ; their own historians, the Calvinist and Lutheran preachers, Schlatter and Muhlenberg, are authority ; there were among them a few schools of low grade ; but the introduction of the public school system among the Germans was resisted by indignation

indignation meetings and litigation. The Tunkers
degenerated so that they did not desire a member-
ship of educated persons, and would have liked to
destroy all books but religious ones. It was said
by these German settlers that schooling made boys
lazy and dissatisfied on the farms, and that religion
would suffer by too much learning. As Bayard
Taylor puts it in his *Pennsylvania Farmer* : —

"Book learning gets the upper hand and work is slow and slack,
  And they that come long after us will find things gone to wrack."

School-teachers in the middle and southern colonies were frequently found in degraded circumstances; many of them were redemptioners and
exported convicts. I have frequently noted such
newspaper advertisements as this from the *Maryland Gazette* : —

"Ran away: A Servant man who followed the occupation of a Schoolmaster, much given to drinking and
gambling."

So universal was drunkenness among schoolmasters that a chorus of colonial "gerund-grinders"
might sing in Goldsmith's words : —

"Let schoolmasters puzzle their brains
    With grammar and nonsense and learning,
  Good liquor, I stoutly maintain,
    Gives genius a better discerning."

Scotland

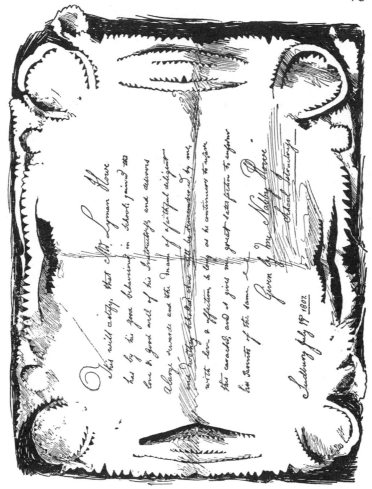

Scotland furnished the best and the largest number of schoolmasters to the colonies.

The first pedagogue of New Amsterdam was one Adam

Adam Roelantsen, and he had a checkered career. His name appears with frequency on the court records of the little town both as plaintiff and defendant. He was as active in slandering his neighbors as they were in slandering him; though, as Miss Van Vechten observes, "It is hard to see what fiction worse than truth could have been invented about him." In spite of the fact that "people did not speak well of him," he married well. But his misdemeanors continued and he was finally sentenced to be flogged. We may contrast the legal records of this gentleman's shortcomings with his duties as set forth in his commission, one of which was "to set others a good example as becometh a devout, pious, and worthy consoler of the sick, church clerk, precentor, and schoolmaster."

Some of the contracts under which teachers were hired still exist. One for the teacher at the Dutch settlement of Flatbush, Long Island, in 1682, is very full in detail, and we learn much of the old-time school from it. A bell was rung to call the scholars together at eight o'clock in the morning, the school closed for a recess at eleven, opened again at one, closed at four; all sessions began and closed with prayer. On Wednesdays and Saturdays the children were taught the questions and answers in the catechism and the common prayers. The master was
                                        paid

paid (usually in wheat or corn) for "a speller or reader" three guilders a quarter, for "a writer" four guilders. He had many other duties to perform besides teaching the children. He rung the church bell on Sunday, read the Bible at service in church, and led in the singing; sometimes he read the sermon. He provided water for baptisms, bread and wine for communion, and in fact performed all the duties now done by a sexton, including sweeping out the church. He delivered invitations to funerals and carried messages. Sometimes he dug the graves, and often he visited and comforted the sick.

Full descriptions exist of the first country schoolhouses in Pennsylvania and New York. They were universally made of logs. Some had a rough puncheon floor, others a dirt floor which readily ground into dust two or three inches thick, that unruly pupils would purposely stir up in clouds to annoy the masters and disturb the school. .The bark roof was a little higher at one side that the rain might drain off. Usually the teacher sat in the middle of the room, and pegs were thrust between the logs around the walls, three or four feet from the ground; boards were laid on these pegs; at these rude desks sat the older scholars with their backs to the teacher. Younger scholars sat on blocks or benches of logs. Until this century many
schoolhouses

"Old Harmony" Schoolhouse, Raritan Township, Hunterdon Co., New Jersey

schoolhouses did not have glass set in the small windows, but newspapers or white papers greased with lard were fastened in the rude sashes, or in holes cut in the wall, and let in a dim light. At one end, or in the middle, a "cat and clay" chimney furnished a fireplace. When the first rough log cabin was replaced by a better schoolhouse the hexagonal shape, so beloved in those states for meeting-houses, meeting-houses, was chosen, and occasionally built in stone. A picture of one still standing and still used as a schoolhouse, in Raritan, New Jersey, is here shown. It retained its old shelf desks till a few years ago.

In a halting way schools in America followed the customs of English schools. The "potation-penny," or "the drinking," was collected in schools in the colonies. In England a considerable sum was often gathered for this treat at the end of the term; but the pennies were doled out more slowly in American schools. Young Joseph Lloyd (of the family of Lloyds Neck on Long Island), in the year 1693, paid out a shilling and sixpence "to the Mistris for feast and wine." A century later, in a school in New Hampshire, the children diligently saved the wood-ashes in the big fireplace and sold them to a neighboring potash works for their treat. They had ample funds to buy rum, raisins, and gingerbread for all who came to the treat, including the ministers and deacons. It was of this school, doubtless attended largely by Scotch-Irish children, that the teacher recorded that the boys, even the youngest, wore leather aprons, while many of the girls took snuff. Another old English custom, the barring-out, occasionally was known here, especially in Pennsylvania.

The

The furnishing of the schoolrooms was meagre; there were no blackboards, no maps, seldom was there a pair of globes. Though Mr. MacMaster asserts that pencils were never used even in the early years of our Federal life, his statement is certainly a mistake. Faber's pencils were made as early as 1761. Peter Goelet advertised lead pencils for sale in New York in 1786, with india rubbers, and as early as 1740 they were offered among booksellers' wares in Boston for threepence apiece, both black and red lead. Judge Sewall had one; perhaps it was not our common lead pencil of to-day.

In 1771 we find the patriot Henry Laurens writing thus to his daughter Martha, "his dearest Patsey," when she was about twelve years old.

". . . I have recollected your request for a pair of globes, therefore I have wrote to Mr. Grubb to ship a pair of the best 18 inch, with caps, and a book of directions, and to add a case of neat instruments, and one dozen Middleton's best pencils marked M. L. When you are measuring the surface of the globe remember you are to cut a part in it, and think of a plum pudding and other domestic duties. Your father,

"Henry Laurens."

Still lead pencils were not in common use even in city schools till this century. The manuscript arithmetics

Samuel Pemberton, Twelve Years Old, 1736

arithmetics or "sum-books" which I have seen were always done in ink. Many a country boy grew to manhood without ever seeing a lead pencil.

In country schools even till the middle of this century copy-books were made of foolscap paper carefully sewed into book shape, and were ruled by hand. For this children used lead plummets instead of pencils. These plummets were made of lead melted and cast in wooden moulds cut out by the ever ready jackknife and were then tied by a hempen string to the ruler. These plummets were usually shaped like a tomahawk, and carefully whittled and trimmed to a sharp edge. Slightly varied shapes were a carpenter's or a woodcutter's axe; also there were cannon, battledores, and cylinders.

Paper was scarce and too highly prized for children to waste; it was a great burden even to ministers to get what paper they needed for their sermons, and they frequently acquired microscopic hand-writing for economy's sake. To the forest the scholars turned for the ever plentiful birch bark, which formed a delightful substitute to cipher on instead of paper. Among the thrifty Scotch-Irish settlers in New Hampshire and the planters in Maine, sets of arithmetic rules were copied by each child on birch bark and made a substantial text-book. Rolls of birch bark resembling in shape the parch-
ment

ment rolls of the Egyptians and lead plummets seem too ancient in appearance to have been commonly employed in schools within a century in this country.

It has been asserted that school slates were not used till this century. Noah Webster says distinctly in a letter written about the schools of his childhood, that "before the Revolution and for some years after no slates were used in common schools." S. Town, attending school in Belchertown, Massachusetts, in 1785, says that slates were unknown.

I have seen but a single reference to them in America and that is in such an ingenuous schoolboy's letter I will quote it in full: —

"To Mr. Cornelius Ten Broeck
                     att Albany.
"Stamford, the 13th Day of October, 1752.

        "Honored Fethar,
                "These fiew Lines comes to let you know that I am in a good State of Health and I hope this may find you also. I have found all the things in my trunk but I must have a pare of Schuse. And mama please to send me some Ches Nutts and some Wall Nutts ; you please to send me a Slate, and som pensals, and please to send me some smok befe, and for bringing my trunk 3/9, and for a pare of Schuse 9 shillings. You please to send me a pare

of

of indin's Schuse.   You please to send me som dride corn.
My Duty to Father and Mother and Sister and to all frinds.
" I am your Dutyfull Son,

" JOHN TEN BROECK.

" Father forgot to send me my Schuse."

In an advertisement of an English bookseller of
the year 1737, one James Marshal of the Bible and
Sun at Stockton are named Slate Pocket Books,
Slates, and Slate Pens.   The first slates were frame-
less, and had a hole pierced at one side on which
a pencil could be hung, or by which they could be
suspended around the neck.   An old gentleman
told me that he distinctly recalled the first time he
ever saw slates in school.   The master brought in
a score that had been ordered to supply his pupils.
He asked if any scholar had a bit of string.   My
old gentleman thrust his hand in his pocket and
confidingly brought out his best fishing-line.   The
master took it, calmly cut it into twenty lengths,
each long enough to go around the neck of a child
and permit the slate when hung on it to lie loosely
in front of his chest.   It was a bitter blow to the
boy to witness the cruel and unexpected severing
of his beloved treasure, and he never forgot it.

In England for centuries existed the custom of
sending young children to the houses of friends,
G   relatives,

relatives, or people of some condition and state to be educated. Young boys were placed in noblemen's households to learn carving, singing, and good manners. Young girls went to learn housewifery, needlework, and etiquette. The work of these children in what would to-day be deemed the

Nathan Hale Schoolhouse

duties of upper servants was given in payment for their board and tuition. The housemistress gained a large corps of orderly, intelligent servitors ; and there was no disgrace in that day in being called a servant. In the time of Henry VII. these customs were universal. *The Italian Relation of England,* of that date, is most severe upon English parents, saying this putting away of young children, though

under

under the guise of having them taught good manners, was done really through lack of affection, through greediness. The *Paston Letters*, the *Verney Papers*, give ample proof that children of good families were thus banished.

A remnant of this custom of the " putting-forth " of children lingered in the colonies. A good education could generally be obtained only in the schools in larger towns, or in the households of learned men. The New England ministers almost universally eked out their meagre incomes by taking young lads into their homes to educate.

When at school in Andover, Josiah Quincy boarded with the minister. The boys, eight in number, slept in a large chamber with four beds, two boys in each. The fare was ample but simple ; of beef, pork, plentiful vegetables, badly baked rye and Indian bread. The minister had white bread as the brown bread gave him the heart-burn.

Children went, if possible, to the house of a kinsman. An old letter in the *Mather Papers* is from Mary Hoar. She writes " To her Esteemed Sister, Mistris Bridget Hoar at Cambridge." One sentence runs thus : —

" I presume our sonn John is left in the hands of a stranger ; which may be of some evel consequence if not timely prevented and therefore I doe look upon myself as
conserned

conserned (soe far as I am capable to diserne ye evel at such a distance) to make my request to you to prevail with my brother to receive him into your own family that he may be under your own ey. And to goe to school in the same town, where you cannot doubtless be destitute of a good schoolmaster, which might be of singular benefit to ye child."

Bridget Hoar was the daughter of Lady Alice Lisle, the martyr, and the wife of Leonard Hoar, president of Harvard College.

Another letter similar in kindly intent is this written to Henry Wolcott, at Windsor, Connecticut : —

"SALEM, April ye 6th, 1695.

" DEAR BRO^R :

" I cannot but be much concerned for your children's disadvantage in your remote livinge (tho' God has blest you with a good Estate which is likely to descend to them) the want of Education being the grand Calamity of this Country, but you have always Been offered no small advantages, besides their diet free, wch I deeme the Leest. I can only Renew the same offer which I have made tenn yeares since and annually, that if you please to send either of your daughters to my House they shall find they are welcome to spend the Summer or a year or as long as you and they please ; and they will be equally welcome to my Wife, also I think it may be to your Sons' advantage to hasten downe to the Colledge while our nephew Price is

there,

Old Brick Schoolhouse, Norwich, Connecticut

there, and if you have anything by you, that you designe
for their Cloathing, let it be made up here; Else it will
not be fit for either of them to ware. Also for the next
Winter if your Son be minded to Retire for a month or
two, as many do in the Dead Season, he may come to my
howse, and Mr. Noyes, I am sure, will be very ready to
oblige him, with the use of his Library and Stoody, he being
Remooved to his own House next weeke, and has a Tenant
in one end of it that dresses his Victualls. I shall not En-
large only to assure you that I shall be happie wherein I
may be serviceable to my father's Children and theirs. I
am Sir your very Aff. Bro^r & Servant,

"J. WOLCOTT."

It

It was the custom of the wealthy planters of the island of Barbadoes to send their children to New England, usually to Boston, to school.   At one time a special school flourished there for the education of the sons of these planters.   Several volumes of letter books of Hon. Hugh Hall, Judge of the Admiralty, are in the possession of his descendant, Miss Margaret Seymour Hall.   He had occasional charge of his younger brothers and sisters, who were sent to Boston from the Barbadoes, and his letters frequently refer to them.   Many of these letters are to and from his grandmother, Madam Lydia Coleman, the daughter of the old Indian fighter, Captain Joshua Scottow.   She had three husbands, — Colonel Benjamin Gibbs, Attorney General Anthony Checkley, and William Coleman.

Richard Hall came to Boston in 1718.   His older brother writes : —

" This Northern Air seems well calculated for Richard's Temperament of body and I am Psuaded he never appeared so Fat and Sanguine while in Barbados.   I am taking all Imaginable Care in Placing him at our best Grammar School and have desir'd the Master and Usher to treat him with the highest Tenderness, Intimating he has a Capacity to go thro ye Exercises of ye School & that a Mild and good Natur'd Treatment will best prevail ; who have promised me their Pticular favour to him."

A

A few months later the grandmother writes in various letters : —

" Richard is well in health, and minds his Learning and likes our Cold country better than I do. . . . I delivered Richard's Master, Mr. Williams, 25 lbs. Cocoa. I spoke with him a little before and asked him what he expected for Richard's schooling. He told me 40 shillings a yeare. As for Richard since I told him I would write to his Father he is more orderly, & he is very hungry, and has grown so much yt all his Clothes is too Little for him. He loves his book and his play too. I hired him to get a Chapter of ye Proverbs & give him a penny every Sabbath day, & promised him 5 shillings when he can say them all by heart. I would do my duty by his soul as well as his body. . . . I hope he does consider ye many inconveniences . yt will attend him if he wont be ruled. He has grown a good boy and minds his School and Lattin and Dancing. He is a brisk Child & grows very Cute and wont wear his new silk coat yt was made for him. He wont wear it every day so yt I don't know what to do with it. It wont make him a jackitt. I would have him a good husbander but he is but a child. For shoes, gloves, hankers & stockens, they ask very deare, 8 shillings for a paire & Richard takes no care of them. . . . I put him in mind of writing but he tells me he don't know what to write."

Then comes Richard's delightful effusion : —

" Boston,

" Boston, New England, July 1, 1719.

" Honour'd Sir :

"I would have wrote now but to tell ye Truth I do not know what to write for I have not had a letter from you since Capt. Beale, and I am very sorry I can't write to you but I thought it my Duty to write these few lines to you to acquaint you of my welfare, and what proficiency I have made in Learning since my Last to you. My Master is very kind to me. I am now in the Second Form, am Learning Castalio and Ovid's Metamorphosis & I hope I shall be fit to go to College in two Years time which I am resolved to do, God willing and by your leave, I shant detain you any longer but only to give my Duty to your good self & Mother & love to my Brothers & Sisters. Please to give my Duty to my God father and to my Uncle & Aunt Adamson & love to Cozen Henry,

" Your dutifull Son,
" Richard Hall."

Soon another letter goes to the father : —

" Richard wears out nigh 12 paire of shoes a year. He brought 12 hankers with him and they have all been lost long ago ; and I have bought him 3 or 4 more at a time. His way is to tie knottys at one end & beat ye Boys with them and then to lose them & he cares not a bit what I will say to him."

Mothers and guardians of the present day who have sent boys off to the boarding school with ample

ple store of neatly marked underclothing, stockings, and handkerchiefs, and had them return at the holidays nearly bereft of underwear, bearing stockings with feet existing only in outlines, and possessing but two or three handkerchiefs, these in dingy wads at the bottom of coat-pockets and usually marked with some other scholar's name — such can sympathize with poor, thrifty old lady Coleman, when naughty Richard tied his good new handkerchiefs in knots, beat his companions, and recklessly threw the knotted strings away.

CHAPTER IV

WOMEN TEACHERS AND GIRL SCHOLARS

A godly young Woman of special parts, who was fallen into a sad infirmity, the loss of her understanding and reason, which had been growing upon her divers years by occasion of giving herself wholly to reading and writing and had written many books. Her husbande was loath to grieve hir; but he saw his error when it was too late. For if she had attended to her household affairs, and such things as belong to women, and not gone out of hir way and calling to meddle in such things as are proper for men whose minds are stronger, she had kept hir Wits, and might have improved them usefully and honorably.
— History of New England. Governor John Winthrop, 1640.

WHILE the education of the sons of the planters in all the colonies was bravely provided and supported, the daughters fared but poorly. The education of a girl in book learning was deemed of vastly less importance than her instruction in household duties. But small arrangement was made in any school for her presence, nor was it thought desirable that she should have any very varied knowledge. That she should read and write was certainly satisfactory, and cipher a little;

little; but many girls got on very well without the ciphering, and many, alas! without the reading and writing.

There had been a time when English girls and English gentlewomen had eagerly studied Latin and Greek; and wise masters, such as Erasmus and Colet and Roger Ascham had told with pride of their intelligent English girl scholars; but all that had passed away with the "good old times." In the seventeenth century English gentlemen looked with marked disfavor on learned women.

Sir Ralph Verney, who adored his own little daughters to the neglect of his sons, and was tender, devoted, and generous to every little girl of his acquaintance, wrote about the year 1690 to a friend: —

" Let not your girle learn Latin or short hand; the difficulty of the first may keep her from that Vice, for soe I must esteem it in a woeman; but the easinesse of the other may bee a prejudice to her; for the pride of taking sermon noates hath made multitudes of woemen most unfortunate. Had St. Paul lived in our Times I am confident hee would have fixt a *Shame* upon our woemen for writing as well as for speaking in church."

Occasionally an intelligent father would carefully teach his daughters. President Colman of Harvard
was

was such a father.   He gave what was called a profound education to his daughter Jane.   A letter of his to her, when she was ten years old, is worthy of full quotation : —

"MY DEAR CHILD: —

"I have this morning your Letter which pleases me very well and gives me hopes of many a pleasant line from you in Time to come if God spare you to me and me to you.   I very much long to see your Mother but doubt whether the weather will permit to-day.   I pray God to bless you and make you one of his Children.   I charge you to pray daily, and read your Bible, and fear to sin.   Be very dutiful to your Mother, and respectful to everybody. Be very humble and modest, womanly and discreet.   Take care of your health and as you love me do not eat green apples.   Drink sparingly of water, except the day be warm. When I last saw you, you were too shamefaced ; look people in the face, speak freely and behave decently.   I hope to bring Nabby in her grandfather's Chariot to see you. The meanwhile I kiss your dear Mother, and commend her health to the gracious care of God, and you with her to His Grace.   Give my service to Mr. A. and family and be sure you never forget the respect they have honoured you with.   "Your loving father.

"BOSTON, Aug. 1, 1718."

Jonathan Edwards was an only son with ten sisters.   In 1711, when he was eight years old, five of these

these sisters had been born. The father, Timothy Edwards, went as chaplain on an expedition to Canada. His letters home show his care and thought for his children, girls and boy : —

" I desire thee to take care that Jonathan dont lose what he hath learnt, but that as he hath got the accidence and about two sides of Propria quæ maribus by heart, so that he keep what he hath got I would therefore have him say pretty often to the girls. I would also have the girls keep what they have learnt of the Grammar, and get by heart as far as Jonathan hath learnt ; he can keep them as far as he had learnt. And would have both him and them keep their writing, and therefore write much oftener than they did when I was at home. I have left paper enough for them which they may use to that end."

Conditions remained the same throughout the century. The wife of President John Adams, born in 1744, the daughter of a New England minister of good family and social position, doubtless had as good an education as any girl of her birth and station. She writes in 1817 : —

" My early education did not partake of the abundant opportunities which the present days offer, and which even our common country schools now afford. I never was sent to any school. I was always sick. Female education, in the best families, went no further than writing and
arithmetic ;

arithmetic; in some few and rare instances music and dancing."

On another occasion she said that female education had been everywhere neglected, and female learning ridiculed, and she speaks of the trifling, narrow, contracted education of American women.

Girls in the other colonies fared no better than New England damsels. The instruction given to girls of Dutch and English parentage in New York was certainly very meagre. Mrs. Anne Grant wrote an interesting account of her childhood in Albany, New York, in a book called *Memoir of an American Lady*. The date was the first half of the eighteenth century. She said : —

" It was at that time very difficult to procure the means of instruction in those districts; female education was in consequence conducted on a very limited scale; girls learned needlework (in which they were indeed both skilful and ingenious), from their mothers and aunts; they were taught, too, at that period to read, in Dutch, the Bible, and a few Calvinistic tracts of the devotional kind. But in the infancy of the settlement few girls read English; when they did they were thought accomplished; they generally spoke it, however imperfectly, and a few were taught writing."

William Smith wrote in 1756 that the schools in New York then were of the lowest order, the teachers

teachers ignorant, and women, especially, ill-educated. It was the same in Virginia. Mary Ball, the mother of George Washington, wrote from her Virginia home when fifteen years old : —

" We have not had a schoolmaster in our neighborhood till now in nearly four years. We have now a young minister living with us who was educated at Oxford, took orders and came over as assistant to Rev. Kemp. The parish is too poor to keep both, and he teaches school for his board. He teaches Sister Susie and me and Madam Carter's boy and two girls. I am now learning pretty fast."

The *Catechism of Health*, an old-time child's book, thus summarily and definitely sets girls in their proper places : —

" *Query :* Ought female children to receive the same education as boys and have the same scope for play ?

" *Answer :* In their earlier years there should be no difference. But there are shades of discretion and regards to propriety which judicious and prudent guardians and teachers can discern and can adjust and apply."

We seldom find any recognition of girls as pupils in the early public schools. Sometimes it is evident that they were admitted at times not devoted to the teaching of boys. For instance, in May, 1767, a school was advertised in Providence for teaching writing and arithmetic to " young ladies." But the
girls

girls had to go from six to half-past seven in the morning, and half-past four to six in the afternoon. The price for this most inconvenient and ill-timed schooling was two dollars a quarter. It is pathetic to read of a learning-hungry little maid in Hatfield, Massachusetts, who would slip away from her spinning and knitting and sit on the schoolhouse steps to listen with eager envy to the boys as they recited within. When it became popular to have girls attend public schools, an old farmer on a country school committee gave these matter-of-fact objections to the innovation. "In winter it's too far for girls to walk; in summer they ought to stay at home to help in the kitchen."

The first school for girls only, where they were taught in branches not learned in the lower schools, was started in 1780 in Middletown, Connecticut, by a graduate of Yale College named William Woodbridge. Boston girls owed much to a famous teacher, Caleb Bingham, who came to that city in 1784 and advertised to open a school where girls could be taught writing, arithmetic, reading, spelling, and English grammar. His school was eagerly welcomed, and it prospered. He wrote for his girl pupils the famous *Young Lady's Accidence*, referred to in another chapter, and under his teaching " newspapers were to be introduced in the school

at

at the discretion of the master." This is the first instance — I believe in any country — of the reading of newspapers being ordered by a school committee.

There were always dame-schools, which were attended by small boys and girls. Rev. John Barnard, of Marblehead, Massachusetts, was born in 1681 and was educated in Boston. He wrote in his old age a sketch of his school life. He says : —

" By that time I had a little passed my sixth year I had left my reading school, in the latter part of which my mistress had made me a sort of usher appointing me to teach some children that were older than myself as well as some smaller ones. And in which time I had read my Bible through thrice. My parents thought me to be weakly because of my thin habit and pale countenance."

The penultimate sentence of this account evidently accounts for the ultimate. It also appears that this unnamed school dame practised the monitorial system a century or more before Bell and Lancaster made their claims of inventing it.

The pay of women teachers who taught the dame-schools was meagre in the extreme. The town of Woburn, Massachusetts, reached the lowest ebb of salary. In 1641 a highly respected widow, one

one Mrs. Walker, kept a school in a room of her own house. The town agreed to pay her ten shillings for the first year; but after deducting seven shillings for taxes, and various small amounts for produce, etc., she received finally from the town *one shilling and three pence* for her pedagogical work.

Elizabeth Wright was the first teacher in the town of Northfield, Massachusetts. She taught a class of young children at her own house for twenty-two weeks each summer; for this she received fourpence a week for each child. At this time she had four young children of her own. She took all the care of them and did all the work of her household, made shirts for the Indians for eightpence each, and breeches for Englishmen for one shilling sixpence a pair, and wove much fine linen to order. For the summer school at Franklin, Connecticut, in 1798, "a qualified woman teacher" had but sixty-seven cents a week pay. Men teachers who taught both girls and boys usually had better pay; but Samuel Appleton, in later life the well-known Boston merchant and philanthropist, was my great-grandfather's teacher in the year 1786. His pay was his board, lodging, and washing, and sixty-seven cents per week, and it was deemed liberal and ample.

There were always in the large cities small classes where

Elizabeth Storer, Twelve Years Old, 1738

where favored girls could be taught the rudiments of an education, and there were many private teachers who taught young misses.   Boston gentlewomen from very early days had a mode of eking out a limited income by taking little girls and young ladies from country homes, especially from the southern colonies and the Barbadoes, to board while they attended these classes and recited to these teachers.

Many honored New England names appear among the advertisements of those desiring boarders.   Mrs. Deming wrote to her niece, Anna Green Winslow, telling her of two boarders she had : —

"Had I time and spirits I could acquaint you of an expedition the two sisters made to Dorchester, a walk begun at sunrise last Thursday morning — dress'd in their dammasks, padusoy, gauze, ribbins, flapetts, flowers, new white hats, white shades, and black leather shoes (Paddington's make) and finish'd, journey, garments, orniments and all quite finish'd on Saturday before noon (mud over shoes) never did I behold such destruction in so short a space — bottom of padusoy coat fring'd quite around, besides places worn entire to floss, and besides frays, dammask from shoulders to bottom not lightly soil'd, but as if every part had rub'd tables and chairs that had long been us'd to wax mingl'd with grease.

" I could have cried, for I really pitied em — nothing left fit to be seen.   They had leave to go, but it never

entered

entered anyone's tho'ts but their own to be dressed in all
(even to loading) of their best.   What signifies it to worry
ourselves about beings that are and will be just so?. I can,
and do, pity and advise, but I shall get no credit by such-
like.   The eldest talks much of learning dancing, musick
(the spinet and guitar) embroidery, dresden, the French
tongue, &c.   The younger with an air of her own advis'd
the elder when she first mention'd French to learn first to
read English and was answer'd, ' Law, so I can well eno'
a'ready.'   You've heard her do what she calls reading, I
believe.   Poor Creature!   Well! we have a time of it!"

There is a beautifully written letter in existence
of Elizabeth Saltonstall, sent to her young daughter
Elizabeth on July 26, 1680, when the latter was
away from home and attending school.   It abruptly
begins: —

" BETTY :

" Having an opportunity to send to you, I could
doe no less than write a few lines to mind you that you
carry yourself very respectively and dutyfully to Mrs.
Graves as though she were your Mother: and likewise
respectively and loveingly to the children, and soberly in
words and actions to the servants : and be sure you keep
yourself diligently imployed either at home or at school, as
Mrs. Graves shall order you. Doe nothing without her
leave, and assure yourself it will be a great preservative from
falling into evill to keep yourself well imployed.   But with
all and in the first place make it your dayly work to pray
earnestly

earnestly to God that he would keep you from all manner of evil. Take heed of your discourse at all times that it be not vaine and foolish but know that for every idle word you must certainly give account another day. Be sure to follow your reading, omit it not one day : your father doth propose to send you some coppies that so you may follow your wrighting likewise. I shall say no more at present but only lay a strict charge upon you that you remember and practise what I have minded you of: and as you desire the blessing of God upon you either in soul or body be careful to observe the counsell of your parents and consider that they are the words of your loving and affectionate mother,

                                    " ELIZ. SALTONSTALL.

Present my best respects to Mistris Graves. Your brothers remember their love to you."

Old Madam Coleman, who had somewhat of a handful in her grandson, Richard Hall, during his school days, was given charge of his sister Sarah, in 1719, to care for and guard while she received an education. When Missy arrived from the Barbadoes she was eight years old. She brought with her a maid. The grandmother wrote back cheerfully to the parents that the child was well and brisk, as indeed she was. All the very young gentlemen and young ladies of Boston Brahmin blood paid her visits, and she gave a feast at a child's dancing party
                                                    with

with the sweetmeats left over from her sea-store.
Her stay in her grandmother's household was surprisingly brief.   She left unceremoniously and un-
bidden with her maid, and went to a Mr. Binning's
to board; she sent home word to the Barbadoes
that her grandmother made her drink water with
her meals.   Her brother wrote at once in return to
Madam Coleman : —

"We were all persuaded of your tender and hearty affection to my Sister when we recommended her to your parental
care.   We are sorry to hear of her Independence in remov-
ing from under the Benign Influences of your Wing & am
surprised she dare do it without our leave or consent or
that Mr. Binning receive her at his house before he knew how
we were affected to it.   We shall now desire Mr. Binning
to resign her with her waiting maid to you and in our Letter
to him have strictly ordered her to Return to your House.
And you may let her know before my Father took his de-
parture for London he desired me peremptorily to enjoin it,
and my Mother and myself back it with our Commands,
which we hope she wont venture to refuse or disobey."

But no brother could control this spirited young
damsel.   Three months later a letter from Madam
Coleman read thus : —

"Sally wont go to school nor to church and wants a nue
muff and a great many other things she don't need.   I tell
her fine things are cheaper in Barbadoes.   She says she will
go

go to Barbados in the Spring.   She is well and brisk, says her Brother has nothing to do with her as long as her father is alive."

Hugh Hall wrote in return, saying his daughter ought to have one room to sleep in, and her maid another, that it was not befitting children of their station to drink water, they should have wine and beer.   The grandmother was not offended with him or the children, but shielded the boy from rebuke when he was sent from one school to another ; said proudly he was " a child of great parts, ye best Dancer of any in town," and could learn as much in an hour as another in three hours.   The bill for the dancing lessons still exists.   Richard's dancing lessons for a year and a quarter cost seven pounds. Sally's for four months, two pounds.   Four months' instruction in writing (and pens, ink, and paper) was one pound seven shillings and four pence.   The entrance fee for dancing lessons was a pound apiece. Sally learned " to sew, floure, write, and dance." The brisk child grew up a dashing belle, and married Major John Wentworth, brother of Governor Benning Wentworth.   Good Brother Richard writes : —

" I heartily rejoice in Sally's good fortune and hope Molly will have her turn also, but it would not have been fair to let Sally dance barefoot which I hear Molly expected would have been done."

                                        Sister

Sister Molly married first Adam Winthrop and then Captain William Wentworth. The two sisters were left widows and lived till great old age in the famous old Wentworth House in Portsmouth, New Hampshire, both dying in 1790.

Mistress Agan Blair of Williamsburg, Virginia, married one Colonel John Banister of Petersburg; her letters, even in old age, are full of a charming freedom of description and familiarity of language, even amounting to slang, which are very unusual in correspondence of that day. They are printed in the *History of the Blair and Braxton Families.* She writes to her sister, Mrs. Braxton, of the latter's little daughter, Betsey, in the year 1769 : —

"Betsey is at work for you. I suppose she will tell you to-morrow is Dancing Day, for it is in her Thoughts by Day & her dreams by Night. Mr. Fearson was so surprised to find she knew so much of the Minuet step, and could not help asking if Miss had never been taught. So you will find she is likely to make some progress that way. Mr. Wray by reason of business has but lately taken her in hand tho' he assures me a little practice is all she wants ; her Reading I hear twice a day. And when I go out she is consigned over to my Sister Blair : we have had some few Quarrels and one Battle. Betsey and her Cousin Jenny had been fighting for several days successively & was threatened to be whipt for it as often but they did not regard

gard us.   Her Mamma & self thought it necessary to let
them see we were in earnest — if they have fought since
we have never heard of it.   She has finish'd her work'd
Tucker, but ye weather is so warm that with all ye pains I
can take with clean hands and so forth she cannot help
dirtying it a little.   I do not observe her to be fond of
negroes company, nor have I heard lately of any bad words :
chief of our Quarrels is for eating of those green Apples in
our garden and not keeping the head smooth. . . . I have
had Hair put on Miss Dolly but find it is not in my power
of complying with my promise in giving her Silk for a
Sacque and Coat.   Some of our pretty Gang broke open a
Trunk in my Absence and stole several Things of which
the Silk makes a part.   So imagine Betsey will petition you
for some.   I am much obliged for the care you have taken
to get all my Duds together, I cannot find you have neglected putting up anything for Betsey."

It will readily be seen from all these letters that
whether the little girl was taught at home or in a
private school, to " sew, floure, write, and dance "
were really the chief things she learned, usually the
only things, save deportment and elegance of carriage.   To attain an erect and dignified bearing
growing girls were tortured as in English boarding
schools by sitting in stocks, wearing harnesses, and
being strapped to backboards.   The packthread
stays and stiffened coats of " little Miss Custis "
were

were made still more unyielding by metal and wood busks; the latter made of close-grained heavy wood. These were often carved in various designs or with

Carved Busks

names and verses, or ornamented with drawings in colored inks, and made a favorite gift.

All these constrainments and accessories contributed to a certain thin-chested though erect appearance,

ance, which is notable in the portraits of girls and women painted in the past century.

The backboard certainly helped to produce an erect and dignified carriage, and was assisted by the quick, graceful motions used in wool-spinning. The daughter of the Revolutionary patriot General Nathanael Greene stated to her grandchildren that in her girlhood she sat every day with her feet in stocks, strapped to a backboard. She was until the end of her long life a straight-backed elegant dame.

Many of the portraits given in this book plainly show the reign of the backboard. The portrait of Elizabeth Storer, facing page 98, is perhaps the best example. It is authenticated as having been painted by Smibert when the subject was but twelve years old, but she is certainly a most mature-faced child.

Another straight-backed portrait, opposite page 108, is the famous one immortalized in rhyme by Dr. Oliver Wendell Holmes, that of " Dorothy Q.," the daughter of Judge Edmund Quincy. The poet's lines are more simply descriptive than any prose.

> " Grandmother's mother : her age, I guess
> Thirteen summers or something less,
> Girlish bust, but womanly air ;
> Smooth square forehead with uprolled hair.

Lips

Lips that lover has never kissed,
Taper fingers and slender wrist.
Hanging sleeves of stiff brocade,
So they painted the little maid."

" Who the painter was none may tell,
One whose best was not over well ;
Hard and dry it must be confessed,
Flat as a rose that has long been pressed.
Yet in her cheek the hues are bright,
Dainty colors of red and white ;
And in her slender shape are seen
Hint and promise of stately mien."

It would be no effort of the imagination to stretch the poet's "thirteen summers or less" to thirty summers.

Of associate interest is the portrait of Elizabeth Quincy, her sister, facing page 112. The faces, hair, and dress are similar, but the parrot is replaced by an impossible little dog. Elizabeth is somewhat fairer to look upon. Dorothy is certainly " nothing handsome." On the back of the portrait is written this inscription: " It pleased God to take Out of Life my Honor'd and dearly Belov'd Mother, Mrs Elizabeth Wendell, daughter to Honble Edmund Quincy, Esqr. March, 1746, aged 39 Years." Her brother Edmund Quincy married her husband's sister Elizabeth (thus the two Elizabeths exchanged

"Dorothy Q."   "Thirteen Summers," 1720 *circa*

exchanged surnames), and Dorothy Q. married Edward Jackson.

The desire of girls and women to be ethereal and slender, delicate and shrinking, began over a century ago, but reached a climax in the early years of this century. To effect this, severe measures were taken in girls' schools. Dr. Holmes wrote in jest, but in truth too : —

> " They braced my aunt against a board
>   To make her straight and tall,
> They laced her up, they starved her down,
>   To make her light and small.
> They pinched her feet, they singed her hair,
>   They screwed it up with pins —
> Oh, never mortal suffered more
>   In penance for her sins."

Though Madam Coleman, a Boston Puritan, told so proudly of her grandchildren's dancing, that accomplishment, or rather intregal part of a little lass's education, had not been quietly promoted in that sober city. In early years both magistrates and ministers had declaimed against it.

In 1684 Increase Mather preached a strong sermon against what he termed " Gynecandrical Dancing or that which is commonly called Mixt or Promiscuous Dancing of Men and Women, be they elder or younger Persons together." He called it
the

the great sin of the Daughters of Zion, and he bursts
forth : —

"Who were the Inventors of Petulant Dancings?
Learned men have well observed that the Devil was the
First Inventor of the impleaded Dances, and the Gentiles
who worshipped him the first Practitioners of this Art."

Of course he could not be silent as to the dancings
of Miriam and David in the Bible, but disposed of
them summarily thus, " Those Instances are not at
all to the Purpose." Preaching against dancing was
as futile as against wig-wearing ; " Horrid Bushes of
Vanity " soon decked every head, and gay young
feet tripped merrily to the sound of music in every
village and town. Dancing could not be repressed
in an age when there was so little other excitement,
so great physical activity, and so narrow a range of
conversation ; and after a time " Ordination-balls "
were given when a new minister was ordained.

Dancing was a pleasant accomplishment, and a
serious one in good society. The regard of it as a
formal function is proved by the story the Marquis
de Chastellux told of the Philadelphia Assembly.
A young lady who was up in a country dance spoke
for a moment to a friend and thus forgot her turn.
The Master of Ceremonies, Colonel Mitchell, immediately came to her side and said severely : " Give
over,

over, Miss.   Take care what you are about.   Do
you think you came here for your pleasure?"

It was a much more varied art than is ordinarily
taught to-day.   Signor Sodi taught rigadoons and
paspies in Philadelphia; John Walsh added the
Spanish fandango.   Other modish dances were
"Allemand vally's, De la cours, Devonshire jiggs,
Minuets." Complicated contra-dances were many in
number and quaint in name: The Innocent Maid,
A Successful Campaign, Priest's House, Clinton's
Retreat, Blue Bonnets, The Orange Tree.

A letter from an interesting little child shows that
dancing was deemed part of a " liberal education."

"PHILADELPHIA, March 30, 1739.

"HONOUR'D SIR :

"Since my coming up I have entered with Mr.
Hackett to improve my Dancing, and hope to make such
Progress therein as may answer to the Expense, and enable
me to appear well in any Public Company.   The great
Desire I have of pleasing you will make me the more
Assiduous in my undertaking, and I arrive at any degree of
Perfection it must be Attributed to the Liberal Education
you bestow on me.

"I am with greatest Respect, Dear Pappa,

"Yr dutiful Daughter,

"MARY GRAFTON.

"RCHD GRAFTON, ESQ.,
New Castle, Delaware."

We

We have much contemporary evidence to show that music, as a formulated study, was rarely taught till after the Revolution. But there never was a time in colonial life when music was not loved and clung to with a sentiment that is difficult of explanation, but must not be underrated.

Dr. John Earle gives in his *Microcosmographie*, the character of a Puritan woman, or a "shee-precise Hypocrite," saying "'shee suffers not her daughters to learne on the Virginalls, because of their affinity with the Organs," yet I find Judge Sewall, a true Puritan, taking his wife's virginals to be repaired. I supposed she played psalm tunes on them. Spinets and harpsichords were brought to wealthy citizens. Copies of old-time music show how very elementary were the performances on these instruments. Listeners were profoundly moved at the sound, but it would seem far from inspiring to-day.

> "The notes of slender harpsichords with tapping, twinkling quills,
> Or carrolling to a spinet with its thin, metallic thrills."

Even the "new Clementi with glittering keys" gave but a tinny sound. Girls "raised a tune," however, to these far from resonant accompaniments, and sung their ballads and sentimental ditties, unhampered by thoughts of technique and methods and

Elizabeth Quincy Wendell, 1720 *circa*

and schools.   Many of these old musical instruments are still in existence.   The harpsichord
bought for " little Miss Custis " is in its rightful
home at Mount Vernon.

By Revolutionary times, girls' boarding schools
had sprung into existence in large towns, and
certainly filled a great want.   One New England
school, haloed with romance, was kept by Mrs.
Susanna Rawson, who was an actress, the daughter of an English officer, and married to a musician.
She was also a play-writer and wrote one novel of
great popularity, *Charlotte Temple*.   Eliza Southgate
Bowne gives some glimpses of the life at this school
in her letters.   She was fourteen years when she
thus wrote to her father : —

   " HON. FATHER :

      " I am again placed at school under the tuition of
an amiable lady, so mild, so good, no one can help loving
her; she treats all her scholars with such tenderness as
would win the affection of the most savage brute.   I learn
Embroiderey and Geography at present, and wish your
permission to learn Musick. . . .   I have described one
of the blessings of creation in Mrs. Rawson, and now I
will describe Mrs. Lyman as the reverse: she is the worst
woman I ever knew of or that I ever saw, nobody knows
what I suffered from the treatment of that woman."

This Mrs. Lyman kept a boarding school at
Medford ;

   I

Medford; eight girls slept in one room, the fare was meagre, and the education kept close company with the fare.

The Moravian schools at Bethlehem, Pennsylvania, were widely popular. President John Adams wrote to his daughter of the girls' school that one hundred and twenty girls lived in one house and slept in one garret in single beds in two long rows. He says, "How should you like to live in such a nunnery?" Eliza Southgate Bowne wrote a pretty account of this school: —

"The first was merely a *sewing school*, little children and a pretty single sister about 30, with her white skirt, white short tight waistcoat, nice handkerchief pinned outside, a muslin apron and a close cap, of the most singular form you can imagine. I can't describe it. The hair is all put out of sight, turned back, and no border to the cap, very unbecoming and very singular, tied under the chin with a pink ribbon — blue for the married, white for the widows. Here was a Piano forte and another sister teaching a little girl music. We went thro' all the different school rooms, some misses of sixteen, their teachers were very agreeable and easy, and in every room was a Piano."

She also tells of the great dormitory; the beds of singular shape, high and covered; a single hanging-lamp lighted at night, with one sister walking patrol.

Though the education given to girls in these boarding

boarding schools was not very profound, they had at the close of the school year a grand opportunity of "showing-off" in a school exhibition. Mary Grafton Dulany wrote when thirteen years old to her father, from a Philadelphia school : —

"I went to Madame B.s exhibition. There were five Crowns, two principal for Eminence in Lessons, and Virtue. They were crowned in great style in the Assembly Rooms in the presence of 500 Spectators."

Mrs. Quincy wrote of a school which she attended in 1784, of what she termed " the breaking up " : —

"A stage was erected at the end of the room, covered with a carpet, ornamented with evergreens and lighted by candles in gilt branches. Two window curtains were drawn aside from the centre before it and the audience were seated on the benches of the schoolroom. The 'Search after Happiness,' by Mrs. More, 'The Milliner,' and 'The Dove,' by Madame Genlis were performed. In the first I acted Euphelia, one of the court ladies, and also sung a song intended in the play for one of the daughters of Urania, but as I had the best voice it was given to me. My dress was a pink and green striped silk, feathers and flowers decorated my head; and with bracelets on my arms and paste buckles on my shoes I thought I made a splendid appearance. The only time I ever rode in a sedan chair was on this occasion, when after being dressed at home, I was conveyed in one to Miss Ledyard's residence. Hackney coaches were then unknown in New York.

York.   In the second piece I acted the milliner and by some
strange notion of Miss Ledyard's or my own was dressed
in a gown, cap, handkerchief and apron of my mother's,
with a pair of spectacles to look like an elderly woman
—a proof how little we understood the character of a
French milliner.   When the curtain was drawn, many of
the audience declared it must be Mrs. Morton herself on
the stage.   How my mother with her strict notions and
prejudices against the theatre ever consented to such pro-
ceedings is still a surprise to me."

All parents did not approve of those exhibitions.
Major Dulany wrote with decision to his daughter
that he lamented the boldness and over-assurance
which accompanied any success in such performances, and which proceeded, he deemed, from cal-
lous feeling.

These plays were merely a revival of an old
fashion when English school children took part in
miracle plays or mysteries.   In the seventeenth
century schoolmasters took great pride in writing
exhibition plays for their pupils.   Dreary enough
these acts or interludes are.   One forced all the
characters to act "anomalies of all the
chiefest parts of grammar" — oh !
the poor lads that therein
played their
parts !

CHAPTER V

HORNBOOK AND PRIMER

To those who are in years but Babes I bow
My Pen to teach them what the Letters be,
And how they may improve their A. B. C.
Nor let my pretty Children them despise.
All needs must there begin, that would be wise,
Nor let them fall under Discouragement,
Who at their Hornbook stick, and time hath spent,
Upon that A. B. C., while others do
Into their Primer or their Psalter go.

— *A Book for Boys and Girls, or Country Rhimes for Children.*
John Bunyan, 1686.

THE English philosopher, John Locke, in his *Thoughts concerning Education*, written in 1690, says the method of teaching children to read in England at that time was always "the ordinary road of Horn-book, Primer, Psalter, Testament, and Bible." These, he said, "engage the liking of children and tempt them to read." The road was the same in New England, but it would hardly be called a tempting method.

The first book from which the children of the

117   colonists

colonists learned their letters and to spell, was not
really a book at all, in our sense of the word. It
was what was called a hornbook. A thin piece of
wood, usually about four or five inches long and two
inches wide, had placed upon it a sheet of paper a
trifle smaller, printed at the top with the alphabet in
large and small letters; below were simple syllables
such as ab, eb, ib, ob, etc.; then came the Lord's
Prayer. This printed page was covered with a thin
sheet of yellowish horn, which was not as transparent as glass, yet permitted the letters to be read
through it; and both the paper and the horn were
fastened around the edges to the wood by a narrow
strip of metal, usually brass, which was tacked down
by fine tacks or nails. It was, therefore, a book
of a single page. At the two upper corners of the
page were crosses, hence to read the hornbook was
often called " reading a criss-cross row." At the
lower end of the wooden back was usually a little
handle which often was pierced with a hole; thus the
hornbook could be carried by a string, which could
be placed around the neck or hung by the side.

When, five years ago, was published my book
entitled *Customs and Fashions in Old New England,*
I wrote that I did not know of the preservation of
a single hornbook in America; though for many
years eager and patient antiquaries, of English and
of

Hornbook owned by Mrs. Anne Robinson Minturn

of American blood, had vainly sought in American historical collections, in American libraries, in American rural homes, for a true American hornbook; that is, one studied by American children of colonial times. The publication of my statement has made known to me three American hornbooks. The first is the shabby little treasure owned by Mrs. Anne Robinson Minturn of Shoreham, Vermont, found hidden under the dusty eaves of a Vermont garret. The illustration shows its exact size. On the back is a paper coarsely stamped in red with a portrait of Charles II., king of England, on horseback. This may indicate its age, but not its exact date. The young colonist who owned it was by this print taught loyalty to the Crown, though in a far land.

The second hornbook is owned by Miss Grace L. Gordon of Flushing, Long Island. It is a family heirloom, having come to its present owner through a great-uncle who was born in 1782, and stated that it was used by his father, who was born in 1736. The tablet is of oak, and the back is covered with a red paper stamped with the design of a double-headed eagle. The third, owned by Mrs. John W. Norton of Guildford, Connecticut, is almost precisely like Miss Gordon's, and is equally well preserved.

From

From these shabby little relics and from thousands of their ill-printed, but useful kinsfolk, childish

Hornbook owned by Miss Gordon

lips in America first read aloud the letters, pointed
firmly out by a knitting needle in some dame's
hand.

hand. Undisturbed by kindergarten inductions and suggestions, unbewildered by baleful processes and diagrams, unthreatened by scientific principles of instruction, did the young colonists stoutly shout their a-b abs, did they spell out their prayer, did they read in triumphal chorus their criss-cross row. Isn't it strange that these three lonely little ghosts of old-time schooling should be the only representatives of their regiments of classmates? Wouldn't it seem that tender association, or miserly hoarding, or even forgetful neglect would have made some greater salvage from the vast number of hornbooks sent to this country in the century after its settlement; that by intent or accident many scores would have survived? But these are all; three little battered oaken backs and stubby handles, three faded paper slips, a splintered sheet or two of horn, a few strips of brass tape, a score of tiny hand-wrought nails — all poor things enough, but shaping themselves into precious and treasured relics. Another of their kindred, a penny hornbook, proved its present value at a sale in London in 1893, by fetching the far from ignoble sum of sixty-five pounds.

One of these little hornbooks filled in its single self what has become a vast item in public school expenses. As Mr. Martin wittily expresses it, " it

was

was in embryo all that the Massachusetts statutes now designate by the formal phrase ' text-books and supplies.' "

The knitting needle of the schooldame could be dignified by the pompous name of fescue, a pointer ; and something of that nature, a straw, a pin, a quill, a skewer of wood, was always used to direct children's eyes to letter or word.

There certainly were plenty of these humble little engines of instruction in America ; old Judge Sewall had them for his fourteen children at the end of the seventeeth century, as we know from his diary ; he wrote in 1691 of his son Joseph going to school " his cousin Jane accompanying him, carrying his horn-book." Waitstill Winthrop sent them to his little Connecticut Plantation nieces in 1716. It is told of one zealous Puritan minister that hating the symbolism of the cross he blotted it out of the criss-cross row of a number of hornbooks imported to Boston.

" Gilt horns " were sold in Philadelphia with Bibles and Primers, as we learn from the *Pennsylvania Gazette* of December 4, 1760, and in New York in 1753, so says the *New York Gazette* of May 14, of that year. Pretty little lesson-toys, these gilded horns must have proved, but not so fine as the hornbooks of silver and ivory used by young

misses

misses of quality in England.   Scores of pictures by
seventeenth-century artists — on canvas and glass –

Back of Hornbook

show demure little maids and masters with hanging
hornbooks.   Even the pictures of the Holy Family

ily show the infant Christ, hornbook in hand, tenderly taught by the Virgin Mother.

The hornbook was called by other names, horngig, horn-bat, battledore-book, absey-book, etc.; and in Dutch it was the *a-b-boordje*. They were worked in needlework, and written in ink, and stamped on tin and carved in wood, as well as printed, and Prior tells in rhyme of a hornbook, common enough in England, which must have proved eminently satisfactory to the student.

> "To master John the English maid
> A horn-book gives of gingerbread ;
> And that the child may learn the better,
> As he can name, he eats the letter."

To this day in England, at certain Fairs and in Kensington bake-shops, these gingerbread hornbooks are made and sold in spite of the solemn warning of British moralists — " No liquorish learning to thy babes extend."   Still

> " All the letters are digested,
> Hateful ignorance detested."

I have seen in New England what were called " cookey-moulds," which were of heavy wood incised with the alphabet, were of ancient Dutch manufacture, and had been used for making those " koeckje " hornbooks.

The

The ROYAL BATTLEDORE: Being the first Introductory Part of the Circle of the Sciences, &c. Publish'd by the KING's AUTHORITY.

LONDON: Printed by J. Newbery, in St. Paul's Church-Yard, and B. Collins, in Sarum, Pr. 2d. Also the Royal Primer, or second Book for Children, Price 3d. bound, adorn'd with Cuts.

He that ne'er learns his A B C,

abcdefghijklmno
pqrstuvwxyz.
ABCDEFGHIJKLMN
OPQRSTUVWXYZ.

ff fi fl ffi ffl ff ct &,

a e i o u y.
ab eb ib ob ub | ba be bi bo bu
ac ec ic oc uc | ca ce ci co cu
ad ed id od ud | da de di do du

IN the Name of the FA-THER, and of the SON, and of the HOLY GHOST. A-men.

I Pray God to bless my Fa-ther and Mo-ther, Bro-thers and Sisters, and all my good Friends, and my E-ne-mies. A-men.

O UR Father which art in Hea-ven, hal-low-ed be thy Name; thy King-dom come; thy Will be done on Earth as it is in Heaven. Give us this Day our daily Bread; and forgive us our Tref-passes, as we for-give them that tref-pass a-gainst us; and lead us not in-to Temp-tation, but deliver us from Evil; for thine is the King-dom, the Power and the Glo-ry, for e-ver and e-ver. A-men. 1 2 3 4 5 6 7 8 9 0.

But he that learns these Letters fair,

For ever will a Blockhead be.

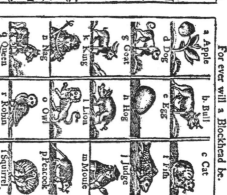

a Apple   b Bull   c Cat
d Dog   e Egg   f Fish
g Goat   h Hog   i Judge
k King   l Lion   m Mouse
n Nag   o Owl   p Peacock
q Queen   r Robin   t Squirrel
t Top   v Vine   w Whale
x Xerxes   y Young Lamb   z Zani

Shall have a Coach to take the Air

The sight of an old hornbook must always be of interest to any one of any power of imagination or of thoughtful mind, who can read between the irregular lines, the ill-shapen letters, its true significance as the emblem, the well-spring of English education and literature. This thought of the symbolism of the hornbook is expressed in quaint words on the back of a shabby battered specimen of questionable age in the British Museum : —

"What more could be wished for even by a literary Gourmand under the Tudors than to be able to Read and Spell; to repeat that holy Charm before which fled all unholy Ghosts, Goblins, or even the Old Gentleman himself, to the very bottom of the Red Sea ; to say that immortal Prayer which seems Heaven to all who *ex animo* use it ; and to have those mathematical powers by knowing units, from which spring countless myriads."

For a fuller account of the hornbook, readers should go to the *History of the Hornbook*, by Andrew W. Tuer, two splendid volumes forming one of the most interesting and exhaustive accounts of any special educational topic that has ever been written.

The printed cardboard battledore was a successor of the hornbook. This was often printed on a double fold of stiff card with a third fold or flap lapping
over

over like an old pocket-book. These battledores were issued in such vast numbers that it is futile to attempt even to allude to the myriad of publishers. An affine of the hornbook is seen in the wooden "reading-boards" which were used a hundred years ago in Erasmus Hall, the famous old academy built in 1786 in Flatbush, Long Island. It is still standing and still used for educational purposes. These "reading-boards" are tablets of wood, fifteen inches long, covered on either side with time-yellowed paper printed in large letters with some simple reading-lesson. The old fashioned long *s* in the type proves their age. Through a pierced hole a loop of string suspended these boards before a class of little scholars, who doubtless all read in chorus. Similar ones bearing the alphabet are still used in Cornish Sunday-schools. They were certainly used in Dutch schools, two centuries ago, as the illustrations of old Dutch books prove.

A prymer or primer was specifically and ecclesiastically before and after the Reformation in England a book of private devotions. As authorized by the Church, and written or printed partially or wholly in the vernacular, it contained devotions for the hours, the Creed, Lord's Prayer, Ten Commandments, some psalms and certain instructions as to the elements of Christian knowledge. These little books

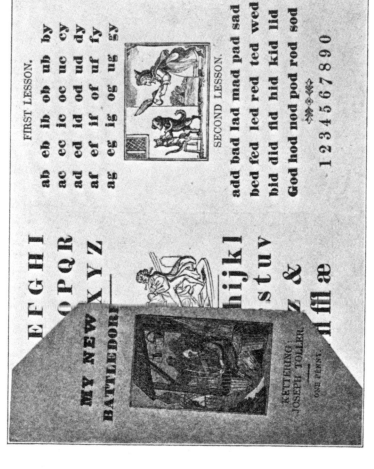

"My New Battledore"

books often opened with the criss-cross row or
alphabet arranged hornbook fashion, hence the term
primer naturally came to be applied to all element-

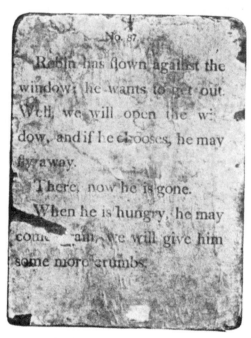

Reading Board. Erasmus Hall

ary books for children's use. A, B, C, the Middle-
English name for the alphabet in the forms apsey,
abce, absie, etc., was also given to what we now call
a primer. Shakespeare called it absey-book. The
list in *Dyves Pragmaticus* runs : —

"I

" I have inke, paper and pennes to lode with a barge,
Primers and abces and books of small charge,
What Lack you Scollers, come hither to me."

The book which succeeded the hornbook in general use was the *New England Primer*. It was the most universally studied school-book that has ever been used in America; for one hundred years it was *the* school-book of America; for nearly another hundred years it was frequently printed and much used. More than three million copies of this *New England Primer* were printed, so declares its historian, Paul Leicester Ford. These were studied by many more millions of school-children. All of us whose great-grandparents were American born may be sure that those great-grandparents, and their fathers and mothers and ancestors before them learned to read from one of these little books. It was so religious in all its teachings and suggestions that it has been fitly called the " Little Bible of New England."

It is a poorly printed little book about five inches long and three wide, of about eighty pages. It contains the alphabet, and a short table of easy syllables, such as a-b ab, e-b eb, and words up to those of six syllables. This was called a syllabarium. There were twelve five-syllable words; of these five were *abomination, edification, humiliation, mortification,* and *purification.*

purification. There were a morning and evening prayer for children, and a grace to be said before meat. Then followed a set of little rhymes which have become known everywhere, and are frequently quoted. Each letter of the alphabet is illustrated with a blurred little picture. Of these, two-thirds represent Biblical incidents. They begin : —

> " In Adam's fall
> We sinned all,"

and end with Z : —

> " Zaccheus he
> Did climb a tree
> His Lord to see."

In the early days of the Primer, all the colonies were true to the English king, and the rhyme for the letter K reads : —

> " King Charles the Good
> No man of blood."

But by Revolutionary years the verse for K was changed to : —

> " Queens and Kings
> Are Gaudy Things."

Later verses tell the praise of George Washington. Then comes a series of Bible questions and answers; then an " alphabet of lessons for youth," consisting of verses of the Bible beginning successively with A, B, C, and so on. X was a difficult initial letter, and had

x   to

to be contented with "Xhort one another daily, etc." After the Lord's Prayer and Apostle's Creed appeared sometimes a list of names for men and

MR. John Rogers, Minifter of the Gofpel in *London*, was the firft Martyr in Queen *Mary's* Reign, and was burnt at *Smithfield, February* 14th 1554. His Wife with nine fmall Children, and one at her Breaft. following him to the Stake; with which forrowful Sight he was not in the leaft daunted, but with woanderful Patience died courageoufly for the Gofpel of Jefus Chrift.   *Some*

John Rogers

women, to teach children to spell their own names. The largest and most interesting picture was that of the burning at the stake of John Rogers; and after this a six page set of pious rhymes which the

martyr

martyr left at his death for his family of small children.

After the year 1750, a few very short stories were added to its pages, and were probably all the children's stories that many of the scholars of that day ever saw. It is interesting to see that the little prayer so well known to-day, beginning " Now I lay me down to sleep," is usually found in the *New England Primer* of dates later than the year 1737. The *Shorter Catechism* was, perhaps, the most important part of this primer. It was so called in contrast to the catechism in use in England called *The Careful Father and Pious Child*, which had twelve hundred questions with answers. The *Shorter Catechism* had but a hundred and seven questions, though some of the answers were long. Usually another catechism was found in the primer, called *Spiritual Milk for Babes*. It was written by the Boston minister, John Cotton, and it had but eighty-seven questions with short answers. Sometimes a *Dialogue between Christ, Youth, and the Devil* was added.

The *Shorter Catechism* was the special delight of all New Englanders. Cotton Mather called it a " little watering pot" to shed good lessons. He begged writing masters to set sentences from it to be copied by their pupils ; and he advised mothers

to

to "continually drop something of the Catechism on their children, as Honey from the Rock." Learning the catechism was enforced by law in New England, and the deacons and ministers visited and examined families to see that the law was obeyed. Thus it may plainly be seen that this primer truly filled the requisites of what the Roxbury school trustees called "scholastical, theological, and moral discipline."

CHAPTER VI

The most worthless book of a bygone day is a record worthy of preservation. Like a telescopic star, its obscurity may render it unavailable for most purposes, but it serves in hands which know how to use it to determine the places of more important bodies.

— *A. de Morgan, 1847.*

WHEN any scholar could advance beyond hornbook and primer he was ready for grammar. This was not English grammar, but Latin, and the boy usually began to study it long before he had any book to con. A bulky and wretched grammar called Lilly's was most popular in England. Locke said the study of it was a religious observance without which no scholar was orthodox. It named twenty-five different kinds of nouns and devoted twenty-two pages of solid print to declensions of nouns ; it gave seven genders, with fifteen pages of rules for genders and exceptions. Under such a régime we can sympathize with Nash's outburst, "Syntaxis and prosodia ! you are

tormentors

tormentors of wit and good for nothing but to get schoolmasters twopence a week."

It was said of Ezekiel Cheever, the old Boston schoolmaster, who taught for over seventy years, "He taught us Lilly and he Gospel taught." But he also wrote a Latin grammar of his own, *Cheever's Accidence*, which had unvarying popularity for over a century. Cheever was a thorough grammarian. Cotton Mather thus eulogized him : —

> "Were Grammar quite extinct, yet at his Brain
> The Candle might have well been Lit again."

There was brought forth at his death a broadside entitled *The Grammarian's Funeral*. A fac-simile of it is here given. Josiah Quincy, later in life the president of Harvard College, wrote an account of his dismal school life at Andover. He entered the school when he was six years old, and on the form by his side sat a man of thirty. Both began *Cheever's Accidence*, and committed to memory pages of a book which the younger child certainly could not understand, and no advance was permitted till the first book was conquered. He studied through the book twenty times before mastering it. The hours of study were long — eight hours a day — and this upon lessons absolutely meaningless.

The

The Grammarians Funeral.

OR,

An ELEGY compofed upon the Death of Mr. *John Woodmancy*,
formerly a School-Mafter in *Bofton* : But now Publifhed upon
the DEATH of the Venerable

Mr. Ezekiel Chevers,

The late and famous School-Mafter of *Bofton* in *New-England* ; Who Departed this Life the
Twenty-firft of *Auguft* 1 7 0 8. Early in the Morning. In the Ninety-fourth Year of his Age.

Eight Parts of *Speech* this Day wear *Mourning Gowns*
Declin'd *Verbs, Pronouns, Participles, Nouns.*
And not declined, *Adverbs* and *Conjunctions,*
In *Lillies* ! orch they ftand to do their functions.
With *Prepofition* ; but the moft affection
Was ftill obferved in the *Interjection.*
The *Subftantive* feeming the limbed beft,
Would fet an hand to bear him to his Reft.
The *Adjective* with very grief did fay,
Hold me by ftrength, or I fhall faint away.
The Clouds of Tears did over-caft their faces,
Yea all were in moft lamentable *Cafes.*
The five *Declenfions* did the Work decline,
And *Told* the *Pronoun Tu*, The work is thine :
But in this cafe thofe have no call to go
That want the *Vocative*, and can't fay O !
The *Pronouns* faid that if the *Nouns* were there,
There was no need of them, they might them fpare :
But for the fake of *Emphafis* they would,
In their Difcretion do what ere they could.
Great honour was confer'd on *Conjugations,*
They were to follow next to the *Relations.*
Amo did love him beft, and *Doceo* might
Alledge he was his Glory and Delight.
But *Lego* faid by me he got his fkill,
And therefore next the *Herfe* I follow will.
Audio faid little, hearing them fo hot,
Yet knew by him much Learning he had got.
O *Verbs* the *Active* were, Or *Paffive* fure,
Sum to be *Neuter* could not well endure:
But this was common to them all to Moan
Their load of grief they could not foon *Depone.*
A doleful Day for *Verbs*, they look fo *moody,*
They drove Spectators to a Mournful Study.
The *Verbs* irregular, 'twas thought by fome,
Would break no rule, if they were pleas'd to come.
Gaudeo could not be found ; fearing difgrace
He had with-drawn, fent *Mæreo* in his Place.
Poffum did to the utmoft he was able,
And bore as Stout as if he'd been A *Table.*

Volo was willing, *Nolo* fome-what ftout,
But *Malo* rather chofe, not to ftand out.
Poffum and *Volo* wifh'd all might afford
Their help, but had not an *Imperative Word.*
Edo from Service would by no means Swerve,
Rather than fail, he thought the *Cakes* to Serve.
Fio was taken in a fit, and faid,
By him a Mournful *P O E M* fhould be made.
Fero was willing for to bear a part,
Altho' he did it with an aking heart.
Feror excus'd, with grief he was fo Torn,
He could not bear, he needed to be born.
Such *Nouns* and *Verbs* as we defective find,
No *Grammar* Rule did their attendance bind.
They were excepted, and exempted hence,
But *Supines*, all did blame for negligence.
Verbs Offspring, *Participles*, hand-in-hand,
Follow, and by the fame direction ftand :
The reft Promifcuoufly did croud and cumber,
Such Multitudes of each, they wanted Number.
Next to the Corps to make th' attendance even,
Jove, Mercury, Apollo came from heaven.
And *Virgil*, *Cato*, gods, men, Rivers, Winds,
With *Elegies*, Tears, Sighs, came in their kinds.
Ovid from *Pontus* haft's Apparrell'd thus,
In Exile-weeds bringing *De Triftibus* :
And *Homer* fure had been among the Rout,
But that the Stories fay his Eyes were out.
Queens, Cities, Countries, Iflands, Come
All Trees, Birds, Fifhes, and each Word in *Um.*
What *Syntax* here can you expect to find ?
Where each one bears fuch difcompofed mind.
Figures of Diction and Conftruction,
Do little : Yet ftand fadly looking on.
That fuch a Train may in their motion *chord,*
Profodia gives the meafure Word for Word.

Sic Mæftus Cecinit,

Benj. Tompfon.

The custom was in Boston — until this century — to study through the grammar three times before any application to parsing.

Far better wit than any found in an old-time jest book was the sub-title of a very turgid Latin grammar, " A delysious Syrupe newly Claryfied for Yonge Scholars yt thurste for the Swete Lycore of Latin Speche."

The first English Grammar used in Boston public schools and retained in use till this century, was *The Young Lady's Accidence, or a Short and Easy Introduction to English Grammar, design'd principally for the use of Young Learners, more especially for those of the Fair Sex, though Proper for Either.* It is said that a hundred thousand copies of it were sold. It was a very little grammar about four or five inches long and two or three wide, and had only fifty-seven pages, but it was a very good little grammar when compared with its fellows, being simple and clearly worded.

The fashion of the day was to set everything in rhyme as an aid to memory ; and even so unpoetical a subject as English Grammar did not escape the rhyming writer. In the *Grammar of the English Tongue*, a large and formidable book in fine type, all the rules and lists of exceptions and definitions were in verse. A single specimen, the definition of

a

a letter, will show the best style of composition, which, when it struggled with moods and tenses, was absolutely meaningless.

> " A Letter is an uncompounded Sound
> Of which there no Division can be Found,
> Those Sounds to Certain Characters we fix,
> Which in the English Tongue are Twenty-Six."

The spelling of that day was wildly varied. *Dilworth's Speller* was one of the earliest used, and the spelling in it differed much from that of the *British Instructor*. A third edition of *The Child's New Spelling Book* was published in 1744. Famous English lesson-books known among common folk as " Readamadeasies," and book traders as " Reading Easies " — really Reading made easy — belied their name. Some had alphabets on two pages because " One Alphabet is commonly worn out before the Scholar is perfect in his Letters." It is interesting to find " Poor Richard's " sayings in these English books, but it is natural, too, when we consider Franklin's popularity abroad, and know that broadsides printed with his pithy and worldly-wise maxims were found hanging on the wall of many an English cottage.

Not until the days of Noah Webster and his famous Spelling Book and Dictionary was there any decided uniformity of spelling. Professor Earle

says

ceeds with all her train ; warm gentle gales begin to blow, and soft falling showers moisten the earth.—The surface of the ground is adorned with young verdent flowers, the cowslip, daisy, primrose, and a thousand pleasing objects spread themselves all around; the trees put forth their green buds. and deck themselves with blossoms ; the birds fill every grove with the charming music of nature; love, tunes their little voices, and they join in pairs to build their nests with care and labour ; which, sometimes the playful, the careless, the giddy boy destroys. The careful farmer now ploughs up his fields. and casts the seeds into the bosom of the earth, and waits for harvest. Now too, the young and harmless lambs skip over the grass in wanton play ! The cuckoo sings—and all nature seems to rejoice.

Trees, which dead did late appear,
Crown with leaves the rising year ;
Ev'ry object seems to say,
Winter's gloom has pass'd away,

SUMMER.

SUMMER succeeds.—The sun now darts his beams with greater force; and the days are at the longest. The flocks and herds not being able to endure the scorching heat of the sun, retire beneath the shade of some spreading tree, or the side of some cooling stream or river. The wanton youths betake themselves to the waters and swim with pleasure over the liquid surface. Early in the morning the careful mower walks forth with his scythe on his shoulder, and sometimes with a pipe in

says the process of compelling a uniform spelling
is a strife against nature. Certainly it took a long
struggle against nature to make spelling uniform in
America. In the same letter, men of high education would spell the same word several different
ways. There was no better usage in England. The
edition of Milton's *Paradise Lost* printed in 1688
shows some very grotesque spelling. Therefore it
is not strange to find a New York teacher advertising to teach " writing and spilling."

To show that a fetich was made of spelling
seventy-five years ago, I give this extract from a
Danbury school notice : —

" The advantages that small children obtain at this school
may be easily imagined when the public are informed that
those who spell go through the whole of Webster's spelling
book twice a fortnight."

The teaching of spelling in many schools was peculiar. The master gave out the word, with a blow
of his strap on the desk as a signal for all to start
together, and the whole class spelled out the word
in syllables in chorus. The teacher's ear was so
trained and acute that he at once detected any mis-
spelling. If this happened, he demanded the name
of the scholar who made the mistake. If there was
any hesitancy or refusal in acknowledgment, he kept
the

the whole class until, by repeated trials of long words, accuracy was obtained. The roar of the many voices of the large school, all pitched in different keys, could be heard on summer days for a long distance. In many country schools the scholars not only spelled aloud but studied all their lessons aloud, as children in Oriental countries do to-day : and the teacher was quick to detect any lowering of the volume of sound and would reprove any child who was studying silently. Sometimes the combined roar of voices became offensive to the neighbors of the school, and restraining votes were passed at town-meetings.

The colonial school and schoolmaster took a firm stand on "cyphering." "The Bible and figgers is all I want my boys to know," said an old farmer. Arithmetic was usually taught without text-books. Teachers had manuscript "sum-books," from which they gave out rules and problems in arithmetic to their scholars. Abraham Lincoln learned arithmetic from a "sum-book" of which he made a neat copy. A page from this sum-book is here given in reduced size. Too often these sums were copied by the pupil without any explanation of the process being offered or rendered by the master. The artist Trumbull recalled that he spent three weeks, unaided in any way, over a single sum in long division.

A

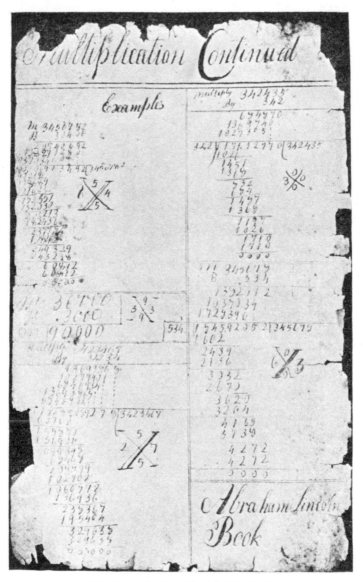

Page from Abraham Lincoln's Sum Book

. A manuscript sum-book in my possession is
marked, "Sarah Keeler her Book, May ye 1st, A.D.
1773, Ridgbury." There are multiplication examples of fifteen figures multiplied by fifteen, and
long division examples of a dividend of quintillions,
chiefly in sevens and nines, divided by a mixed
divisor of billions in eights and fives — a thing to
make poor Sarah turn in her grave. There are
Reductions Ascending and Reductions Descending
and Reductions both Ascending and Descending
at the same time, as complicated as the computa-
tions of the revolutions of the celestial spheres.
There are miserable catch-examples about people's
ages and others about collections of excises, with
" Proofs," and still others about I know not what,
for there are within their borders mysterious abbre-
viations and signs, like some black magic. Sainted
Sarah Keeler! a melancholy sympathy settles on me
as I regard this book and all the extended sums
you knew, and think of the paths of pleasantness of
the present pupils of kindergartens; and wonder
what kind of a mathematical song or game or
allegory could be invented to disguise these very
" plain figures."

Sometimes a zealous teacher would write out
tables of measures and a few blind rules for his
scholars. This amateur arithmetic would be copied
and

and recopied until it was punctuated with mistakes.

Many scholars never saw a printed arithmetic;

Cocker's
ARITHMETICK:

BEING

A plain and familiar Method, suitable to the meaneſt Capacity, for the full underſtanding of that incomparable Art, as it is now taught by the ableſt School-Maſters in City and Country.

COMPOSED

By *Edward Cocker*, late Practicioner in the Arts of Writing, Arithmetick, and Engraving. Being that ſo long ſince promiſed to the World.

PERUSED and PUBLISHED

By *John Hawkins*, Writing-Maſter near St. George's Church in *Southwark*, by the Author's correct Copy, and commended to the World by many eminent Mathematicians and Writing-Maſters in and near *London*.

This Impreſſion is corrected and amended, with many Additions throughout the whole.

Licenſed, *Sept.* 3. 1677. *Roger L'Eſtrange.*

L O N D O N,

Printed by *R. Holt*, for *T. Paſſinger*, and ſold by *John Back*, at the black Boy on *London-Bridge*, 1688.

Title Page

and when the master had one for circulation it was scarcely more helpful than the sum-book. One of the most ancient arithmetics was written by the mathematician Record, who lived from the year 1500 to 1558. He is said to have invented the sign of equality =, but there is nothing in his book to indicate this fact. The terms "arsemetrick" and "augrime" are

No. 1. First Picture Alphabet.
No. 2. Second Picture Alphabet.
No. 3. Third Picture Alphabet.

No. 4. Lessons in One Syllable.
No. 5. Lessons in Numbers.
No. 6. Words in Common Use.

One   I.   1
Two   II.   2
Three III. 3
Four   IV.   4
Five   V.   5
Six   VI.   6
Seven VII. 7
Eight VIII. 8
Nine   IX.   9
Ten   X.   10
Eleven XI.   11
Twelve XII. 12

The Clock has two hands; a long one and a short one. The short hand is the hour hand, and the long one is the minute hand.

The short or hour hand moves very slowly, and the long or minute hand goes all round the Clock face while the hour hand goes from one figure to the next one.

Two and two added together make . . . 2 | 2 | 4

One and four together make . . . . 1 | 4

Five and two together make . . . . 5 | 2

Seven and two together make . . . 7 | 1

What are eight and two?—They make . 8 | 2

Twice ten make . . . . 10 | 10

Twenty is a score, and five score . . . 20 | 5 | 100

are used in it, instead of arithmetic.   Many curious
and obsolete rules are given, among them, " The
Golden Rule," " Rule of Falsehood," " The Re-
deeming of Pawnes of Geams," " The Backer
Rule of Thirds." Here is a simple problem under
the latter : —

"I did lend my friend 3/4 of a Porteguise 7 months
upon promise that he should do as much for me again,
and when I should borrow of him, he could lend me but
5/12 of a Porteguese, now I demand how long time I
must keep his money in just Recompence of my loan,
accounting 13 months in the year."

Rhyme is used in this book, in dialogues between
the master and scholar. Copies of *Cocker's Arithmetick* are said to be very rare in England, but I
have seen several in America. An edition was published in Philadelphia in 1779. The frontispiece
of English and American editions shows the picture
of the mathematician surrounded by a wreath of
laurel with the droll apostrophe : —

"Ingenious Cocker !   Now to Rest thou 'rt Gone
Noe Art can Show thee fully but thine Own
Thy rare *Arithmetick* alone can show
What vast Sums of Thanks wee for Thy Labour owe."

"Ingenious Cocker," as one would say " Most
noble Shakespeare !" It is hard indeed to idealize or
write poetical tributes to one by the name of Cocker.
It

It gives us a sense of pleasant familiarity with any one to know that he is "well acquaint" with one of our intimate friends, so I feel much drawn to ingenious Cocker by knowing that he was well known of Sam Pepys.   He was a writing master, and did some mighty fine engraving for Pepys, who calls him ingenuous, not ingenious.   It is rather a facer to learn from the notes in the Diary that Cocker had nothing whatever to do with his Arithmetic, which was a forgery by John Hawkins.

The age that would rhyme a grammar would rhyme an arithmetic, and Record's example was followed and enlarged upon.   Thomas Hylles published one in 1620, *The Arte of Vulgar Arithmiteke*, written in dialogue, with the rules and theorems in verse.   This is an example of his poesy : —

"THE PARTITION OF A SHILLING INTO HIS ALIQUOT PARTES.

"A farthing first finds forty-eight
A Halfpeny hopes for twentiefoure
Three farthings seeks out 16 streight
A peny puls a dozen lower
Dicke dandiprat drewe 8 out deade
Twopence took 6 and went his way
Tom trip a goe with 4 is fled
But Goodman grote on 3 doth stay
A testerne only 2 doth take
Moe parts a Shilling cannot make."

In

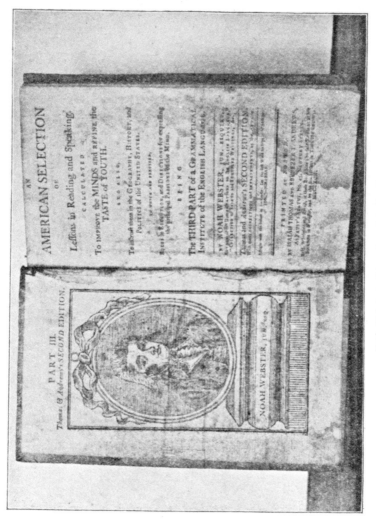

Noah Webster's "American Selection"

In 1633 Nicholas Hunt added to his rules and tables an "Arithmetike-Rithmeticall or the Handmaid's Song of Numbers," which rhymes are simply unspeakable. These attempts did not end with the seventeenth century. In 1801 Richard Vyse had a *Tutor's Guide* with problems in rhyme.

> "When first the Marriage Knot was tied
>   Between my Wife and Me
> My age did hers as far exceed
>   As three times three does three.
> But when Ten years and half ten Years
>   We man and wife had been
> Her age came up as near to mine
>   As eight is to sixteen.
> Now tell me I pray
>   What were our Ages on our Wedding Day?"

The earliest date of the old rhyme, —

> "Thirtie daies hath September, Aprill, June and November,
> Februarie eight and twentie alone, all the rest thirtie and one."

is given by Halliwell as 1633. I have found it in an old arithmetic printed in London in 1596. The lines beginning "Multiplication is vexation," are not an outburst of modern students. They are found in a manuscript dated 1570 circa.

> "Multiplication is mie vexation
>   And Division quite as bad,
> The Golden rule is mie stumbling stule,
>   And Practice makes me mad."

After

After the Revolution, in new and zealous Americanism, text-books by American authors outsold English books. The blue-backed spelling book of Noah Webster drove Perry and Dilworth from the field. Bingham and Webster took advantage of the need of suitable school-books and divided the field between them. Webster's Spelling Book outstripped Bingham's *Child's Companion*, but Bingham's Readers, such as *The American Preceptor* and *The Columbian Orator* held their ground against Webster's. Not one of Bingham's books proved a failure. *The Columbian Orator* contained seven extracts from speeches of Pitt in opposition to the measures of George III., it had speeches by Fox and Sheridan, part of the address of President Carnot at the establishment of the French Republic, and the famous speech of Colonel Barré on the Stamp Act.

Nicholas Pike of Newburyport, Massachusetts, wrote an arithmetic that routed the English books of Cocker and Hodder. It was studied by many persons now living. It had three hundred and sixty-three barren rules, and not a single explanation of one of them. Many of them would now be wholly unintelligible to scholars, though no more antiquated than are the methods; for instance, this rule in Tare and Trett: —

" Deduct

THE

William Shelton Jun.

LITTLE READER'S

ASSISTANT;

CONTAINING

I. A number of Stories, mostly taken from the history of America, and adorned with Cuts.

II. Rudiments of English Grammar.

III. A Federal Catechism, being a short and easy explanation of the

Constitution of the United States.

IV. General principles of Government and Commerce.

V. The Farmer's Catechizm, containing plain rules of husbandry.

All adapted to the capacities of children.

THE SECOND EDITION.

By NOAH WEBSTER, Jun.

Attorney at Law.

HARTFORD,

Printed by ELISHA BABCOCK,

M,DCC,XCI.

[*Published according to Act of Congress.*]

"The Little Reader's Assistant," by Noah Webster

"Deduct the Tare and Trett. Divide the Suttle by amount given; the Quotient will be the Cloff which subtract from the Suttle the Remainder will be the Neat."

The tables of measures were longer than ours to-day; in measuring liquids were used the terms anchors, tuns, butts, tierces, kilderkins, firkins, puncheons, etc. In dry measure were pottles, strikes, cooms, quarters, weys, lasts. Examples in currency were in pounds, shillings, and pence; and doubtless helped to retain the use of these terms in daily trade long after dollars had been coined in America. This labored book, aided by the flattering testimonials of Governor Bowdoin, of the Presidents of Harvard, Yale, and Dartmouth Colleges, and of that idolized American, George Washington, gained wide acceptance.

I have examined with care a *Wingate's Arithmetic* printed in 1620, which was used for over a century in the Winslow family in Massachusetts. "Pythagoras his Table," is, of course, our multiplication table. Then comes, the "Rule of Three," the "double Golden Rule," the "Rule of Fellowship," the "Rule of False," etc., etc., ending with "Pastimes, a collection of pleasant and polite Questions to exercise all the parts of Vulgar Arithmetick." Here is one : —

L   " This

"This Problem is usually propounded in this manner, viz. fifteen *Christians* and fifteen *Turks* being at Sea in one and the same Ship in a terrible Storm, & the Pilot declaring a necessity of casting the one half of those Persons into the Sea, that the rest might be saved; they all agreed that the persons to be cast away should be set out by lot after this manner, viz. the thirty persons should be placed in a round form like a *Ring*, and then beginning to count at one of the Passengers, and proceeding circularly, every ninth person should be cast into the Sea, until of the thirty persons there remained only fifteen. The question is, how those thirty persons ought to be placed, that the lot might infallibly fall upon the fifteen *Turks* & not upon any of the fifteen *Christians?* For the more easie remembering of the rule to resolve this question shall presuppose the five vowels, a, e, i, o, u, to signifie five numbers to wit, (a) one, (e) two, (i) three, (o) four, and (u) five; then will the rule it self be briefly comprehended in these two following verses: —

> From numbers, aid and art
> Never will fame depart.

In which verses you are principally to observe the vowels, with their correspondent numbers before assigned, and then beginning with the *Christians* the vowel *o* (in *from*) signifieth that four *Christians* are to be placed together; next unto them, the vowel *u* (in *num*) signifieth that five *Turks* are to be placed. In like manner *e* (in *bers*) denoteth 2 *Christians*, *a* (in *aid*) 1 *Turk*, *i* (in *aid*) 3 *Christians*, *a* (in *and*) 1 *Turk*, *a* (in *art*) 1 *Christian*, *e* (in *ne*) 2 *Turks*, *e* (in *ver*) 2 *Christians*,

tians, i (in *will*) 3 *Turks, a* (in *fame*) 1 *Christian, e* (in *fame*)
2 *Turks, e* (in *de*) 2 *Christians, a* (in *part*) 1 *Turk.*

"The invention of the said Rule and such like, de-
pendeth upon the subsequent demonstration, viz. if the
number of persons be thirty, let thirty figures or cyphers be
placed circularly or else in a right line as you see : —

oooooooooooooooo."

I trust the little Winslows and their neighbors
understood this sum, and its explanation, and that
the Christians were all saved, and the Turks were
all drowned.

Geography was an accomplishment rather than
a necessary study, and was spoken of as a diversion for a winter's evening.   Many objections were
made that it took the scholar's attention away from
"cyphering."   It was not taught in the elementary
schools till this century.   *Morse's Geography* was
not written till after the Revolution.   It had a
mean little map of the United States, only a few
inches square.   On it all the land west of the Mis-
sissippi River was called Louisiana, and nearly all
north of the Ohio River, the Northwestern Terri-
tory.   Small as the book was, and meagre as was
its information, many of its pages were devoted to
short, stilted dialogues between a teacher and pupil,
in which the scholar was made to say such priggish
sentences : —

"I

" I am very thankful, sir, for your entertaining instruction, and I shall never forget what you have been telling me.

" I long, sir, for to-morrow to come that I may hear more
of your information.

" I am truly delighted, sir, with the account you have
given me of my country.   I wish, sir, it may be agreeable
to you to give me a more particular description of the
United States.

" I hope, sir, I have a due sense of your goodness to me.
I have, sir, very cheerfully, and I trust very profitably,
attended your instructions."

A rather amusing *Geographical Catechism* was
published in 1796, by Rev. Henry Pattillo, a Pres-
byterian minister of North Carolina, for the use
of the university students.   It is properly and
Presbyterianly religious.   It gives this explanation
of comets : —

" Their uses are mere conjecture.   Some judge them
the seats of punishment where sinners suffer the extremes
of heat and cold.   Mr. Whiston says a comet approaching
the sun brushed the earth with its tail and caused the
deluge, and that another will cause the conflagration."

Let us not be too eager to jeer at these ancient
school-books.   Pope wrote nearly two centuries ago :

" Still is to-morrow wiser than to-day
We think our fathers fools so wise we grow.
Our wiser sons no doubt will think us so."

Perhaps

Perhaps the series of text-books which have chased each other in and out of our nineteenth-century public schools under the successive boards of commissioners and school committees who have also flashed briefly on our educational horizon, may cut no better figure two centuries hence than do those of
Lilly and Pike and
Cocker.

CHAPTER VII

PENMANSHIP AND LETTERS

Ink alwais good store on right hand to stand
Brown paper for great haste or else box of sand.
Dip pen and shake pen and touch pen for haire
Wax, quills and penknife see alwais ye beare.
— *A New Book of Hands, 1650 circa.*

IN glancing over old school contracts it will be noted that in a majority of cases the teacher is specified as a writing-master; without doubt the chief requisite of a satisfactory teacher in colonial days was that he should be a good teacher of penmanship.

We have seen in our own day distinct changes in the handwriting of an entire generation; the colonists whose lives ended with the seventeenth century had a characteristic handwriting which retained certain elements of old English, even of mediæval script. It was a handsome and dignified chirography and an impressive one, and was usually easy to read. The writing of the first Pilgrim and Puritan fathers was not over-good. Governor John Winthrop's

was

was not much better than Horace Greeley's. Bradford's we are familiar with through the beautiful facsimiles of his *Relation*.

The first half of the succeeding century did not send forth such good writers; nor did it send forth writers so universally; the proportion of signatures to public documents by cross instead of writing increased. Our grandparents and great-grandparents all wrote well. In hundreds of century-old letters which I have examined an ill-written letter is an exception. Children at the close of the eighteenth century wrote beautifully rounded, clear, and uniform hands, if we can judge from their copybooks. Little Anna Green Winslow, writing in 1771, showed page after page in a hand far better than that of most girls of her age to-day.

Claude Blanchard was commissary of supplies for the French army which landed in Newport in 1780. He visited the Newport school and gave this tribute to the scholars : —

"I saw the writing of these children, it appeared to me to be handsome; among others that of a young girl nine or ten years old, very pretty and very modest, and such as I would like my own daughter to be when she is so old; she was called Abigail Earle, as I perceived upon her copy-book, on which her name was written. I wrote it myself, adding to it ' very pretty.' "

An

An "exhibition piece" is here given of the penmanship of Anne Reynolds, a little girl of Norwich, Connecticut, who died shortly after this "piece" was written.

Writing-masters were universally honored in every community. A part of the funeral notice of one in Boston, who died in 1769, reads thus: —

"Last Friday morning died Mr. Abiah Holbrook in this town. He was looked upon by the best Judges as the Greatest Master of the pen we ever had among us, of which he has left a beautiful Demonstration."

This "beautiful demonstration" of his penmanship was a most intricate piece of what was known as fine knotting, or knotwork. It was said to be "written in all the known hands of Great Britain," and was valued at £100. It was bequeathed to Harvard College unless it was bought by the Revolutionary patriot, John Hancock, who had been one of Master Holbrook's pupils and, as we know from the fine bold signature of his own name to the Declaration of Independence, was a very creditable scholar.

This work had occupied every moment of what Abiah Holbrook called his "spare time" for seven years. As he had, in the year 1745, two hundred and twenty scholars at one time in one school, his
                                                        spare

Exhibition "Piece" of Anne Reynolds

spare time must have been very short. He and
other writing-masters of the Holbrook family left
behind a still nobler demonstration than this knotwork in the handwriting of their scholars — Boston
ministers, merchants, statesmen, and patriots —
whose elegant penmanship really formed a distinct
style, and was known as " Boston Style of Writing."

The " hands of Great Britain " were many in
number; among them Saxon, Old Mss., Chancery,
Gothic, Running Court, Exchequer, Pipe Office,
Engrossing, Running Secretary, Round Text, and
the " Lettre Frisee," which was minutely and regu-
larly zigzagged.

A well-known Boston writing-master was famil-
iarly known as Johnny Tileston. He was born in
1738 and taught till 1823, when he was pensioned
off. He was a rough-mannered old fellow; his
chief address to the scholars being the term, "You
gnurly wretch." His ideal was his own teacher,
Master Proctor, and when late in life he saw a
scholar wipe his pen on a bit of cloth, he approached
the desk, lifted the rag and said, " What's this ?
Master Proctor had no such thing." Tileston himself always wiped his pens with his little finger and
in turn dried his finger on his own white hairs under
his wig. An old spelling-book has these lines for a
" writing-copy " : —

" X things a penman should have near at hand —
    Paper, pomice, pen, ink, knife, horn, rule, plummet, wax,
    sand."

It will be noted that a penwiper is not upon the list.

In olden times but one kind of a pen was used, one cut from a goose-quill with the feathers left

Writing-master's Initial

on the handle. The selection and manufacture of these goose-quill pens was a matter of considerable care in the beginning, and of constant watchfulness and " mending" till the pen was worn out. One of the indispensable qualities of a colonial schoolmaster was that he was a good pen maker and pen mender. It often took the master and usher two hours to make the pens for the school. Boys studied arithmetic at eleven years of age, but were not allowed to make pens in school till they were twelve years old.

Ink was not bought in convenient liquid form as at present; each family, each person had to be an ink manufacturer. The favorite method of ink-making was through the dissolving of ink-powder. Liquid ink was but seldom seen for sale. In remote districts of Vermont, Maine, and Massachu-setts, _the PEN._

these command

ye Rank of Fame shall stand

𝕲od makes the PEN his Herald to proclaim

𝕿he Splendid Glories of his Works and Name.

Abiah Holbrook Scripsit 1767.

Writing of Abiah Holbrook

setts, home-made ink, feeble and pale, was made by steeping the bark of swamp-maple in water, boiling the decoction till thick, and diluting it with copperas. Each child brought to school an ink-bottle or ink-horn filled with the varying fluid of domestic manufacture.

A book called *The District School,* written as late as 1834, shows the indifferent quality of the ink used. The writer complains that the parents made a poor ink of vinegar, water, and ink-powder, which the child could not use, and permitted to dry up while he borrowed of the teacher. The inkstand is then " used at the evening meetings as a candlestick." Other inkstands with good ink are seized and used for the same purpose and the ink ruined with grease and nothing left to write with when the teacher sets his scholars to work.

There are no remains of olden times that put us more closely in touch with the men, women, and children who moved and lived in these shadowy days than do the letters they wrote. Old James Howell said over two centuries ago: " Letters are the Idea and the truest Miror of the Mind ; they shew the Inside of a Man." Certainly the most imaginative mind must be touched with a sense of nearness to the heart of the writer whose yellowed pages he unfolds and whose fading words he deciphers.

ciphers. The roll of centuries cannot dim the power of written words.

In the Prince Library, in Boston, are the manuscripts known under the various titles of the *Mather Papers*, the *Cotton Papers*, the *Torrey Papers*, etc. They are delightful to see and to read, for the ink is still clear and black, the paper firm and good, the letters well-formed, and the text breathes a spirit of kindness, affection, and loving thoughtfulness that speaks of the beauty of Puritan home life. Some of the letters are written by Puritan women ; and these letters are uniformly well spelt, well written, and intelligent. Perhaps only intelligent women were taught to write. These letters are on fine Dutch paper ; there was no English writing-paper till the time of William and Mary. They are carefully folded with due regard to the etiquette of letter-folding, and plainly and neatly addressed.

The letters are very tender and gentle ; sometimes they are written to children ; they begin, " My deare Child " ; " My Indear'd Sonn " ; " To my dearly loved Friend and Child." One ends, " With my Indeared Love, committing thyself and thy duty and service to all our friends, and to the protection of the Almighty, I am thine." A mother addresses on the outside her letter to her son in these words, " To my very good friend, These

These Present," etc. John Cotton addresses a letter externally thus: " These, For the Reverend, his very deare Brother, Mr. Increase Mather, Teacher of a Church at Boston, Present." Sometimes the address ran, " Messenger present these to, etc." Hence it may be seen that the word " Present " sometimes seen on modern letters properly is the imperative verb Present. Occasionally the words " Haste! post haste!" were seen, as on English letters, but I have never seen the old postal inscription, " Haste! post, haste! on your Life! on your Life!"

A very genuine and pleasing letter was written by John Quincy Adams when he was nine years old to his father, President John Adams:—

" BRAINTREE, June the 2nd, 1777.

" DEAR SIR: I love to receive letters very well, much better than I love to write them. I make but a poor figure at composition, my head is much too fickle, my thoughts are running after bird's eggs, play, and trifles till I get vexed with myself. I have but just entered the 3rd vol of Smollett tho' I had design'd to have got it half through by this time. I have determined this week to be more diligent, as Mr. Thaxter will be absent at Court, & I cannot persue my other studies. I have set myself a Stent & determine to read the 3rd Volume Half out. If I can but keep my resolution, I will write again at the end of the

week

week and give a better account of myself. I wish, Sir,
you would give me some instructions with regard to my
time & advise me how to proportion my Studies & my
Play, in writing I will keep them by me & endeavour to
follow them. I am, dear Sir, with a present determination
of growing better yours. P. S. Sir, if you will be so good
as to favour me with a Blank Book, I will transcribe the
most remarkable occurrences I meet with in my reading
which will serve to fix them upon my mind."

We cannot wonder at the precision and elegance
of the letter-writing of our forbears, when we know
the "painful" precepts of parents in regard to their
children's penmanship and composition. In the
letters written by Ephraim Williams, a plain New
England farmer, from his home in Stockbridge in
the years 1749 *et seq.* to his son Elijah, while the
latter was in Princeton College, is shown the respect
felt for a good handwriting. Nearly every letter
had some such sentences as these : —

"I would intreat you to endeavour daily to Improve
yourself in writting and spelling; they are very ornimentall
to a scholar and the want of them is an exceeding great
Blemish."

"I desire you would observe in your Wrighting to make
proper Distances between words; don't blend your words
together use your utmost endeavours to spell well; con-
sult all Rules likely to help you; Such words as require

it

David Waite, Seven Years Old

it allways begin with a capitoll Letter, it will much Grace your wrighting.   Try to mend your hand in wrighting every day all Opportunities you can possibly get.   Observe strictly Gentlemen's meathod of wrighting and superscribing, it may be of service to you: you can scarce conceive what a vast disadvantage it will be to leave the Colledg and not be able to write and spell well.   Learn to write a pretty fine Hand as you may have Ocation."

He urges him to study the spelling rules laid down in the *Youth's Instructor in the English Tounge*, and tells him not to follow his (the father's) writing for an example as he has " but common English learning."   He reproves, admonishes, and finally says Elijah's sisters will prove better scholars than he is if he does not have a care, which was a bitter taunt.

Major Dulany of Maryland wrote to his little daughter some very intelligent advice, of which these lines are a portion : —

" In letter writing as in conversation it will be found that those who substitute the design of distinguishing themselves for that of giving pleasure to those whom they address must ever fail.   Having decided upon what is proper to be said accustom yourself to express it in the best possible manner. Always use the words that most exactly correspond with the ideas you mean to express.   There are fewer synonymous words in our language than is generally supposed, as

you

you will find in looking over your Dictionary. It has been remembered upon as a great excellence of Gen'l Washington's writings that no one could substitute a single word which could so well express his meaning. I have heard (whether it be true or not I cannot say) that for seven years of his life he never wrote without having his Dictionary before him."

The letters of Aaron Burr, written at a little later period to his beloved daughter Theodosia, show as unvarying and incessant pains to form perfection in letter-writing, as was displayed by Lord Chesterfield in his letters to his son. When she was but ten or twelve we find Burr giving her minute instruction as to her penmanship; its size, shape, the formation of sentences, the spelling, the exact use of synonyms. He sends her sentences bidding her return them in a more elegant form, to translate them into Latin. He exhorts her to study the meaning, use, and etymology of every word in his letter. He has her keep for him a daily journal written in a narrative style. Even when on trial for treason in 1808 he still instructed her, reproving her for her negligent failure to acknowledge letters received. He commended her style, saying she had energy and aptitude of expression; altogether I can fancy no rule of correct epistolary conduct left unsaid by Burr to his daughter. That he had a high opinion of her

powers

powers we cannot doubt; but the specimens of her composition that exist show no great brilliancy or originality.

As books multiplied after the Revolution, many letters were modelled on effusions that had been seen and admired in print: this at a loss of much naturalness and quaintness of expression. Letter-writing guides formed the most pernicious influence. Miss Stoughton of East Windsor inviting sprightly Nancy Williams of East Hartford to a gay party began her note in this surprising way: "Worthy Lady."

Children (and grown people too) had a very reprehensible habit of scribbling in their books. Of course each owner wrote his name, with more or less elegance and accompanying flourishes, according to his capacity. Some very valuable autographs have by this means been preserved. A single title-page will often bear the names of several owners. They also wrote various rhymes and sentiments, which might be gathered under the head of title-page lore.

The most ancient rhyme I have seen is dated 1635 and is in an ancient *Cocker's Arithmetic* : —

> " John Greene (or Graves), his book
> God give Him Grace theirein to look
> Not oneley to look, but to Understand
> That Larning is better than House or Land."

M   This

This rhyme is frequently seen, sometimes with the added lines : —

> "When Land is Gone and Money Spent
> Then Larning is most excellent.
>   If this you See
>   Remember Me."

Another rhyme is : —

> "Steal not this Book for if You Do
> The Devil will be after You."

Longer and more formal rhymes are found in the books of older owners. Occasionally a child's book had a valentine sentiment, or a riddle, or a drawing of hearts and darts ; crude pictures of Indians and horses are many. I have seldom found verses from the Bible or religious sentiments written in childish hands. Whether this is the result of profound respect or of indifference I cannot tell. As a special example of book scribbling, one of historical interest is given, a page of the famous " White Bible,"
which contains the entry, much disputed
of genealogical and historical societies,
that John Howland married
Governor Carver's
" grand-darter."

Page from " White " Bible

CHAPTER VIII

DIARIES AND COMMONPLACE BOOKS

And such his judgment, so exact his text
As what was best in bookes as what bookes best,
That had he join'd those notes his labours tooke
From each most praised and praise-deserving booke,
And could the world of that choise treasure boast
It need not care though all the rest were lost :
And such his wit, he writ past what he quotes
And his productions farre exceed his notes.

        — *Eglogue on the Death of Ben Jonson.*
        Lucius Cary, Lord Falkland, 1637.

GROWN folk had in colonial days a habit of keeping diaries and making notes in interleaved almanacs, but they are not of great value to the historian; for they are not what Wordsworth declared such compositions should be, namely, "abundant in observation and sparing of reflection." They are instead barren of accounts of happenings, and descriptions of surroundings, and are chiefly devoted to weather reports and moral and religious reflections, both original and in the form of sermon and lecture notes. The note-taking

taking habit of Puritan women was held up by such
detractors as Bishop Earle as one of their most
contemptible traits. To-day we can simply deplore
it as having been such a vain thing; for it is certainly true, no matter how deeply religious in feeling any one of the present day may be, that to the
modern mind a long course of the pious sentiments
and religious aspirations of others is desperately tiresome reading. Such records were not˜ tiresome,
however, to those of Puritan faith; there were but
few old-time diaries which were not composed on
those lines. The chief exception is that historical
treasure-house, Judge Sewall's diary, which shows
plainly, also, the deep religious feeling of its author.
Another of more restricted interest, but of value, is
that of Dr. Parkman, the Westborough minister.
Governor Winthrop's *History* has much of the diary
element in it. Naturally, the diaries of children
copied in quality and wording those of their elders.
A unique exception in these youthful records is the
journal of a year or two of the life of a Boston
schoolgirl, Anna Green Winslow. Fortunately,
little Anna's desire to report the sermons she had
heard at the Old South Church, and to moralize
in ambitious theological comments thereon, was
checked by the sensible aunt with whom she lived,
who said, "A Miss of 12 years cant possibly do
justice

Anna Green Winslow

justice to nice Subjects in Divinity, and therefore had better not attempt a repetition of particulars." We, therefore, have a story of her life, not of her thoughts; and many references to her diary appear in this volume.

It is curious and interesting to note how Puritan traits and habits lingered in generation after generation, and outlived change of environment and mode of living. In 1630, Rev. John White of Dorchester, England, brought out a Puritan colony which settled in Massachusetts, and named the village Dorchester, after their English home. In 1695, a group of the descendants of these settlers once more emigrated to " Carolina." Tradition asserts that they were horrified at the persecution of witches in Massachusetts. Upham names one Daniel Andrew as a man who protested so vigorously against the prevailing folly and persecution, that he was compelled to fly to South Carolina. Thomas Staples was fearless enough to sue and obtain judgment against the Deputy Governor for saying Goodwife Staples was a witch, and members of his family went also to South Carolina.

With loyalty to their two Dorchester homes, a third Dorchester, in South Carolina, was named. They built a good church which is still standing, though the village has entirely disappeared, and the

site

site is overgrown with large trees. Indian wars, poor
government, church oppression, and malaria once
more drove forth these undaunted Puritans to found
a fourth Dorchester in Georgia.   In 1752, they left
in a body, took up a grant of twenty-two thousand
acres in St. John's Parish, and formed the Midway
Church.   Their meeting-house was headquarters for
the Whigs during the Revolution, was burned by
the British, rebuilt in 1790, and is still standing.
In it meetings are held every spring by hundreds
of the descendants of its early members, though it
is remote from railroads, and swamps and pine bar-
rens have taken the place of smiling rice and cotton
fields.

Stories of the rigidity of church government of
these people still exist.   The tradition of one child
who smiled in Midway Church was for generations
held up with horror, "as though she had hoofs and
horns."   There attended this church a descendant
of both Andrew and Staples, the scoffers at witches,
one Mary Osgood Sumner.   She had a short and
sad life.   Married at eighteen she was a widow at
twenty, and with her sister, Mrs. Holmes (an
aunt of Oliver Wendell Holmes), and another
sister, Anne, sailed from Newport to New York,
"and were never heard of more."

She left behind her sermon notes and a " Monitor,"

Black Leaf.

July 8 I left my chaise on the bed.

9 Misplaced Sister's Lock.

10 Spoke in haste to my little Sister spilt the Cream on the floor in the Closet

11

12 Left Sister Cynthia's frock on the bed

White Leaf.

8 I went and said my Catechism &c Came home and wrote down the Questions and Answers then dressed and went to the Lawn endeavoured to be more sedate

Aug 9 Nothing perfect in school than common spent the evening in writing the Questions and Answers.

10 I got all my things before break fast and put them on the landing from whence I finished writing down my Questions.

11 Composed my time before break fast, after break fast wrote some fairly and did all my work before sundown

12 I went to meeting and paid good attention to the sermon came home and wrote down as much of it as I could remember.

Pages from the Diary of Mary Osgood Sumner.

tor," or diary, which had what she called a black list of her childish wrong-doings, omissions of duty, etc., while the white list showed the duties she performed. Though she was evidently absolutely conscientious these are the only entries on the " Black Leaf" : —

" July 8. I left my staise on the bed.

   "   9. Misplaced Sister's sash.

   " 10. Spoke in haste to my little Sister, spilt the cream on the floor in the closet.

   " 12. I left Sister Cynthia's frock on the bed.

   " 16. I left the brush on the chair; was not diligent in learning at school.

   " 17. I left my fan on the bed.

   " 19. I got vexed because Sister was a-going to cut my frock.

   " 22. Part of this day I did not improve my time well.

   " 30. I was careless and lost my needle.

Aug. 5. I spilt some coffee on the table."

Not a very heinous list.

Here are entries from the good page of her little " Monitor " : —

White Leaf.

" July 8. I went and said my Catechism to-day. Came home and wrote down the questions and answers, then dressed and went to the dance, endeavoured to behave myself decent.

   " 11.

" 11. I improved my time before breakfast; after breakfast made some biscuits and did all my work before the sun was down.

" 12. I went to meeting and paid good attention to the sermon, came home and wrote down as much of it as I could remember.

" 17. I did everything before breakfast; endeavored to improve in school; went to the funeral in the afternoon, attended to what was said, came home and wrote down as much as I could remember.

" 25. A part of this day I parsed and endeavored to do well and a part of it I made some tarts and did some work and wrote a letter.

" 27. I did everything this morning same as usual, went to school and endeavored to be diligent; came home and washed the butter and assisted in getting coffee.

" 28. I endeavored to be diligent to-day in my learning, went from school to sit up with the sick, nursed her as well as I could.

" 30. I was pretty diligent at my work to-day and made a pudding for dinner.

Aug. 1. I got some peaches for to stew after I was done washing up the things and got my work and was midlin Diligent.

" 4. I did everything before breakfast and after breakfast got some peaches for Aunt Mell and then got my work and stuck pretty close

to

> to it and at night sat up with Sister and nursed her as good as I could.
>
> " 8. I stuck pretty close to my work to-day and did all that Sister gave me and after I was done I swept out the house and put the things to rights.
>
> " 9. I endeavored to improve my time to-day in reading and attending to what Brother read and most of the evening I was singing."

I have given this record of this monotonous young life in detail, simply to prove the simplicity of the daily round of a child's life at that time. The pages prove with equal force the domination of the Puritan temperament, a nervous desire and intent to be good, and industrious, and attentive, and helpful. We seldom meet that temperament in children nowadays; and when we do it is sure to be, as in this case, a Puritan inheritance.

John Quincy Adams, when eleven years old, determined to write a Journal, and he thus lucidly and sensibly explains his intentions to his mother : —

"HONOURED MAMMA : My Pappa enjoins it upon me to keep a journal, or diary of the Events that happen to me, and of objects I see, and of Characters that I converse with from day to day ; and altho' I am convinced of the utility, importance, & necessity of this Exercise, yet I have not patience & perseverance enough to do it so Constantly

as

as I ought.   My Pappa, who takes a great deal of Pains to put
me in the right way, has also advised me to Preserve copies
of all my letters, and has given me a Convenient Blank
Book for this end ; and altho' I shall have the mortification
a few years hence to read a great deal of my Childish nonsense, yet I shall have the Pleasure and advantage of Re-
marking the several steps by which I shall have advanced
in taste judgment and knowledge.   A journal Book & a letter
Book of a Lad of Eleven years old can not be expected to
contain much of Science, Litterature, arts, wisdom or wit,
yet it may serve to perpetuate many observations that I may
make & may hereafter help me to recolect both Persons &
things that would other ways escape my memory. · · · My
father has given me hopes of a Pencil & Pencil Book in
which I can make notes upon the spot to be transferred
afterwards to my Diary, and my letters, this will give me
great pleasure, both because it will be a sure means of im-
provement to myself & make me to be more entertaining to
you.

"I am my ever honoured and revered Mamma your
Dutiful & Affectionate Son.

"JOHN QUINCY ADAMS."

I believe this diary, so carefully decided upon,
does not now exist.   The Adams family preserved a
vast number of family papers, but this was not among
them.   I am sorry ; for I find John Quincy Adams
a very pleasing child.   When he was about seven
years old, his father was away from home as a dele-
gate

Joshua Carter, Four Years Old, 1765

gate to a Congress in Philadelphia which sought to
secure unity of action among the rebellious colonies.
His patriotic mother taught her boy in their retreat
at Braintree to repeat daily each morning, with
the Lord's Prayer, Collins' inspiring ode beginning,
" How sleep the brave who sink to rest," etc. Later
in life Adams wrote to a Quaker friend : —

" For the space of twelve months my mother with her
infant children dwelt, liable every hour of the day and of
the night to be butchered in cold blood, or taken and carried
into Boston as hostages. My mother lived in unintermitted
danger of being consumed with them all in a conflagration
kindled by a torch in the same hands which on the seventeenth of June (1775) lighted the fires of Charlestown. I
saw with my own eyes those fires, and heard Britannia's
thunders in the Battle of Bunker Hill, and witnessed the
tears of my mother and mingled them with my own."

The mother took her boy by the hand and
mounted a height near their home and showed him
the distant signs of battle. Thus she fixed an impression of a war for liberty on his young memory.
Two years later, to relieve her anxious and tedious
waiting for intelligence from her husband, the boy
became " post rider " for her between Braintree and
Boston, which towns were eleven miles apart — not
a light or easy task, for the nine-year-old boy with
the unsettled roads and unsettled times. The spirit
of

of patriotism which filled the mind of all grown folk was everywhere reflected in the minds of the children.   Josiah Quincy was at school in Andover from 1778 to 1786, and he stated that he and his schoolmates had as a principle, as a schoolboy law, that every hoop, sled, etc., should in some way bear *thirteen* marks.   This was evidence of the good political character of the owner; and if the marks were wanting the article was contraband, was seized and forfeited without judge, jury, or power of appeal.

Besides journal keeping, folks of that day had a useful custom of keeping a commonplace book; that is, they wrote out in a blank-book memorable sentences or words which attracted their attention or admiration in the various books they read, or made abstracts or notes of the same.   Cotton Mather tells of such note making by young students.   This writing out of aphorisms, statements, etc., not only fixed them in the memory, but kept them where the memory, if faulty, could easily be assisted.   It also served as practice in penmanship.   A verb, to commonplace, came from this use of the word.   The biography of Francis North, Baron Guildford, gave an account which explains fully commonplacing : —

" It was his lordship's constant practice to commonplace as he read.   He had no bad memory but was diffident
and

and would not trust it. He acquired a very small but legible hand, for where contracting is the main business (of law) it is not well to write as the fashion now is, in uncial or semi-uncial letters to look like a pig's ribs. His writing on his commonplaces was not by way of index but epitome : because he used to say the looking over a commonplace book on any occasion gave him a sort of survey of what he had read about matters not then inquisited, which refreshed them somewhat in his memory."

People invented methods of keeping common-place books and gave rules and instructions in com-monplacing. I have seen several commonplace books, made by children of colonial times ; pathetic memorials, in every case, of children who died in early youth. Tender and loving hearts have saved those little unfinished records of childish reading, after the way of mothers and fathers till the pres-ent day, whose grieved affections cannot bear the thought even of reverent destruction of the irregu-lar writing of a dearly loved child whose hands are folded in death. One of these books with scantily filled pages was tied with a number of note-books of an old New England minister, and in the father's handwriting on the first leaf were these words : —

"Fifty years ago died my little John. A child of promise. Alas ! alas ! January 10th, 1805."

The

The matter read by those children is clearly indicated by their commonplace books.   One entry shows

I hope aunt wont let one wear the black hatt with the red Dominie— for the people will ask one what I have got to sell as I go along street if I do. or, how the folk at Newguinie do? Dear mamma, you dont know the fation here— I beg to look like other folk. You dont kno what a stir would be made in Sudbury street were I to make my appearance there in my red Domi nie & black Hatt. But the old cloak & bonnett together will make me a decent Bonnet for common ocation (I like that aunt says, its a pitty some of the ribbin you sent wont do for the Bonnet— I must now close up this Journal. With Duty, Love, & Compli ments as due, perticularly to my Dear little brother, (I long to se him) & Mrs. Law, I will write to her soon I am, Honl. Poppa & mama,

Yr. ever Dutiful Daughter

N. B. my aunt Deming   *Anna Green Winslow.*
dont approve of my English.
it has not the fear that you will think has concernd in the Diction

Page from Diary of Anna Green Winslow

evidence of light reading.   It is of riddles which are headed " GUESSES " ; they are the ones familiar to us all in *Mother Goose's Melodies* to-day.   The

answers

answers are written in a most transparent juvenile shorthand.   Thus the answer, " Well," is indicated by the figures 23, 5, 12, 12, referring to the position of the letters in the alphabet.

The usual entries are of a religious character; extracts from sermons, answers from the catechism, verses of hymns, accompany stilted religious aspirations and appeals.   In them a painful familiarity with and partiality for quotations bearing on hell and the devil show the religious teaching of the times.

CHAPTER IX

CHILDISH PRECOCITY

Where babies, much to their surprise,
Were born astonishingly wise;
With every Science on their lips,
And Latin at their finger-tips.
                    — Bab Ballads. W. S. Gilbert, 1877.

THE seventeenth century was in Europe a
period of eager development and hasty har-
vesting; English boys were made serious-
minded by the conditions they saw around them,
as well as by a forcing-house system of education,
begun at very early years. This early ageing is
reflected in the writings of the times. The
Religio Medici, apparently the composition of a man
of the large experience and serene contemplation of
extreme age, was written by Sir Thomas Browne
when he was but thirty.

There are many records of the precocity of children, preserved for us many times, alas! through
the sad recounting of early deaths. One of the

most

Samuel Torrey, Twelve Years Old, 1770

most pathetic records of a father's blasted hopes may be found in the pages of the diary of John Evelyn. In December, 1658, died his little son, Richard, five years and three days old. He was a prodigy of wit and learning, as beautiful as an angel, and of rare mental endowment. His father's account of his acquirements runs thus: —

" He had learned all his catechism at two years and a half old; he could perfectly read any of the English, Latin, French, or Gothic letters, pronouncing the first three languages exactly. He had, before the fifth year, or in that year, not only skill to read most written hands, but to decline all the nouns, conjugate the verbs regular, and most of the irregular; learned out Puerelis, got by heart almost the entire vocabulary of Latin and French primitives and words, could make congruous syntax, turn English into Latin, and vice versa, construe and prove what he read, and did the government and use of relatives, verbs, substantives, ellipses and many figures and tropes, and made a considerable progress in Comenius' Janua; begun himself to write legibly and had a strong passion for Greek. The number of verses he could recite was prodigious, and what he remembered of the parts of plays which he would also act; and, when seeing a Plautus in one's hand, he asked what book it was, and being told it was comedy and too difficult for him, he wept for sorrow. Strange was his apt and ingenious application of fables and morals, for he had read Æsop; he had a wonderful disposition to mathe-

N   matics,

matics, having by heart divers propositions of Euclid that were read to him in play, and he would make lines and demonstrate them.   He had learned by heart divers sentences in Latin and Greek which on occasion he would produce even to wonder.   He was all life, all prettiness, far from morose, sullen, or childish in any thing he said or did."

Of course this is not given as an ordinary education of an every-day child.   It is an extraordinary record of a very unusual child, but it shows what an intelligent child could be permitted to do. Evelyn was a man of great good sense; not the sort of man who would force a child; indeed he averred that he abhorred precocity.   But in truth it was a time in England's history when such a child could easily be overstimulated, when public events, the course of history, was so exciting that every child of keen wit must have felt the effects.

The crowding of young minds did not end with the seventeenth century.   A striking example of the desire to press education is found in the letters of Lord Chesterfield to his son, beginning in 1738, when the boy was not six years old.   The language and subjects would be deemed to-day suited only to mature minds.   In 1741 the father wrote: —

" This is the last letter I shall write to you as a little boy, for to-morrow you will attain your ninth year; so that
for

for the future, I shall treat you as a youth. You must now commence a different course of life, a different course of studies. No more levity. Childish toys and playthings must be thrown aside, and your mind directed to serious objects. What was not unbecoming to a child would be disgraceful to a youth" etc.

Letter after letter continued in this tone. For years was the process carried on. The result was a striking proof of the futility of such methods. The son died when but little past his youth, a failure in everything the father had most fondly desired and striven for. The crowded brain ever stumbled and hesitated when put to any important test.

It was inevitable that New England parents, with their fairly passionate intensity of zeal for the education of their children, should in many cases over-stimulate and force the infant minds in their charge. It seems somewhat anomalous with the almost universal distrust and hindrance of female education that one of the most precocious flowers of Puritanism should have been a girl, the "pious and ingenious Mrs. Jane Turell," who was born in Boston in 1708. Before her second year was finished she could speak distinctly, knew her letters, and " could relate many stories out of the Scriptures to the satisfaction and pleasure of the most judicious." Governor Dudley and other " wise and polite "
New

New England gentlemen were among those entitled "judicious," who placed her on a table to show off her acquirements. When she was three years old she could recite the greater part of the *Assembly's Catechism*, many of the psalms, many lines of poetry, and read distinctly ; at the age of four she "asked many astonishing questions about divine mysteries."

As her father was President of Harvard College, it may be inferred she had an extended reading course ; but in a catalogue of Harvard College library printed a year or two later there is not a title in it of any of the works of Addison, or any of the poems of Pope, nothing of Dryden, Steele, Young, or Prior. In 1722, when Jane Turell was twenty years old, the works of Shakespeare were first advertised for sale in Boston.

In many families of extreme Puritanical thought, the children developed at an early age a comprehension of religious matters which would seem abnormal to-day, but was natural then. A striking instance of this youthful development (as he was of highly sensitive thought of every description) was Jonathan Edwards. A letter of his written when he was twelve years old is certainly precocious in its depth, though there is a certain hint of humor in it. Some one had stated the belief that the soul was material and

The Copley Family

and remained in the body until after the resurrection.   Young Edwards wrote : —

"I am informed y^t you have advanced a notion y^t the soul is material and keeps wth y^e body till y^e resurrection. As I am a profest lover of novelty you must alow me to be much entertained by this discovery.   1st. I w^d know whether this material soul keeps wth in ye Coffin, and if so whether it might not be convenient to build a repository for it in order wch I w^d know w^t shape it is of whether round, triangular or foresquare or whether it is a number of long fine strings reaching from ye head to ye foot, and whether it does not live a very discontented life.   I am afraid when ye Coffin gives way ye Earth will fall in and crush it, but if it should chuse to live above Ground and hover above ye Grave how big it is, whether it covers all ye body, or is assined to ye Head or Breast, w^t it does when another Body is laid upon it.   Souls are not so big but y^t 10 or a dozen of y^m may be about one body whether yy will not quarrill for ye highest place."

His paper on spiders, written when he was but twelve, has become famous as a bit of childish composition.   It shows great habits of observance, care in note-taking, and logical reasoning ; and bears no evidence of youth either in matter or manner.

A typical example of the spirit of the times in regard to juvenile education is found in the letters of Mrs. Pinckney.   She writes to a friend : —

"Shall

"Shall I give you the trouble my dear Madam to buy my son a new toy (a description of which I inclose) to teach him according to Mr. Locke's method (which I have carefully studied) to play himself into learning. Mr. Pinckney (his father) himself has been contriving a sett of toys to teach him his letters by the time he can speak. You perceive we begin betimes for he is not yet four months old."

This toy may have been what is known to-day as a set of alphabet blocks, a commonplace toy. Locke speaks of a game of dice with letters with which children could play a game like "royal-oak," and through which they would learn to spell. He was not the inventor of these "letter-dice," as is generally asserted. It was a stratagem of Sir Hugh Plat, fully explained and illustrated in his *Jewel House of Art and Nature*, printed in London in 1653, a portion of a page of which is shown here.

The toy seems to have been a success, for the following year Mrs. Pinckney writes to her sister:—

"Your little nephew not yet two and twenty months old prattles very intelligibly: he gives his duty to you and thanks for the toys, and desires me to tell his Aunt Polly that if she don't take a care and a great deal of pains in her learning, he will soon be the best scholar, for he can tell his letters in any book without hesitation, and begins to spell before he is two years old."

This

This precocious infant, afterward General Charles Cotesworth Pinckney of Revolutionary fame, declared in his later life that this early teaching was sad stuff, and that the haste to make him a very

A ready way for children to learn their A.B.C.

CAufe 4 large dice of bone or wood to be made, and upon every fquare, one of the fmal letters of the crofs row to be graven, but in fome bigger fhape, and the child ufing to play much with them,

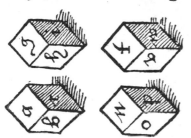

and being alwayes told what letter chanceth, will foon gain his Alphabet, as it were by the way of fport or paftime. I have heard of a pair of cards, whereon moft of the principall Grammer rules have been printed, and the School-Mafter hath found good fport thereat with his fchollers.

Facsimile from *Jewel House of Art and Nature*

clever fellow nearly made him a very stupid one.

Little Martha Laurens, born in Charleston, South Carolina, in 1759, could, in her third year, "read any book"; and like many another child since her day learned to read holding the book upside down.

Joseph

Joseph T. Buckingham declared that when he was four years old he knew by heart nearly all the reading lessons in the primer and much of the *Westminster Catechism*.

Boys entered the Boston Latin School when as young as but six years and a half old. They began to study Latin frequently when much younger. Zealous and injudicious parents sometimes taught infants but three years old to read Latin words as soon as they could English ones. It redounds to the credit of the scholarship of one of my kinsmen, rather than to his good sense or good temper (albeit he was a minister of the Gospel) that each morning while he shaved, his little son, five years of age, stood by his dressing-table, on a footstool, and read Latin to his father, who had also a copy of the same book open before him, that he might note and correct the child's errors. And the child when grown to old age told his children and grandchildren that his father, angered at what he deemed slowness of progress, frequent errors of pronunciation, and poor attempts at translation, would throw the book at the child, and once felled him from the footstool to the floor.

It is told of Timothy Dwight, President of Yale College, that he learned the alphabet at a single lesson, and could read the Bible before he was four

years

Polly Flagg, One Year Old, 1751

years old, and taught it to his comrades. At the age of six he was sent to the grammar school and importuned his father to let him study Latin. Being denied he studied through the Latin grammar twice without a teacher, borrowing a book of an older boy. He would have been prepared for college when but eight years old, had not the grammar school luckily discontinued and left him without a teacher.

The curriculum at Harvard in olden times bore little resemblance to that of to-day. Sciences were unknown, and the requirements in mathematics were meagre. Still a boy needed even then to be clever to know enough Greek and Latin to enter at eleven. Paul Dudley did so in 1686. His father wrote to the president a quaint letter of introduction : —

"I have humbly to offer you a little, sober, and well-disposed son, who, tho' very young, if he may have the favour of admittance, I hope his learning may be tollerable: and for him I will promise that by your care and my care, his own Industry, and the blessing of God, this mother the University shall not be ashamed to allow him the place of a son — Appoint a time when he may be examined."

There were still younger college students. In 1799 there was graduated from Rhode Island College

lege (now Brown University) a boy named John Pitman, who was barely fourteen.

There is no evidence that the early marriages, that is, marriages of children and very young lads and girls, which were far from rare in England during the first years of our colonial life, ever were permitted in the new world. Nor were they as common at that date in England as during the previous century, for there had been severe legislation against them, especially against the youthful marriages of poor folk.

Many have known of the juvenile weddings of English princes and princesses and marriages by proxy for reasons of state; but few know of these unions being general among English people. An interesting and authoritative book on this subject was published in 1897 by the *Early English Text Society*. Dr. Furnivall made a careful study of the old court records of the town of Chester, England, and published this account of trials and law cases concerning child-marriages, divorces, ratifications, troth-plights, affiliations, clandestine marriages, and other kindred matters. It is, as the editor says, a "most light-giving" volume. It ranges over all classes, from people of wealth, the manor owners and squires, to ale-house keepers, farmers, cobblers, maids, and men. It tells of the
marriages

marriages of little children in their nurses' arms, some but two or three years old, so young that their baby tongues could not speak the words of matrimony. Various arrangements, chiefly relating to lands and maintenance, led to these marriages, also a desire to evade the Crown's guardianship of orphans. In one case, a " bigge damsell " of twelve "intysed with two apples " a younger boy to marry her. " The woman tempted me and I did eat." One little bridegroom of three was held up in the arms of an English clergyman, who coaxed him to repeat the words of the service. Before it was finished the child said he would learn no more of his lesson that day. The parson answered, " You must speak a little more and then go play yon." The child-marriage of the Earl and Countess of Essex in 1606, resulting in the poisoning of Sir Thomas Overbury, and the Countess' marriage to the Earl of Somerset, is a well-known historical example of the unhappy result of such marriages. The Earl of Anglesey's grandson was married in 1673, when he was eight years old. Mary Hewitt of Danton Basset was wedded in 1669, when three years old. In 1672 John Evelyn was present " at the marriage of Lord Arlington's only daughter, a sweet child if there ever was any, aged five, to the Duke of Grafton."

I

I have given the dates of these later child-marriages to show that they were not unusual in England long after America was settled. As late as 1729 a little English girl of some wealth and but nine years old was taken from her boarding school by her guardian and married to his son. Very differently did the upright New Englander regard the duties of guardianship. A little girl named Rebecca Cooper was left an orphan in early colonial days at Salem, Massachusetts. She was "a verie good match," an "inheritrice," and the sharp eyes of Emanuel Downing and his wife were upon her to "make a motion of marriage" for their son. Both wrote to Governor Winthrop, Madam Downing's brother, to gain his intercession in the matter, though the maid had not been spoken to. Madam wrote : —

"The disposition of the mayde and her education with Mrs. Endicott are hopefull, her person tollerable, the estate very convenient, and that is the state of the business."

Governor Endicott was the guardian and his answering letter to Winthrop has a manly and honorable ring which might well have sounded in the ears of all English guardians.

"I am told you are sollicited in a busniss concerninge the girle which was putt to my warde and trust. I have not

been

James Flagg, Five Years Old, 1744

been made acquainted with it by you know whome, which, if there had been any such intendment, I think had been but reason. But to let that passe, I pray you advise not to stirre in it, for it will not be affected for reasons I shall show you. · · ·

" The Lord knows I have alwais resolved (and so hath my wife ever since the girl came to vs) to yielde her vp to be disposed by yourself to any of yours if ever the Lord should make her fitt and worthie.

" Now for the other for whom you writt. I confesse I cannot freelie yeald thereunto for the present, for these grounds. ffirst: The girle desires not to mary as yet. 2ndlee: Shee confesseth (which is the truth) hereselfe to be altogether yett vnfitt for such a condition, shee beinge a veric girl and but 15 yeares of age. 3rdlie: Where the man was moved to her shee said shee could not like him. 4thlie: You know it would be of ill reporte that a girl because shee hath some estate should bee disposed of soe young, espetialie not having any parents to choose for her. ffifthlie: I have some good hopes of the child's coming on to the best thinges. And on the other side I fear — I will say no more. Other things I shall tell you when we meet. If this will not satisfy some, let the Court take her from mee and place with any other to dispose of her. I shall be content. Which I heare was plotted to accomplish this end; but I will further enquire about it, and you shall know if it be true, ffor I know there are many passages about this busniss which when you heare of you will not like."

It

It is pleasant to record that all this match-making and machination came to naught. It would not have been strange if Governor Winthrop had deemed this girl old enough to be married. He had been but seventeen years old himself when he was married, but he was, so he writes, "a man in stature and understanding." He evidently was of the opinion that a child of fourteen or fifteen was of mature years. When his son John was but fourteen the governor made a will making the boy the executor of it.

These child-marriages were not abolished in America because maturity or majority was established at a greater age; for up to the Revolution boys reached man's estate at sixteen years of age, became tax-payers, and served in the militia. Early unions were controlled by restrictive laws, such as the one enacted in Massachusetts in 1646, that no female orphan during her minority should be given in marriage by any one except with the approbation of the majority of the selectmen of the town in which she resided. Another privilege of the girl orphan was that at fourteen she could choose her own guardian. Thus were children protected in the new world, and their rights conserved.

CHAPTER X

OLDTIME DISCIPLINE

My child and scholar take good heed
unto the words that here are set,
And see thou do accordingly
or else be sure thou shalt be beat.
— *The English Schoolmaster. Edward Coote, 1680.*

THE manner of oldtime children differed as much from the carriage of children to-day as the severe and arbitrary modes of discipline of colonial days differed from the persuasive explanations, the moral inculcations and exhortations by which modern youth are influenced to obedience. Parents, teachers, and ministers chanted in solemn and unceasing chorus, " Foolishness is bound up in the heart of a child," and they believed the only cure for that foolishness was in stern repression and sharp correction — above all in the rod. They found abundant support for this belief in the Bible, their constant guide.

John Robinson, the Pilgrim preacher, said in his essay on *Children and Their Education* : —

" Surely

"Surely there is in all children (though not alike) a stubbernes and stoutnes of minde arising from naturall pride which must in the first place be broken and beaten down that so the foundation of their education being layd in humilitie and tractablenes other virtues may in their time be built thereon. It is commendable in a horse that he be stout and stomackfull being never left to his own government, but always to have his rider on his back and his bit in his mouth, but who would have his child like his horse in his brutishnes ? "

The chief field of the "breaking and beating down" process was in school. English schoolmasters were proverbial for their severity, and from earliest days; though monks with their classes are never depicted with the rod.

We find Agnes Paston, in 1457, writing to London for word to be delivered to the schoolmaster of her son Clement, who was then sixteen years old : —

"If he hath nought do well, nor wyll nought amend, pray hym that he wyll trewly belassch hym, tyll he wyll amend ; and so did the last master, and the best that ever he had, at Cambridge. And say I wyll give hym X marks for hys labor, for I had lever he were beryed than lost for defaute."

She herself had "borne on hand" on her marriageable daughter; beating her every week, sometimes

Katherine Ten Broeck, Three Years Old, 1719

times twice a day, "and her head broken in two or three places." This seems to have been the usual custom of the British matron in high life. Lady Jane Grey, when she was fifteen years old, never came into the presence of her father and mother but she was "sharply taunted, cruelly threatened, yea, punished sometimes with pinches, nips, bobs, and other way." Elizabeth, Lady Falkland, as long as her mother lived, always spoke to that rigid lady while kneeling before her, " sometimes for more than an hour together, though she was but an ill kneeler, and worse riser." Poor Elizabeth! she was an only child, "an inheritrice"; but she could truthfully aver she never was spoiled.

An early allusion to school discipline is in the *Boy Bishop's Sermon* from the press of Wynkyn de Worde, who died in 1535. It runs thus:—

"There is no fault he doth but he is punished. Sometimes he wringeth him by the ear, sometimes he giveth him a strype on the hand with the ferrul, sometimes beateth him sharply with the rod."

Great Cromwell was sent off to school with injunctions to the master, Dr. Beard, to flog the boy soundly "for persisting in the wickedness of the assertion" that he had had a vision and prophecy of his future greatness. Dr. Johnson told of the

o   unmerciful

unmerciful beating he had by one Master Hunter,
who was "very wrong-headedly severe." He said
the man never distinguished between ignorance and
negligence, and beat as hard for not knowing a thing
as for neglecting to know it, and as he whipped
would shout, "This I do to save you from the
gallows." Still the Doctor was grateful for the
beatings, as he felt to them he owed his knowledge
of Latin; and he approved of the rod, saying of
some well-behaved young ladies whose mother had
whipped them oft and heavily, in variation of one
of Shakespeare's lines, " *Rod*, I will honor thee for
this thy duty." His creed of correction was this : —

"I would rather have the rod to be the general terror
to all, to make them learn, than to tell a child, if you do
this, or thus, you will be more esteemed than your brothers
and sisters. The rod produces an effect which terminates
in itself. A child is afraid of being whipped, and gets his
task, and there's an end on't. Whereas, by exciting emu-
lation and comparisons of superiority, you lay the foundation
of lasting mischief; you make brothers and sisters hate
each other."

The illustrations of old Dutch books that show
school furniture, have the odd ferules of monkish
days, the flat ladle-shaped pieces of wood which
were distinctly for striking the palm of the scholar's
hand.

hand. The derivation of the word " ferule " is interesting. It is from *ferula*, fennel. The tough stalks
of the giant fennel of Southern Europe were used

Illustration from *Plain Things for Little Folks*

by the Roman schoolmasters as an instrument of
castigation.

Old English lesson books of the seventeenth and
eighteenth centuries, many, even, of the early years
of this century, that have any illustrations of classes,
schoolmasters, or school interiors, invariably picture
the

the master with a rod or bunch of birch twigs.   An old herbalist says : —

" I have not red of any vertue byrche hath in physick, howbeit it serveth many good uses, and none better than for the betynge of stubborn boyes, that either lye or will not learn."

Birch rods were tauntingly sold on London streets with a cry by pedlers of " Buy my fine Jemmies ; Buy my London Tartars."   Even that miserable *Dyves Pragmaticus* enumerated " Fyne Rod for Children of Wyllow and Burche" among his wares. A crowning insult was charging the cost of birch rod on schoolboys' bills ; and in some cases making the boy pay for the birch out of his scant spending money.

Birch trees were plentiful in America — and whippings too.   Scholars in New England were not permitted to forget the methods of discipline of " the good old days."   Massachusetts schools resounded with strokes of the rod.   Varied instruments of chastisement were known, from

" A besomme of byrche for babes verye fit
  To a long lasting lybbet for lubbers as meet."

A lybbet was a billet of wood, and the heavy walnut stick of one Boston master well deserved the name.   A cruel inquisitor invented an instrument

ment of torture which he termed a flapper.   It was
a heavy piece of leather six inches in diameter, with
a hole in the middle.   This was fastened by an edge
to a pliable handle.   Every stroke on the bare flesh
raised a blister the size of the hole in the leather.
Equally brutal was the tattling stick, a cat-o'-nine-
tails with heavy leather straps.   The whipping with
this tattling stick was ordered to be done upon
" a peaked block " — whatever that may be.   That
fierce Boston disciplinarian and patriot, Master
Lovell, whipped with strong birch rods, and made
one culprit mount the back of another scholar to
receive his lashing.   He called these whippings
trouncings, the good old English word of the
Elizabethan dramatists.   Another brutal Boston
master struck his scholars on the head with a ferule,
until this was forbidden by the school directors ; he
then whipped the soles of the scholars' feet, and
roared out in an ecstasy of cruelty, " Oh ! the Cai-
tiffs ! it is good for them."

There was sometimes an aftermath of sorrow,
when our stern old grandfathers whipped their
children at home for being whipped at school, so
told Rev. Eliphalet Nott.

Many ingenious punishments were invented.   A
specially insulting one was to send the pupil out to
cut a small branch of a tree.   A split was made by
the

the teacher at the severed end of the branch, and the culprit's nose was placed in the cleft end.   Then

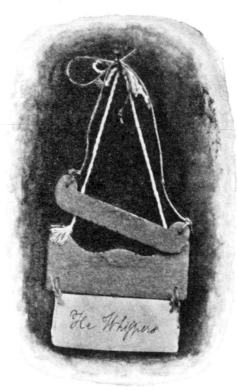

Whispering Sticks

he was forced to stand, painfully pinched, an object of ridicule. A familiar punishment of the dame school, which lingered till our own day, was the smart tapping of the child's head with a heavy thimble; this was known as "thimell-pie." Another was to yoke two delinquents together in a yoke made with two bows like an ox yoke. Sometimes a boy and girl were yoked together — a terrible disgrace. "Whispering sticks" were used to preserve quiet in the schoolroom.   Two are shown here, wooden gags to be tied in the mouth with strings, some-

what

what as a bit is placed in a horse's mouth. Children were punished by being seated on a unipod, a stool with but a single leg, upon which it was most tiring to try to balance; they were made to stand on dunce stools and wear dunce caps and heavy leather spectacles; they were labelled with large placards marked with degrading or ridiculous names, such as "Tell-Tale," "Bite-Finger-Baby," "Lying Ananias," "Idle-Boy," and "Pert-Miss-Prat-a-Pace."

One of Miss Hetty Higginson's punishments in her Salem school at the beginning of this century was to make a child hold a heavy book, such as a dictionary, by a single leaf. Of course any restless motion would tear the leaf. Her rewards of merit should be also told. She would divide a single strawberry in minute portions among six or more scholars; and she had a "bussee," or good child, who was to be kissed.

Many stories have been told of special punishments invented by special teachers. The schoolmaster at Flatbush was annoyed by the children in his school constantly using Dutch words, as he was employed to teach them English. He gave every day to the first scholar who used a Dutch word a little metal token or medal. This scholar could promptly transfer the token to the next child who spoke a Dutch word, and so on; thus it went from hand

hand to hand through the day. But the unlucky scholar who had the token in his possession at the close of school, received a sound whipping.

An amusing method of securing good lessons and good behavior was employed by old Ezekiel Cheever, and was thus told by one of his pupils, Rev. John Barnard : —

"I was a very naughty boy, much given to play, in so much that Master Cheever openly declared, ' You, Barnard, I know you can do well enough if you will, but you are so full of play you hinder your classmates from getting their lessons, therefore if any of them cannot perform their duty, I shall correct you for it.'   One day one of my classmates did not look at his book, and could not say his lesson, though I called upon him once and again to mind his book. Whereupon our master beat me. . . .   The boy was pleased with my being corrected and persisted in his neglect for which I was still beaten and that for several days.   I thought in justice I ought to correct the boy and compel him to a better temper ; therefore after school was done I went to him and told him I had been beaten several times for his neglect and since master would not correct him, I would, and then drubbed him heartily."

The famous Lancasterian system — that of monitorial schools — discountenanced the rod, but the forms of punishment were not wholly above criticism. They were the neck-and-hands pillory, familiar up

to

to that date in England and America as a public
punishment of criminals; wooden shackles; hanging in a sack; tying the legs together; and label-
ling with the name of the offence against rules.

12. Falsehood Punished.

Illustration from *Early Seeds to Produce Spring Flowers*

I have found nothing to show that Dutch schoolmasters were as severe as those of the English
colonies.   Dr. Curtius, the first master of the Latin
School in New Amsterdam, complained that " his
hands

hands were tied as some of the parents of his scholars forbade him punishing their children," and that as a result these unruly young Dutchmen "beat each other and tore the clothes from each other's backs." The contract between the Flatbush Church and schoolmaster, dated 1682, specifies that he shall "demean himself patient and friendly towards the children."

The discipline of Master Leslie, a New York teacher of the next century, is described by Eliza Morton Quincy in her delightful *Memoirs*. The date is about 1782 : —

"His modes of punishment would astonish children of the present day. One of them was to hold the blocks. They were of two sizes. The large one was a heavy block of wood, with a ring in the centre, by which it was to be held a definite number of minutes, according to the magnitude of the offence. The smaller block was for the younger child. Another punishment was by a number of leathern straps, about an inch wide and a finger long, with which he used to strap the hands of the larger boys."

One German schoolmaster, Samuel Dock, stands out in relief in this desert of ignorance and cruelty. With simplicity and earnestness he wrote in 1750 the story of his successful teaching, as in simplicity and earnestness he had taught in his school at Shippack. His story is as homely as his life : —

"How

"How I Receive the Children in School.

"It is done in the following manner. The child is first welcomed by the other scholars, who extend their hands to it. It is then asked by me whether it will learn industriously and be obedient. If it promises me this, I explain to it how it must behave; and if it can say its A. B. C.'s in order, one after the other, and also by way of proof, can point out with the forefinger all the designated letters, it is put into the A-b, Abs. When it gets thus far, its father must give it a penny and its mother must cook for it two eggs, because of its industry; and a similar reward is due to it when it goes further into words; and so forth."

He made them little presents as prizes; drew pictures for them; taught them singing and also musical notation; and he had a plan to have the children teach each other. He had a careful set of rules for their behavior, to try to change them from brutish peasants to intelligent citizens. They must be clean; and delinquents were not punished with the rod, but by having the whole school write and shout out their names with the word "lazy" attached. Letter-writing was carefully taught, with exercises in writing to various people, and to each other. Profanity was punished by wearing a yoke, and being told the awful purport of the oaths. He taught spelling and reading with much Bible instruction; but he did not teach the Catechism, since he

he had scholars of many sects and denominations;
however, he made them all learn and understand
what he called the "honey-flowers of the New
Testament."

In order to appreciate his gentleness and intelligence, one should know of the drunken, dirty,
careless, and cruel teachers in other Pennsylvania
schools.   One whipped daily and hourly with a
hickory club with leather thongs attached at one
end; this he called the "taws."   Another had a
row of rods of different sizes which, with ugly
humor, he termed his "mint sticks."   Another,
nicknamed Tiptoe Bobby, always carried a raccoon's
tail slightly weighted at the butt-end; this he would
throw with sudden accuracy at any offender, who
meekly returned it to his instructor and received a
fierce whipping with a butt-end of rawhide with
strips of leather at the smaller end.   One Quaker
teacher in Philadelphia, John Todd, had such a
passion for incessant whipping that, after reading
accounts of his ferocious discipline, his manner and
his words, the only explanation of his violence and
cruelty is that of insanity.

There is no doubt that the practice of whipping
servants was common here, not only children who
were bound out, and apprentices and young redemptioners, but grown servants as well.   Occasionally
the

Cathalina Post, Fourteen Years O!d, 1750

the cruel master was fined or punished for a brutal over-exercise of his right of punishment. At least one little child died from the hand of his murderous master. In Boston and other towns commissioners were elected who had power to sentence to be whipped, exceeding ten stripes, children and servants who behaved " disobediently and disorderly toward their parents, masters, and governours, to the disturbance of families and discouragement of such parents and governours." In Hartford, Connecticut, a topping young maid felt the force of a similar law : —

" Susan Coles for her rebellious cariedge towards her mistris is to be sent to the house of correction, and be kept to hard labour and coarse dyet, to be brought forth the next Lecture Day to be publicquely corrected and so to be corrected Weekly until Order be given to the Contrary."

Scores of similar records might be given. Judge Sewall, in his diary, never refers to punishing his servants, nor to any need of punishing them. There is some evidence of their faithfulness and of his satisfaction in it, especially in the references to his negro man servant, Boston, who, after a life of faithful service, was buried like a gentleman, with a ceremonious funeral, a notice of his death in the *News Letter*, a well-warmed parlor, chairs set in in orderly rows, cake and wine, and doubtless gloves.

John Wynter was the head agent of a London company at a settlement at Richmond's Island, in Maine. His wife had an idle maid, and some report of her beating this maid was sent back to England. Wynter writes : —

" You write of some yll reports is given of my Wyfe for beatinge the maide : yf a faire way will not doe yt, beatinge must sometimes vppon such idle girrels as she is. Yf you think yt fitte for my Wyfe to do all the work and the maide sitt still, and shee must forbear her hands to strike then the work will lye vndonn. . . . Her beatinge that she hath had hath never hurt her body nor limes. She is so fatt and soggy shee can hardly doe any work. Yf this maide at her lazy tymes when she hath bin found in her yll accyons doe not disserve 2 or 3 blowes I pray you who hath the most reason to complain my Wyfe or maide. My Wyfe hath an vnthankful office."

It has surprised me that this complaint — and others — should have been sent home to England, where (as we have abundant evidence) the whipping of servants was excessive and constant. Pepys and other old English authors make frequent note of it. Pepys whipped his boy till his arm was lame. The *Diary of a Lady of Quality* gives some glimpses of this custom. On January 30, 1760, Lady Frances

Illustration from " Young Wilfrid "

Frances Pennoyer writes at her home at Bullingham Court, Herefordshire, that one of her maids spoke in the housekeeper's room about a matter that was not to the credit of the family. My lady knew there was truth in what the girl said, but it was not her place to speak of it, and she must be taught to know and keep her place.

The diarist writes : —

" She hath a pretty face, and should not be too ready to speak ill of those above her in station. I should be very sorry to turn her adrift upon the world, and she hath but a poor home. Sent for her to my room, and gave her choice, either to be well whipped or to leave the house instantly. She chose wisely I think and with many tears said I might do what I liked. I bade her attend my chamber at twelve.

" Dearlove, my maid, came to my room as I bade her. I bade her fetch the rod from what was my mother-in-law's rod-closet, and kneel and ask pardon, which she did with tears. I made her prepare, and I whipped her well. The girl's flesh is plump and firm, and she is a cleanly person, such a one, not excepting my own daughters who are thin, and one of them, Charlotte, rather sallow, as I have not whipped for a long time. She hath never been whipped before, she says, since she was a child (what can her mother and the late lady have been about I wonder ?), and she cried out a great deal."

Poor little Dearlove, fair and plump, and in bitter

tears

tears — you make a more pleasing picture seen through the haze of a century than fierce my lady with her rod.

The many hundred pages of Judge Sewall's diary give abundant testimony of his tender affection for his children. In this record of his entire married life he but twice refers to punishing his children; once his son was whipped for telling a lie, a second time he notes the punishment thus : —

" 1692, Nov. 6. Joseph threw a knob of Brass, and hit his sister Betty upon the forehead so as to make it bleed; upon which, and for his playing at Prayer-time, and eating when Return Thanks I whip'd him pretty smartly. When I first went in, call'd by his Grandmother, he sought to shadow and hide himself from me behind the head of the Cradle, which gave me the sorrowful remembrance of Adam's carriage."

It was natural that Judge Sewall, ever finding symbols of religious signification in natural events, should see in his son Joseph's demeanor a painful reminder of original sin; and we can imagine with what sad sense of duty he whipped him.

It is the standard resort of ignorant writers upon Puritanism, and especially upon Puritanic severity, to give the name of Cotton Mather as a prime expositor of cruel discipline. I have before me a magazine illustration which represents him, lean, lank,

lank, violent, and mean of aspect, with clipped head, raising a heavy bunch of rods over a cowering child. He was in reality exceedingly handsome, very richly bewigged, with the full, distinctly sensual countenance of the Cottons, not the severe ascetic features of the Mathers, and he as strongly opposed punishment by the rod as most of his friends and neighbors favored and practised it. His son wrote of him : —

"The slavish way of education carried on with raving and kicking and scourging, in schools as well as in families, he looked upon as a dreadful judgment of God on the world : he thought the practice abominable and expressed a mortal aversion to it.

"The first chastisement which he would inflict for any ordinary fault, was to let the child see and hear him in an astonishment, and hardly able to believe that the child would do so base a thing. He would never come to give the child a blow, except in case of obstinacy, or something very criminal. To be chased for a while out of his presence he would make to be looked upon as the sorest punishment in his family."

There can be found episodes of colonial history where the disprejudiced modern mind can perceive ample need of the sharp whippings so freely bestowed upon dull or idle scholars and slow servants. Cotton Mather was too gentle and too forbearing

P toward

toward certain children with whom he had close
relations. A "warm birch" applied in the early
stages of that terrible tragedy, the Salem Witchcraft, to Ann Putnam, the protagonist of that drama,
would doubtless so quickly have ended
it in its incipiency as to obliter-
ate it entirely from
the pages of
history.

William Verstile, 1769

CHAPTER XI

MANNERS AND COURTESY

A child should always say what's true,
And speak when he is spoken to,
And behave mannerly at table,
At least as far as he is able.
— *A Child's Garden of Verse.   Robert Louis Stevenson, 1895.*

IN ancient days in England, manners and courtesy, manly exercises, music and singing, knowledge of precedency and rank, heraldry and
ability to carve, were much more important elements
in education than Latin and philosophy.   Children
were sent to school, and placed in great men's houses
to learn courtesy and the formalities of high life.

Of all the accomplishments and studies of the
Squire as recounted by Chaucer in the *Canter-*
bury Tales, but one would now be taught in English college — music.   Of all which were taught,
courtesy was deemed the most important.

> " Aristotle the Philosopher
> this worthye sayinge writ
> That manners in a chylde
> are more requisit

Than

Than playinge on instrumentes
and other vayne pleasure ;
For virtuous manners
is a most precious treasure."

The importance given to outward forms of courtesy was a natural result of the domination for centuries of the laws of chivalry and rules of heraldry. But they were something more than outward show. Emerson says, "The forms of politeness universally express benevolence in a superlative degree." They certainly developed a regard for others which is evinced in its highest and best type in the character of what we term a gentleman and gentlewoman.

It is impossible to overestimate the value these laws of etiquette, these conventions of customs had at a time when neighborhood life was the whole outside world. Without them life would have proved unendurable. Even savage nations and tribes have felt in their isolated lives the need of some conventions, which with them assume the form of taboos, superstitious observances, and religious restrictions.

The laws of courtesy had much influence upon the development of the character of the colonial child. Domestic life lacked many of the comforts of to-day, but save in formality it did not differ in essential elements from our own home life. Everything

thing in the community was made to tend to the preservation of relations of civility; this is plainly shown by the laws. Modern historians have been wont to wax jocose over the accounts of law-suits for slander, scandal-monging, name-calling, lying, etc., which may be found in colonial court records. Astonishingly petty seem many of the charges; even the calling of degrading nicknames, making of wry faces, jeering, and "finger-sticking" were fined and punished. But all this rigidity tended to a preservation of peace. The child who saw a man fined for lying, who beheld another set in the stocks for calling his neighbor ill names, or repeating scandalous assertions, grew up with a definite knowledge of the wickedness and danger of lying, and a wholesome regard for the proprieties of life. These sentiments may not have made him a better man, but they certainly made him a more endurable one.

The child of colonial days had but little connection with, little knowledge of, the world at large. He probably never had seen a map of the world, and if he had, he didn't understand it. Foreign news there was none, in our present sense. Of special English events he might occasionally learn, months after they had happened; but never any details nor any ordinary happenings. European information was of the scantiest and rarest kind; knowledge of
the

the result of a war or a vast disaster, like the Lisbon earthquake, might come. From the other great continents came nothing.

Nor was his knowledge of his own land extended. There was nothing to interest him in the news-letter, even if he read it. He cared nothing for the other colonies, he knew little of other towns. If he lived in a seaport, he doubtless heard from the sailors on the wharves tales of adventure and romantic interest, and he heard from his elders details of trade, both of foreign and native ports.

The boy, therefore, grew up with his life revolving in a small circle ; the girl's was still smaller. It had its advantages and its serious disadvantages. It developed an extraordinarily noble and pure type of neighborliness, but it did not foster a general broad love of humanity. Perhaps those conditions developed types which were fitted to receive and absorb gradually the more extended views of life which came through the wider extent of vision, which has been brought to us by newspapers, by steam, and by electricity. At any rate children were serenely content, for they were unconscious.

Among early printed English books are many containing rules of courtesy and behavior. Many of these and manuscripts on kindred topics were carefully reprinted in 1868 by the *Early English Text*

The Pepperell Children

Text Society of Great Britain. Among these are: *The Babees Book; The Lytill Children's Lytil Boke; The Boke of Nurture,* 1577.; *The Boke of Curtasye,* 1460; *The Schole of Vertue,* 1557. From those days till the present, similar books have been written and printed, and form a history of domestic manners.

It certainly conveys an idea of the demeanor of children of colonial days to read what was enjoined upon them in a little book of etiquette which was apparently widely circulated, and doubtless carefully read. Instructions as to behavior at the table run thus : —

" Never sit down at the table till asked, and after the blessing. Ask for nothing; tarry till it be offered thee. Speak not. Bite not thy bread but break it. Take salt only with a clean knife. Dip not the meat in the same. Hold not thy knife upright but sloping, and lay it down at right hand of plate with blade on plate. Look not earnestly at any other that is eating. When moderately satisfied leave the table. Sing not, hum not, wriggle not. Spit no where in the room but in the corner, and —"

But I will pursue the quotation no further, nor discover other eighteenth-century proneneses painfully revealed in lurid light in other detailed " Don'ts."

It is evident that the ancient child was prone to eat as did Dr. Samuel Johnson, hotly, avidly, with

strange

strange loud eager champings; he was enjoined to
more moderation : —

"Eat not too fast nor with Greedy Behavior.   Eat
not vastly but moderately.
Make not a noise with thy
Tongue, Mouth, Lips, or
Breath in Thy Eating and
Drinking.   Smell not of
thy Meat ; nor put it to
Thy Nose ; turn it not the
other side upward on Thy
Plate."

THE
SCHOOL
OF
MANNERS.
OR
RULES for Childrens
Behaviour:

AtChurch,at Home,atTable,
inCompany,inDifcourfe,at
School,abroad, and among
Boys. With fome other
fhort and mixt Precepts.

By the Author of the *Englifh*
Exercifes.

The Fourth Edition.

LONDON.

Printed for *Tho. Cockerill*, at the
ThreeLegs andBible againft Gro-
cers-Hall in the *Poultrey*, 1701.

Title-page of *The School of Manners*

In many households
in the new world chil-
dren could not be
seated at the table,
even after the blessing
had been asked. They
stood through the en-
tire meal.   Sometimes
they had a standing
place and plate or
trencher;   at other
boards they stood be-
hind the grown folk and took whatever food was
handed to them.   This must have been in families
of low social station and meagre house furnishings.
In

In many homes they sat or stood at a side-table, and trencher in hand, ran over to the great table for their supplies. A certain formality existed at the table of more fashionable folk. Children were given a few drops of wine in which to drink the health of their elders. In one family the formula was, " Health to papa and mamma, health to brothers and sisters, health to all my friends." In another, the father's health only was named. Sometimes the presence of grandparents at the table was the only occasion when children joined in health-drinking.

The little book teaches good listening : —

" When any speak to thee, stand up. Say not I have heard it before. Never endeavour to help him out if he tell it not right. Snigger not; never question the Truth of it."

The child is enjoined minutely as to his behavior at school : to take off his hat at entering, and bow to the teacher; to rise up and bow at the entrance of any stranger ; to " bawl not in speaking "; to "walk not cheek by jole," but fall respectfully behind and always " give the Wall to Superiors."

The young student's passage from his home to his school should be as decorous as his demeanor at either terminus : —

" Run

" Run not Hastily in the Street, nor go too Slowly. Wag not to and fro, nor use any Antick Postures either of thy Head, Hands, Feet or Body.   Throw not aught

(9)

17. Bite not thy bread, but break it, but not with flovenly Fingers, nor with the fame where-with thou takeſt up thy meat,

18 Dip not thy Meat in the Sawce.

19. Take not falt with a greazy Knife.

20 Spit not, cough not, nor blow thy Noſe at Table if it may be avoided ; but if there be ne-ceſſity, do it aſide, and without much noiſe.

21. Lean not thy Elbow on the Table, or on the back of thy Chair.

22. Stuff not thy mouth fo as to fill thy Cheeks ; be content with fmaller Mouthfuls.

23. Blow not thy Meat, but with Patience wait till it be cool.

24. Sup not Broth at the Ta-ble, but eat it with a Spoon.

Page of *The School of Manners*

on the Street, as Dirt or Stones.   If thou meetest the scholars of any other School jeer not nor affront them, but show them love and respect and quietly let them pass along."

Boys

Boys took a good deal from their preceptors, and took it patiently and respectfully; but I can well imagine the roar of disgust with which even a much-hampered, eighteenth-century schoolboy read the instructions to show love and respect to the boys of a rival school and not to jeer or fire stones at them.

This book of manners was reprinted in Worcester by Isaiah Thomas in 1787. I have seen an earlier edition, called *The School of Manners*, which was published in London in 1701. The title-page and a page of the precepts are here reproduced. The directions in these books of etiquette are plainly copied from a famous book entitled *Youths' Behaviour, or Decency in Conversation Amongst Men*, a book unsurpassed in the seventeenth century as an epitome of contemporary manners, and held in such esteem that it ran through eleven editions in less than forty years after its first appearance. Not the least remarkable thing about this volume was the fact that the first edition in English was by an " ingeniose Spark " not then eight years of age, one Francis Hawkins, who rendered it from " the French of grave persons." The bookseller begs the reader to " connive at the stile," on the plea that it was " wrought by an uncouth and rough file of one in green years." Green years! we cannot fancy sober young Francis as ever green or as anything but a

scre

sere and prematurely withered leaf. We can see him in sad colored attire, carefully made quill pen in hand, seated at desk and standish, his poor little shrunken legs hanging pitifully down, inditing on foolscap with precision and elegance his pompous precepts. After all he only translated these maxims ; hence, perhaps, was the reason that he managed to live to grow up. For translating did not tax his "intellectuals" as would have composition.

The *Youths' Behaviour* contained many rules and instructions worded from still older books on courtesy, such as *The Babees Book*, and *The Boke of Nurture*, and traces of those hackneyed rules lingered even in the etiquette books of Isaiah Thomas, long after the house-furnishings and household conditions indicated by them and sometimes necessitated by them had become as obsolete as the formal duties of the squire's sons, "the younkers of account, youths of good houses, and young gentlemen henxmen," for whom they had originally been written. Let us believe that the habits pointed out by such rules were obsolete also. I cannot think, for instance, that the boy born after our Revolutionary war was in the habit of casting poultry and meat bones under dining tables, even though he is so seriously enjoined not to do so. This rule is a survivor from the earthen floors and dirty ways of old England.

A

A famous book of rules of etiquette, entitled *The Mirror of Compliments*, was printed in 1635 in England, and as late as 1795 many pages of it were reprinted in America by Thomas under the title *A New Academy of Compliments*. The teachings in this book were· fearfully and wonderfully polite. This is the sort of thing enjoined upon children and grown folk as correct phrases to be exchanged on the subject of breaking bread together : —

" Sir, you shall oblige me very much if you will do me the honour to take my poor dinner with me.

" Sir, you are too courteous and persuasive to be refused and therefore I shall trouble you.

" Sir, pray excuse your bad entertainment at the present dinner and another time we will endeavour to make you amends.

" Truly, Sir, it has been very good, without any defect, and needs no excuse."

The child who sought to be mannerly certainly must have felt rather discouraged at the prospect laid before him. These superfluities of politeness were equalled by the absurdities of restraint. It would certainly have been a study of facial expression to see the average schoolboy when he read this dictum, " It is a wilde and rude thing to lean upon ones elbow."

In Brinsley's *Grammar Schoole*, written in 1612, he

he enumerates the "bookes to bee first learned of children." First were "abcies" and primers, then the Psalms in metre, then the Testament.

"Then if any other require any little booke meet to enter Children, the *Schoole of Virtue* is one of the Principall, and easiest for the first enterers being full of precepts of ciuilitie. . . . And after the *Schoole of Good Manners*, leading the child as by the hand, in the way of all good manners."

The constant reading of these books, and the persistent reprinting of their formal rules of behavior, may have tended to conserve the old-fashioned deportment of children which has been so lamented by aged grumblers and lovers of the good old times. It was certainly natural that children should be affected by the regard for etiquette, the distinctions of social position which they saw heeded all around them, and in all departments of life. No man could enlist in the Massachusetts Cavalry unless he had a certain amount of property. Even boys in college had their names placed in the catalogues, not by classes, years, scholarship, or alphabetical order, but by the dignity and wealth of their family and social position; and a college boy at Harvard had to give the baluster side of the staircase to any one who was his social superior.

Of

Thomas Aston Coffin, Three Years Old

Of course the careful "seating of the meeting" was simply an evidence of this regard of rank and station.

It was a profound distance between Mr. and Goodman. Mistress and Goody marked a distinction as positive if not as great as between a duchess and a milkmaid. Unmarried women and girls, if deemed worthy any title at all, were not termed Miss, but were also Mrs. Rev. Mr. Tompson wrote a funeral tribute to a little girl of six, entitled, " A Neighbour's Tears dropt on ye Grave of an amiable Virgin ; a pleasant Plant cut down in the blooming of her Spring, viz: Mrs. Rebecka Sewall August ye 4th, 1710." Cotton Mather wrote of " Mrs. Sarah Gerrish, a very beautiful and ingenious damsel seven years of age." Miss was not exactly a term of reproach, but it was not one of respect. It denoted childishness, flippancy, lack of character, and was not applied in public to children of dignified families. In *Evelina* the vulgar cousins, the Braughtons, call the heroine Miss. " Lord ! Miss, never mind that ! " " Aunt has told you all hant she, Miss ? "

A certain regard for formality obtained even in very humble households. The childhood of David and John Brainerd, born respectively in 1718 and 1720, in East Haddam, Connecticut, who later in life

life were missionaries to the New Jersey Indians, has been written by a kinsman. They were nurtured under the influences of Connecticut Puritanism, in a simple New England home. Their biographer writes of their rearing : —

"A boy was early taught a profound respect for his parents, teachers, and guardians, and implicit prompt obedience. If he undertook to rebel his will was broken by persistent and adequate punishment. He was taught that it was a sin to find fault with his meals, his apparel, his tasks or his lot in life. Courtesy was enjoined as a duty. He must be silent among his superiors. If addressed by older persons he must respond with a bow. He was to bow as he entered and left the school, and to every man and woman, old or young, rich or poor, black or white, whom he met on the road. Special punishment was visited on him if he failed to show respect for the aged, the poor, the colored, or to any persons whatever whom God had visited with infirmities."

All children in godly households were taught personal consideration of the old and afflicted, a consideration which lasted till our present days of organized charities. As a lesson of patience and kindness, read Mrs. Silsbee's account of the blind piano tuner in Salem. He was employed in many households and ever treated with marked attention. His tuning instrument had to be placed for
him

him on each piano-screw by some member of the
family. He was paid, given cake and wine, then
humored by being given a tangled skein of silk to
unravel and thus show his dexterity, and finally led
tenderly home.

Sir Francis Doyle says, " It is the intention of
the Almighty that there should exist for a certain
time between childhood and manhood, the natural
production known as a boy." This natural production existed two centuries ago as well as to-day.
Though children were certainly subdued and silent
in the presence of older folk, still they were boys
and girls, not machine-like models of perfection.
We know of their turbulence in church; and boys
in colonial days robbed orchards, and played ball
in the streets, and tore down gates, and frightened
horses, and threw stones with as much vim and
violence as if they had been born in the nineteenth
century. Mather, in his *Vindication of New England*, referring to the charge of injuring King's
Chapel, shows us Boston schoolboys in much the
same mischief that schoolboys have been in since : —

" All the mischief done is the breaking of a few Quarels
of Glass by idle Boys, who if discover'd had been chastis'd
by their own Parents. They have built their Chapel in a
Publick burying place, next adjoining a great Free School,
where the Boyes (having gotten to play) may, some by
Accident,

Accident, some in Frolick, and some perhaps in Revenge for disturbing their Relatives' Graves by the Foundation of that Building, have broken a few Quarels of the Windows.''

Children did not always pose either as models of decorum or propriety in their relations with each other. In a little book called *The Village School*, we read of their beating and kicking each other, and that there was one bleeding nose. Worse yet, when the girls went forth to gather "daisies and butter-flowers," the ungal- lant boys kicked the girls "to make them pipe."

CHAPTER XII

Puritanism is not of the Nineteenth Century, but of the Seventeenth, the grand unintelligibility for us lies there. The Fast Day Sermons, in spite of printers, are all grown dumb. In long rows of dumpy little quartos they indeed stand here bodily before us; by human volition they can be read, but not by any human memory remembered. The Age of the Puritans is not extinct only and gone away from us, but it is as if fallen beyond the capabilities of memory itself; it is grown what we may call incredible. Its earnest Purport awakens now no resonance in our frivolous hearts, . . . the sound of it has become tedious as a tale of past stupidities.

— *Oliver Cromwell's Life and Letters. Thomas Carlyle, 1845.*

THE religious aspect of the life of children, especially in early colonial days, and most particularly in New England, bore a far deeper relation to the round of daily life than can be accorded to it in these pages. The spirit of the Lord, perhaps I should say the fear of the Lord, truly filled their days. Born into a religious atmosphere, reared in religious ways, surrounded on every side by religious influences, they could not escape the

the impress of deep religious feeling; they certainly had a profound familiarity with the Bible. The historian Green says that the Englishman of that day was a man of one book, and that book the Bible. It might with equal truth be said that the universal child's book of that day was the Bible. There were few American children until after the Revolution who had ever read from any book save the Bible, a primer, or catechism, and perhaps a hymn book or an almanac.

The usual method at that time of reading the Bible through was in the regular succession of every chapter from beginning to end, not leaving out even Leviticus and Numbers. This naturally detracted from the interest which would have been awakened by a wise selection of parts suited to the liking of children; and many portions doubtless frightened young children, as we have abundant record in the writings of Sewall and Mather. J. T. Buckingham stated in his *Memoirs* that he read the Bible through at least a dozen times before he was sixteen years old. Some portions, especially the Apocalypse or Revelation of St. John, filled him with unspeakable terror, and he called the enforced reading of them " a piece of gratuitous and unprofitable cruelty." He was careful, however, to pay due tribute to the influence of the Bible upon his literary composition and phraseology.

Mrs. John Hesselius and her Children, John and Caroline

phraseology.   The constant reading of the beautiful
English wording of the Bible influenced not only
the style of writing of that day, but controlled the
everyday speech of the people, keeping it pure and
simple.

There was one important reason for the unfailing
desire of English folk for the Bible and the employment of its words and terms ; it was not only the
sole book with which most English readers were
familiar, — the book which supplied to them sacred
hymns and warlike songs, the great voices of the
prophets, the parables of the Evangelists, stories of
peril and adventure, logic, legends, history, visions, —
but it was also a new book.   The family of the
seventeenth century that read the words of the small
Geneva Bibles in the home circle, or poorer folk
who listened to the outdoor reading thereof, heard
a voice that they had longed for and waited for and
suffered for, and that their fathers had died for, and
a treasure thus acquired is never lightly heeded.
The Pilgrim Fathers left England for Holland
before King James' Bible, our Authorized Version,
had been published.   The Puritans of the Boston
and Salem settlements had seen the importation of
Geneva Bibles forbidden in England by Laud in
1633, and the reading prohibited at their meetings.
They revelled in it in their new homes, for custom
had

had not deadened their delight, and they were filled with it; it satisfied them; they needed no other literature.

Though Puritanism in its anxious and restricted religionism denied freedom to childhood, yet the spirit of Puritanism was deeply observant and conservative of family relations. The meagre records of domestic life in Puritan households are full of a pure affection, if not of grace or good cheer. The welfare, if not the pleasure of their children, lay close to the heart of the Pilgrims. Their love was seldom expressed, but their rigid sense of duty extended to duty to be fulfilled as well as exacted.

Governor Bradford wrote in his now world-famous *Log-book*, in his lucid and beautiful English, an account of the motives of the emigration from Holland, and in a few sentences therein he gives one of the most profound reasons of all, their intense yearning for the true welfare of their children : —

"As necessitie was a taskmaster over them, so they were forced to be such, not only to their servants but in a sorte, to their dearest children; the which as it did not a little wound ye tender harts of many a loving father and mother, so it produced likewise sundrie sad and sorrowful effects. For many of theier children, that were of best dispositions and gracious inclinations, having lernde to bear the yoake in their youth and willing to beare parte of their

parents

parents burden, were often times so oppressed with their
hevie labours, that though their minds were free and willing yet their bodies bowed under ye weight of ye same,
and became decrepid in their early youth, the vigor of
nature being consumed in ye very budd as it were.   But
that which was more lamentable and of all sorrows most
heavie to be borne was that many of their children, were
drawne away by evill examples into extravagant and dangerous coarses, getting ye raines off their necks, and depart-
ing from their parents."

This country was settled at a time when all English people were religious.   The Puritan child was
full of religious thoughts and exercises, so also was
the child of Roman Catholic parents, or one reared
in the Established Church.   The diarist Evelyn
was a stanch Church of England man, no lover of
Puritan ways, but he could write thus of his little
child : —

"As to his piety, astonishing were his applications of
Scripture upon occasion and his sense of God.   He had
learned all his Catechism early, and understood all the
historical part of the Bible and New Testament to a
wonder, how Christ came to redeem mankind, and how
comprehending those messages himself, his godfathers were
discharged of his promises.

"He would of himself select the most pathetic psalms
and chapters out of Job, to read to his maid during his
sickness,

sickness, telling her, when she pitied him, that all God's children must suffer affliction. He declaimed against the vanities of the world before he had seen any. Often he would desire those who came to see him to pray by him, and a year before he fell sick to kneel and pray with him alone in some corner."

It was not of a Puritan dame that this was written : —

" Her Maids came into her Chamber early every morning, and ordinarily shee passed about an howr with them ; In praying, and catechizing, and instructing them : To these secret and private Praiers, the publick Morning and Evening praiers of the Church, before dinner and supper, and another form, together with reading Scriptures, and singing Psalms, before bed-time, were daily and constantly added."

This zealous Christian was Letice, Lady Falkland, a devoted Church of England woman ; so strict was she that if she missed any from the religious services, she " presently sent for them and consecrated another howr of praier there purposely for them." A strenuous insistence showed inself in all sects in the new world. The " Articles Lawes and Orders Divine Politique and Martiall for the colony of Virginea" were unrivalled in their mingling of barbarity and Christianity by any other code of laws issued in America. No Puritan dared go farther than did the good Episcopalian Sir Thomas Dale.

Dale.   For irreverence to " any Preacher or Minister of Gods Holy Word " the offender was to be
whipped three times and thrice to ask public for-
giveness.   Any one who persistently refused to be
instructed and catechized could be whipped every
day.   Rigidly were all forced to attend the Sunday
exercises.

There is one name which must appear constantly
on the pages of any history of New England of the
half century from 1680 to 1728,—that of Cotton
Mather.   This reference is due him not only
because he was prominent in the history of those
years, but because he is the preserver of that
history for us.   From his multitudinous pages —
full though they be of extraordinary religious sentiments, strained metaphors, and unmistakable slang
— we also gain much to show us the life of his day.
The man himself was not only a Puritan of the
Puritans, but the personification of a passionate desire to do good.   This constant thought for others
and wish to benefit them frequently led him to perform deeds which were certainly officious, ill-timed,
and unwelcome, though inspired by noble motives.

His son Samuel wrote a life of him, which has justly
been characterized by Professor Barrett Wendell as
the most colorless book in the English language ;
but even from those bleached and dried pages we
learn

learn of Cotton Mather's love of his children, and his earnest desire for their education and salvation. His son's words may be given as evidently truthful : —

" He began betimes to entertain them with delightful stories, especially Scriptural ones ; and he would ever conclude with some lesson of piety bidding them to learn that lesson from the story. Thus every day at the table he used himself to tell some entertaining tale before he rose ; and endeavor to make it useful to the olive plants about the table. When his children accidentally at any time came in his way, it was his custom to let fall some sentence or other that might be monitory or profitable to them.

" He betimes tried to engage his children in exercises of piety, and especially secret prayer. . . . He would often call upon them, ' Child, don't you forget every day to go alone and pray as I have directed you.' He betimes endeavoured to form in his children a temper of kindness. He would put them upon doing services and kindnesses for one another and other children. He would applaud them when he saw them delight in it. He would upbraid all aversion to it. He would caution them exquisitely against all revenges of injuries and would instruct them to return good offices for evil ones. . . . He would let them discover he was not satisfied, except when they had a sweetness of temper shining in them."

His thought for the young did not cease with those of his own family; he never failed to instil good

Charlotte and Elizabeth Hesselius

good lessons everywhere ; and a special habit of his on visiting any town was to beg a holiday for the school children, asking them to perform some religious task in return.

Another Puritan preacher, Rev. Ezekiel Rogers, was so laden with the fruit of the tree of knowledge that " he stoopt for the very children to pick off the apple ready to drop into their mouths." When they came to his study, he would examine them, " How they walked with God ? How they spent their time, what good books they read ? Whether they prayed without ceasing?" He wrote to a brother minister in 1657 : —

" Do your children and family grow more godly ? I find greatest trouble and grief about the rising generation. Young people are little stirred here ; but they strengthen one another in evil by example and by counsel. Much ado have I with my own family ; hard to get a servant that is glad of catechizing or family duties. I had a rare blessing of servants in Yorkshire, and those that I brought over were a blessing, but the young brood doth much afflict me. Even the children of the godly here, and elsewhere make a woful proof."

These ministers lived at a time when New England Puritanism in its extreme type was coming to a close ; but parents and households thus reared clung more rigidly and exactly to it and instilled

in

in it a fervent hope of giving permanency to what seemed to their sad eyes in danger of being wholly thrust aside and lost. Such religionists were both Cotton Mather and Samuel Sewall, "true New-English Christians" they called and deemed themselves. They were very gentle with their children; but a profound anxiety for the welfare of those young souls made them most cruel in the intensity of their teaching and warning; especially displeasing to modern modes of thought are their constant reminders of death.

When Cotton Mather's little daughter was but four years old he made this entry in his diary:—

"I took my little daughter Katy into my Study and then I told my child I am to dye Shortly and shee must, when I am Dead, remember Everything I now said unto her. I sett before her the sinful Condition of her Nature, and I charged her to pray in Secret Places every Day. That God for the sake of Jesus Christ would give her a New Heart. I gave her to understand that when I am taken from her she must look to meet with more humbling Afflictions than she does now she has a Tender Father to provide for her."

The vanity of all such painful instruction, harrowing to the father and terrifying to the child, is shown in the sequel. Cotton Mather did not die till thirty years afterward, and long survived the
                                                        tender

tender little blossom that he loved yet blighted with the chill and dread of death.

The pages of Judge Sewall's diary sadly prove his performance of what he believed to be his duty to his children, just as the entries show the bewilderment and terror of his children under his teachings. Elizabeth Sewall was the most timid and fearful of them all ; a frightened child, a retiring girl, a vacillating sweetheart, an unwilling bride, she became the mother of eight children ; but always suffered from morbid introspection, and overwhelming fear of death and the future life, until at the age of thirty-five her father sadly wrote, " God has delivered her now from all her fears."

The process which developed this unhappy nature is plainly shown by many entries in the diary. This was when she was about five years old : —

"It falls to my daughter Elizabeth's Share to read the 24 of Isaiah which she doth with many Tears not being very well and the Contents of the Chapter and Sympathy with her draw Tears from me also."

The terrible verses telling of God's judgment on the land, of fear, of the pit, of the snare, of emptiness and waste, of destruction and desolation, must have sunk deep into the heart of the sick child, and produced

produced the condition shown by this entry when she was a few years older : —

" When I came in, past 7 at night, my wife met me in the Entry and told me Betty had surprised them. I was surprised with the Abruptness of the Relation. It seems Betty Sewall had given some signs of dejection and sorrow; but a little while after dinner she burst into an amazing cry which caus'd all the family to cry too. Her Mother ask'd the Reason, she gave none; at last said she was afraid she should go to Hell, her Sins were not pardon'd. She was first wounded by my reading a sermon of Mr. Norton's; Text, Ye shall seek me and shall not find me. And these words in the Sermon, Ye shall seek me and die in your Sins, ran in her Mind and terrified her greatly. And staying at home, she read out of Mr. Cotton Mather —Why hath Satan filled thy Heart? which increas'd her Fear. Her Mother asked her whether she pray'd. She answered Yes, but fear'd her prayers were not heard, because her sins were not pardoned."

Poor little wounded Betty! her fear that she should go to hell because she, like Spira, was not elected, was answered by her father who, having led her into this sad state, was but ill-fitted to comfort her. Both prayed with bitter tears, and he says mournfully, " I hope God heard us." Hell, Satan, eternal damnation, everlasting torments, were ever held up before these Puritan children. We could truthfully

truthfully paraphrase Wordsworth's beautiful line
" Heaven lies about us in our infancy," and say of
these Boston children, " Hell lay about them in
their infancy." The lists in their books of the
proper names in the Bible had an accompanying list
— that of names of the devil.

A most painfully explicit account of one of the
ultra-sensitive natures developed by these methods
is given by Cotton Mather in his most offensive
style in a short religious biography of Nathaniel
Mather. The boy died when he was nineteen years
old, but unhappily he kept a diary of his religious
sentiments and fears. He fasted often and prayed
constantly even in his sleep. He wrote out in
detail his covenant with God, and I cannot doubt
that he more than lived up to his promises, as he
did to the minute rules he laid out for his various
religious duties. Still this young Christian was full
of self-loathing, horrible conceptions of God, unbounded dread of death, and all the horrors of a
morbid soul.

A letter written by an older Mather (about 1638),
when he was twelve years old, shows an ancestral
tendency to religious fears : —

" Though I am thus well in body yet I question
whether my soul doth prosper as my body doth, for I perceive yet to this very day, little *growth* in grace; and this

makes

makes me question whether grace be in my heart or no. I feel also daily great unwillingness to good duties, and the great ruling of sin in my heart; and that God is angry with me and gives me no answers to my prayers; but many times he even throws them down as dust in my face; and he does not grant my continued request for the *spiritual blessing of the softening of my hard heart.* And in all this I could yet take some comfort but that it makes me to wonder what God's *secret decree* concerning me may be: for I doubt whether even God is wont to deny grace and mercy to his chosen (though *uncalled*) when they seek unto him by prayer for it; and therefore, seeing he doth thus deny it to me, I think that the reason of it is most like to be because I belong not unto *the election of grace.* I desire that you would let me have your prayers as I doubt not but I have them, and rest

" Your Son, SAMUEL MATHER."

A strong characteristic of English folk at the time of the settlement of the American colonies was superstition. This showed not only in scores of petty observances but in serious beliefs, such as those about comets and thunder-storms. It controlled medical practice, and was displayed in the religious significance attributed to trifling natural events. It was evinced in the dependence on dreams, and the dread of portents. Naturally children were imbued with the beliefs and fears of their parents,

Charles Spooner Cary, Eight Years Old, 1786

parents, and multiplied the importance and the terror of these notions.   It can readily be seen that religious training and thought, such as was shown in the families of Samuel Sewall and Cotton Mather, joined to hereditary traits and race superstitions, could naturally produce a condition of mind and judgment which would permit such an episode as that known as the Salem Witchcraft.   Nor is it anything but natural to find that those two prominent Bostonians took such important parts in the progress of that tragedy.

It was my intent to devote a chapter of this book to the results of the study of the part borne by children in that sad tale of psychological phenomena and religious fanaticism.   The study proved most fascinating, and research was faithfully made; but a stronger desire was that children might find some pleasure in these pages in reading of the child life of their forbears.   Such a chapter could neither be profitable to the child nor comprehended by him, nor would it be to the taste of parents of the present day.   It was a sad tale, but was not peculiar to Salem nor to New England.   The Salem and Boston settlers came largely from the English counties of Suffolk and Essex, where witches and witch-hunters and witch-finders abounded, and Salem children and parents had seen in their Eng-

R   lish

lish homes or heard the tales of hundreds of similar obsessions and possessions.

New England children were instilled with a familiarity with death in still another way than through talking and reading of it. Their presence at funerals was universal. A funeral in those days had an entirely different status as a ceremony from to-day. It was a social function as well as a solemn one; it was a reunion of friends and kinsfolk, a ceremonial of much expense and pomp, a scene of much feasting and drinking.

Judge Sewall tells of the attendance of his little children when five and six years old at funerals. When Rev. Thomas Shepherd was buried "scholars went before the Herse" at the funeral. Sargent, in his *Dealings with the Dead*, tells of country funerals in the days of his youth : —

"When I was a boy and at an academy in the country everybody went to everybody's funeral in the village. The population was small, funerals rare; the preceptor's absence would have excited remark and the boys were dismissed for the funeral. . . . A clergyman told me that when he was settled at Concord, N.H., he officiated at the funeral of a little boy. The body was borne in a chaise, and six little nominal pall-bearers, the oldest not thirteen, walked by the side of the vehicle. Before they left the house a sort of master of ceremonies took them

to

to the table and mixed a tumbler of gin, sugar and water for each."

A crisis was reached in Boston when funerals had to be prohibited on Sundays because the vast concourse of children and servants that followed the coffin through the streets became a noisy rabble that profaned the sacred day.

Little girls were pall-bearers also at the funerals of their childish mates, and young unmarried girls at those of their companions. Dressed in white with uncovered heads, or veiled in white, these little girls made a touching sight.

Religious expression naturally found its highest point in Puritan communities in the strict and decorous observance of Sunday. Stern were the laws in ordering this observance. Fines, imprisonment, and stripes on the naked back were dealt out rigorously for Sabbath-breaking. The New Haven Code of Laws with still greater severity enjoined that profanation of the Lord's Day, if done "proudly and with a high hand against the authority of God," should be punished with death. This rigid observance fell with special force and restriction on children. A loved poet, Oliver Wendell Holmes, wrote of the day : —

> " Hush, 'tis the Sabbath's silence-stricken morn,
> No feet must wander through the tasselled corn,

No

No merry children laugh around the door,
No idle playthings strew the sanded floor.
The law of Moses lays its awful ban
On all that stirs.   Here comes the Tithing-man.''

There were many public offices in colonial times which we do not have to-day, for we do not need them.   One of these is that of tithing-man; he was a town officer, and had several neighboring families under his charge, usually ten, as the word " tithing " would signify.   He enforced the learning of the church catechism in these ten homes, visited the houses, and heard the children recite their catechism.   These ten families he watched specially on Sundays to see whether they attended church, and did not loiter on the way.   In some Massachusetts towns he watched on week days to keep " boys and all persons from swimming in the water."   Ten families with many boys must have kept him busy on hot August days.   He inspected taverns, reported disorderly persons, and forbade the sale of intoxicating liquor to them.   He administered the " oath of fidelity " to new citizens, and warned undesirable visitors and wanderers to leave the town. He could arrest persons who ran or rode at too fast a pace when going to meeting on Sunday, or who took unnecessary rides on Sunday, or otherwise broke the Sunday laws.

Within

Within the meeting-house he kept order by beating out dogs, correcting unruly and noisy boys, and waking those who slept.   He sometimes walked up and down the church aisles, carrying a stick which had a knob on one end, and a dangling foxtail on the other, tapping the boys on the head with the knob end of the stick, and tickling the face of sleeping church attendants with the foxtail.   Some churches had tithing-men until this century.

A Puritanical regard of the Sabbath still lingers in our New England towns.   There are many Christian old gentlemen still living of whom such an anecdote as this of old Deacon Davis of Westborough might be told.   A grandson walked to church with him one Sabbath morning and a gray squirrel ran across the road.   The child, delighted, pointed out the beautiful little creature to his grandfather.   A sharp twist of the ear was the old Puritan's rejoinder, and the caustic words that "squirrels were not to be spoken of on the Lord's Day."

With all the religious restriction, and all the religious instruction, with the everyday repression of youth and the special Sabbath-day rigidity of laws, it is somewhat a surprise to the reader of the original sources of history to find that girls sometimes laughed, and boys behaved very badly in meeting.   The latter condition would be more surprising

prising to us did we not see so plainly that the method of "seating the meeting" in colonial days was not calculated to produce or maintain order. Boys were not separated from each other into various pews in the company of their parents as to-day; they were all huddled together in any undignified or uncomfortable seats. In Salem, in 1676, it was ordered that all the boys of the town "sitt upon ye three paire of stairs in ye meeting-house"; and two citizens were deputed to assist the tithing-man in controlling them and watching them, and if any proved unruly "to psent their names as the law directs." Sometimes they were seated on the pulpit stairs, under the eyes of the entire audience; more frequently in a "boys pue" in a high gallery remote from all other Christians, the "wretched boys" were set off as though they were religious lepers.

In Dorchester the boys could not keep still in meeting; the selectmen had to appoint some "meet person to inspect the boys in the meeting house in time of divine service." These guardians had to tarry at noon and "prevent disorder" then. By 1776 the boys were so turbulent, the spirit of independence was so rife and riotous, that six men had to be appointed to keep order, and they had authority to "give proper discipline" if necessary.

It

Margaret Graves Cary, Fourteen Years Old, 1786

It is not necessary to multiply examples of the badness of the boys, nor of the unsophisticated art-lessness of their parents.   Scores of old town and church records give ample proof of the traits of both fathers and sons.   These accounts are often as amusing as they are surprising in their hopeless-ness.   The natural remedy of the isolation of the inventors of mischief, and separation of conspira-tors and quarrellers, did not enter the brains of our simple old forefathers for over a century.   Indeed, these "Devil's play-houses," as Dr. Porter called them, were not entirely abolished until fifty years ago.   The town of Windsor, Connecti-

cut, suffered and suffered from

"boys pews" until

the year

1845.

CHAPTER XIII

RELIGIOUS BOOKS

Lisping new syllables, we scramble next
Through moral narrative, or sacred text,
And learn with wonder how this world began ;
Who made, who marred, and who has ransomed man.
                    — Tyrocinium.   William Cowper, 1784.

IT was inevitable, since the colonization of America was in the day of Puritanism, that the first modern literature known by American children should be the distinctive literature of that sect and period.   These were religious emblems, controversial treatises, records of martyrdoms, catechismic dialogues, and a few accounts of precociously pious infants who had died.   Thomas White, a Puritan minister, wrote thus : —

" When thou canst read, read no ballads and romances and foolish books, but the Bible and the Plaine Man's Pathway to Heaven, a very plaine holy book for you.   Get the Practice of Piety, Mr. Baxter's call to the Unconverted, Allen's Alarm to the Unconverted, The Book of Martyrs."

                                                    The

The two books which he named after the Bible had the distinction of being the only ones owned by the wife of John Bunyan.   The confiding Puritan child who read *The Plain Man's Pathway to Heaven,* under the promise that it was a " plaine and perfite " book, must have been sorely disappointed. But if it wasn't plain it was popular.   The twelfth edition is dated 1733.   Foxe's *Book of Martyrs* was found in many colonial homes, and was eagerly read by many children.   Neither this nor any of the books on the Rev. Mr. White's list were properly children's books.

A special book for children was written by a Puritan preacher whose sayings were very dull in prose, and I am sure must have been more so in verse.   It was called, *Old Mr. Dod's Sayings; composed in Verse, for the better Help of Memory; and the Delightfulness of Children reading them, and learning them, whereby they may be the better ingrafted in their memories and Understanding.*   Cotton Mather also wrote *Good Lessons for Children, in Verse.*

Doubtless the most popular and most widely read of all children's books in New England was one whose title-page runs thus : *A Token for Children, being an Exact Account of the Conversion, Holy and Exemplary Lives and Joyful Deaths of Several Young Children, by James Janeway.   To which is added*

added A Token for the Children of New England or Some Examples of Children in whom the Fear of God was remarkably Budding before they died; in several Parts of New England. Preserved and Published for the Encouragement of Piety in other Children.

The first portion of this book was written by an English minister and was as popular in England as in America. The entire book with the title as given went through many editions both in England and America, even being reprinted in this century. In spite of its absolute trustfulness and simplicity of belief, it is a sad commentary on the spiritual conditions of the times. I will not give any of the accounts in full, for the expression of religious thought shown therein is so contrary to the sentiment of to-day that it would not be pleasing to modern readers. The New England portion was written by Cotton Mather, and out-Janeways Janeway. Young babes chide their parents for too infrequent praying, and have ecstasies of delight when they can pray *ad infinitum.* One child two years old was able " savingly to understand the mysteries of Redemption " ; another of the same age was " a dear lover of faithful ministers." One poor little creature had " such extraordinary meltings that his eyes were red and sore from weeping on his sins."

Anne

The Custis Children, 1760, *circa*

Anne Greenwich, who died when five years old,
"discoursed most astonishingly of great mysteries";
Daniel Bradley, who had an "Impression and in-
quisitiveness of the State of Souls after Death,"
when three years old; Elizabeth Butcher, who,
"when two and a half years old, as she lay in the
Cradle would ask her self the Question What is my
corrupt Nature? and would answer herself It is
empty of Grace, bent unto Sin, and only to Sin,
and that Continually," were among the distressing
examples.

Jonathan Edwards' *Narratives of Conversions* contained similar records of religious precocity. There
is a curious double light in all these narratives: the
premature sadness of the children, who seem as old
as original sin, is equalled by the absolute childishness of the reverend gentlemen, Mr. Janeway, Mr.
Mather, Mr. Edwards, who tell the tales. There
were other similar collections of examples, — one of
children in Siberia, others in Silesia, and another of
*Pious Motions and Devout Exercises of Jewish Chil-
dren in Berlin.* Siberia was apparently as remote and
inaccessible to Boston in those days as the moon,
and the incredulous mind cannot help wondering
who sent and how were sent these accounts to those
trusting Boston ministers.

Another child's book, by James Janeway, was
The

The Looking Glass for Children. There had been a previous book with nearly the same title. Janeway's book was certainly popular, perhaps because it was in verse, and children's poetry was very scanty and rare in those days. It was reprinted many times, and parts appeared in selections and compilations until this century. A few lines run thus : —

> " When by Spectators I behold
>   What Beauty doth adorn me
> Or in a glass when I behold
>   How sweetly God did form me,
> Hath God such comeliness bestowed
>   And on me made to dwell
> What pity such a pretty maid
>   As I should go to Hell."

A book of similar title was *Divine Blossoms, a Prospect or Looking Glass for Youth.*

The lack of poetry may also account in some degree for the astonishing popularity of a poem which appeared in 1662, written by a Puritan preacher named Michael Wigglesworth, and entitled, *The Day of Doom ; or a Poetical description of the Great and Last Judgement.* This "epic of hell-fire and damnation" was reprinted again and again, and was sold in such large numbers that it is safe to assert that every New England household, whose members could read, was familiar with it. It was printed

printed as a broadside, and children committed it to
memory; teachers extolled it; ministers quoted it.
Its horrible descriptions of hell and the sufferings
of the damned are weakened to the modern mind
by the thought of the presumptuous complacence
of the author who would dare to give page after
page of what he conceived the great Judge would
say on the Day of Judgment.   But of course no
child, certainly no child of Puritan training, would
note either absurdity or impropriety in assigning
such words, and it is sad to think what must have
been the climax of horror with which a sensitive
child read God's answer to the plea for salvation
made by " reprobate infants"; the terrible words
running on through many stanzas, and ending
thus : —

> " Will you demand Grace at my hand,
> and challenge what is mine ?
> Will you teach me whom to set free
> and thus my Grace confine ?
> You sinners are, and such a share
> as sinners may expect ;
> Such you shall have ; for I do save
> none but my own Elect.

> " Yet to compare your sin with their's
> who liv'd a longer time,
> I do confess yours is much less,
> though every sin's a crime.

A

A Crime it is, therefore in bliss
    you may not hope to dwell ;
But unto you I shall allow
    the easiest room in Hell."

Thomas White wrote a book for children which certainly comes under the head of religious books, though its pages held also those frivolous lines " A was an archer who shot at a frog," etc. This dreary volume was entitled a *Little Book for Little Children*. It contained accounts of short-lived and morbid young Christians, much like those of James Janeway's book. One child of eight wept bitter and inconsolable tears for his sins. One wicked deed was lying. His mother asked him whether he were cold. He answered "Yes" instead of "Forsooth," and afterward doubted whether he really was cold or not. Another sin was whetting his knife on the Sabbath day. Poor Nathaniel Mather whittled on the Lord's day — and hid behind the door while thus sinning. A boy's jack-knife was a powerful force then as now. This book also had accounts of the Christian martyrs and their tortures. This was an English book, first reprinted in Boston in 1702. An edition of *Pilgrim's Progress* was printed in Boston in 1681, another in 1706, and an illustrated edition in 1744, but I doubt that these were the complete book. Many shortened
copies

The Holy Bible Abridged

copies and imitations appeared. One was called *The Christian's Metamorphosis Unfolded*. Another *The Christian Pilgrim*. Dr. Neale edited it for children, making, says a modern critic, " a most impudent book." Bunyan also wrote *Divine Emblems*, which the young were enjoined to read, and he also " bowed his pen to children " and wrote *Country Rhimes for Children*. For many years no copy of this was known to exist, but one was found in America in recent years, and is now in the British Museum. It is an uncouth mixture of religious phrases and similes and very crude natural history.

Pilgrim's Progress was the first light reading of Benjamin Franklin. Other books of his boyhood were Plutarch's *Lives*, Defoe's *Essays upon Projects*, Cotton Mather's *Essays to do Good*, and Burton's *Historical Collections*. Another patriot, at a later day — Abraham Lincoln — learning little but the primer at school, read slowly and absorbed into his brain, his heart, and his everyday speech the Bible, *Pilgrim's Progress*, Æsop's *Fables* and Plutarch's *Lives*, — a good education, — to which a *Life of Washington* added details of local patriotism.

Another book for young people — which might be termed a story-book, though its lesson was deemed deeply religious — was called, *A Small Book*

Book in Easy Verse Very Suitable for Children, entitled The Prodigal Daughter or the Disobedient Lady Reclaimed. It was a poem of about a hundred

Illustration from *Original Poetry for Young Minds*

stanzas, relating the story of a very wilful young woman who, on being locked up in her room by her father to check her extravagance, made a league with the Devil, attempted to poison her father and mother, dropped dead apparently on her wickedness being discovered, was carried to the grave, but revived just as the sexton was about to lower her coffin in the ground. She recovered, repented, related her experiences with unction, and lived ever after

after happy.   The title-page bears a picture of the
devil as a fine gentleman wearing his tail as a
sword, and having one high-topped cloven-footed
boot.   This book enjoyed unbounded popularity
even during the early years of this century.

It was similar in teaching to a chap-book which
was entitled *The Afflicted Parents, or the Undutiful
Child Punished*.   In this tale the daughter gave some
very priggish advice to her wicked brother, who
promptly knocks her down and kills her.   He is
captured, tried, condemned, sentenced, and at last
executed by two pardoned highwaymen.   But upon
being cut down he comes to life, pompously dis-
courses at much length, and then is executed a second
time, as a warning to all disobedient children.

Death-bed scenes continued to be full of living
interest.   *The Good Child's Little Hymnbook* represents the taste of the times.   One poem is on the
death and burial of twins, and thus is doubly interesting.   Another is on " Dying."   The child asks
whether he is going to die and " look white and
awful and be put in the pithole with other dead
people."   And yet the preface runs : —

> " Mamma See what a Pretty Book
>   At Day's Pappa has bought,
> That I may at the pictures look
>   And by the words be taught."

s   After

After a time some attempts were made to render the Bible in a form specially for children's reading. There was a rhymed adaptation called the *Bible in Verse*. This was not the Bible versification of Samuel Wesley, printed in 1717, of which he says condescendingly, "Some passages here represented are so barren of Circumstances that it was not easy to make them shine in Verse." Older hands had essayed to rhyme the Bible; one was called *A Briefe Somme of the Bible*.

These Bible abridgments were literally little books, usually three or four inches long, covered with brown or mottled paper. One tiny, well-worn book of Bible stories was but two inches long and an inch wide. It had two hundred and fifty pages, each of about twenty words.

There was also the famous *Thumb Bible* printed by the Boston book printers, Mein and Fleming. A copy of this may be seen at the Lenox Library in New York City. *The Hieroglyphick Bible with Emblematick Figures* was illustrated with five hundred tiny pictures set with the print, which helped to tell the story after the manner of an illustrated rebus. Bewick made the cuts for the English edition. Tiny catechisms were widely printed and sought after, and used as gifts to good and godly children. There were also dull little books of parables,

parables, modelled on the parables of the Bible.
Those were profoundly religious, but were so darkly

Page of Hieroglyphick Bible

and figuratively expressed as to be frequently entirely
incomprehensible ; and they fully realized the definition

nition of a parable given by a child I know — "a heavenly story with no earthly meaning."

An extremely curious and antiquated religious panada was entitled the *History of the Holy Jesus.* The seventh edition was printed in New London in 1754. The illustrations in this stupid little book were more surprising than the miserable text. No attempt was made to represent Oriental scenery. The picture of an earthquake showed a group of toy houses and a substantial church of the type of the Old South in perfect condition, tipped over and leaning solidly on each other. The Prodigal Son returned to an English manor-house with latticed windows, and the women wore high commodes and hoop-skirts. In the cut intended to represent to the inquiring young Christian in New England the Adoration of the Magi, the wise men of the East appear in the guise of prosperous British merchants; in cocked hats, knee breeches, and full-skirted coats with great flapped pockets, they look wisely at the star-spotted heavens, and a mammoth and extremely conventionalized comet through British telescopes mounted on tripods. The Slaughter of the Innocents must have seemed painfully close at hand when Yankee children looked at the trim military platoons of English-clad infants, each waving an English flag; while Herod, in a modern uniform,

on

on a horse with modern trappings, charged upon
them.   Perhaps some of the fathers and mothers
born in England and in the Church of England
had a still more vivid realization of Herod's crime,
for it was the custom in some English parishes at
one time to whip all the children on Holy Innocent's Day.   As Gregory said : —

" It hath been a custom to whip up the children upon
Innocent's Day morning, that the memorie of this murther
might stick the closer; and in a moderate proportion to act
over the crueltie again in kind."

The book was in rhyme.   Here are a few of the
verses : —

> " The Wise Men from the East do come
>   Led by a Shining Star.
> And offer to the new born King
>   Frankincense, Gold and Myrrh.
> Which Herod hears & wrathful Grows
>   And now by Heavn's Decree
> Joseph and Mary and her Son
>   Do into Ægypt flee.
> The Bloody Wretch enrag'd to think
>   Christ's Death he could not gain,
> Commands that Infants all about
>   Bethlehem should be slain.
> But O ! to hear the awful cries
>   Of Mothers in Distress,
> And Rachel mourns for her first-born
>   Snatch'd from her tender Breast."

The

The History of the Holy Jesus was told by Rev.
Mr. Instructwell to Master Learnwell.   The book
contained also the *Child's Body of Divinity*, and
some of Dr. Watts' hymns.   These *Divine Songs
for Children* appear in many forms.   The *Cradle
Hymn* is the one most frequently seen, and I
recently have heard it extolled as " a perfect lullaby for a child."   A curious study it is, showing
how absolutely traditional religious conception could
usurp the mind and obscure the impulses of the
heart.   Its sweet and tender lines, which begin —

> " Hush my dear, lie still and slumber.
> Holy angels guard thy bed,"

are soon contrasted with the vehement words which
tell of the lot of the infant Jesus; and at the mother's
passionate expressions of " brutal creatures," " cursed
sinners," that " affront their Lord," the child apparently cries, for the mother sings : —

> " Soft, my child, I did not chide thee,
> Though my song may sound too hard."

In the next stanza, however, theological venom
again finds vent to the poor wondering baby : —

> " Yet to read the shameful story
> How the Jews abused their King —
> How they served the Lord of Glory,
> Makes me angry while I sing."

This

This certainly seems an ill-phrased and exciting
lullaby, but is perhaps what might be
expected as the notion of a sooth-
ing cradle hymn from
a bigoted old
bachelor.

CHAPTER XIV

STORY AND PICTURE BOOKS

If we are to consider that the condition of the human mind at any particular juncture is worth studying, it is certainly of importance to know on what food its infancy is fed.

— *The Book Hunter.* *John Hill Burton, 1863.*

LOCKE says in his *Thoughts on Education* that "the only book I know of fit for children is Æsop's ' Fables ' and ' Reynard the Fox.'" By this he means the only story-books. A chap-book, a cheap, ill-printed edition of Æsop's *Fables*, was read in New England, but I have found nothing to indicate that these fables were specially printed or bought for children, or that children were familiar with them.

There seem to have been absolutely no books for the special delight of young men and maids in the first years in the new world, no romances or tales of adventure ; nor were there any in England. One Richard Codrington, a Puritan, and a tiresome old bore, wrote a book " For the Instructing of the Younger Sort of Maids and Boarders at Schools."

It

It is about as void of instruction as a book well could be; and this is his pleasant notion of a "girl's own book":—

"To entertain young Gentlewomen in their hours of Recreation we shall commend unto them God's Revenge against Murther and Artemidorous his Interprctation of Dreams."

It isn't hard to guess which one of these two was "taken out" most frequently from the school library. Speculation about dreams was one of the few existing outlets to youthful imagination, and many happy hours were spent in elaborate interpretations. Thus tired Nature's sweet restorer, balmy Sleep, supplied the element of romance which the dull waking hours denied, and made life worth living.

Though no great books wcrc written for children during all these years, three of the great books of the world, written with dccp purpose, for grown readers, were calmly appropriated by children with a promptness that would seem to prove the truth of the assertion that children are the most unerring critics of a story. These books were *Pilgrim's Progress*, first published in 1688; *Robinson Crusoe*, in 1714; and *Gulliver's Travels*, in 1726. The religious, political, and satirical purposes of these books

books have been wholly obscured by their warm adoption as stories. They have been loved by hundreds of thousands of English-reading children, and translated into many other languages.

MERRY TALES.
OF THE
Wife Men of GOTHAM.

Printed and Sold in London,

Title-page of *Merry Tales*

Hundreds of other books, chiefly for children, have been written, that have been inspired by or modelled on these books — thus the debt of children to them is multiplied.

The history of children's storybooks in both England and America begins with the life of John Newbery, the English publisher, who settled in London in 1744. His life and his work have been told at length by Mr. Charles Welsh in the book entitled *A Book Seller of the Last Century.* Newbery was the first English bookseller who made any extended attempt to publish books especially

for

for children's reading. The text of these books was written by himself, and by various English authors, among them no less a genius than Oliver Goldsmith. His books were promptly exported to America, where they were doubtless as eagerly welcomed as in England. The meagre advertisements of colonial newspapers contain his lists. During Newbery's active career as a publisher — and activity was his distinguishing characteristic—he published over two hundred books for children. One of the earliest was announced in

TALE III.

ON a time the men of Gotham fain would have pinned the cuckoo, that she might sing all the year; all in the midst of the town they had a hedge made in a round compass, and got a cuc-

boo, and put her into it, and said, Sing here and you shall lack neither meat nor drink all the year. The Cuckoo when she see herself encompassed within the hedge, flew away. A vengeance on her said the Wife Men, we made not teh hedge high enough.

Page of *Merry Tales of Wise Men of Gotham*

1744 as "a pretty little pocket book." It contained the story of Jack the Giant Killer.

An amusing, albeit thrifty, intermezzo of all children's books was the publisher's persistent advertisement of his other juvenile literary wares. If a generous

generous godfather is introduced, he is at once importuned to buy another of good Mr. Newbery the printer's books.   When Tommy Truelove is to have his reward of virtue and industry, he implores that it may be a little book sold at the Book Shop over against Aldermary Churchyard, Bow Lane. If a kind mamma sets out to "learn Jenny June to read," she does it with one of Marshall's " Universal Battledores, so beloved of young masters and misses."   The old-time reader was never permitted to forget for over a page that the good, kind, thoughtful gentleman who printed this book had plenty of others to sell.

Newbery was the most ingenious of these advertisers.   This is an example of one of his newspaper eye-catchers printed in 1755 : —

" This day was published Nurse Truelove's New Years Gift or the book of books for children, adorned with cuts, and designed as a present for every little boy who would become a great man, and ride upon a fine horse; and to every little girl who would become a great woman and ride in a lord-mayor's gilt coach.   Printed for the author who has ordered these books to be given gratis to all boys and girls, at the Bible and Sun in St. Paul's Churchyard, they paying for the binding which is only twopence for each book."

Other books were sold "with a Ball and Pincushion, the use of which will infallibly make Tommy

Tommy a good boy, and Polly a good girl." The juvenile characters in the books are always turning aside to read or buy some one of Mr. Newbery's little books; or pulling one of Mr. Newbery's "nice gilded library" out of their pockets, or taking Dr. James' Fever Powder, which was also one of Mr. Newbery's popular specialities.

The Revolutionary patriot and printer, Isaiah Thomas, was said to be very "ingenious in spirit." I do not know the exact significance of this term unless it means that he was a wide-awake publisher, which he certainly was. He was a bright, stirring man of quick wit and active intelligence in all things. He brought out just after the Revolution many little books for children. Few of them have any pretence of originality, even in a single page. Nearly all are wholesale reprints of various English books for children, chiefly those of John Newbery.

I don't know what made Thomas so ready to catch up the reprinting of these children's books in advance of other American printers. Perhaps his attention was led to it by the fact that his "Prentice's Token," or specimen of his work when he was a printer's 'prentice, was one of those little books. It was issued in 1761 by A. Barclay in Cornhill, Boston, and a copy now in the possession of the American Antiquarian Society at Worcester, Massachusetts,

Massachusetts, is indorsed in Thomas' own handwriting as being by his 'prentice hand. The book is entitled, *Tom Thumbs Play Book. To Teach Children their letters as soon as they can speak.* It contains the old rhyme, " A, Apple pye, B, bit it, C, cut it," etc. Then came the rhymes beginning, " A, was an Archer and shot at a frog ; " also a short catechism.

Isaiah Thomas lived in Worcester, printed these books there, and founded there the American Antiquarian Society ; in the library of that society now in that city may be seen copies of nearly all these children's books which he reprinted ; and a collection of pretty, quaint little volumes they are.

It is the universal decision of the special students of juvenile literature, that Goldsmith wrote *Goody Two Shoes.* Washington Irving thought the title-page plainly " bore the stamp of the sly and playful humour" of the author of the *Vicar of Wakefield.* It reads thus : —

" The History of Little Goody Two Shoes, otherwise called Mrs. Margery Two Shoes, with the means by which she acquired her Learning and Wisdom, and in consequence thereof, her Estate ; set forth at large for the Benefit of those

　　" Who from a state of Rags and Care
　　　And having Shoes but half a pair,
　　　Their fortune and their fame would fix
　　　And gallop in a Coach and Six.

" See

your rooks do. You see they are going to rest already.

Do you so likewise, and get up with them in the morning; earn, as they do, every day what you eat, and and drink no more than you can; and you'll get health and keep it. What should induce the rooks in frequent gentlemen's houses, only but to tell them how to lead a...

about life? They never build over cottages or farm houses, because they fear these people know how to live without their admonition.

The foolish and wise you may improve,
Taught by the tenants of the grove.

The gentleman laughing gave Mary sixpence, and told her she was a sensible hussey.

CHAP. VI.

Now the whole Parish was frightened.

WHO does not know Lady Buckington, or who does not know that she was buried at this parish church?

Well,

The Renowned History of Goody Two Shoes

" See the original manuscript in the Vatican at Rome, and the Cuts by Michael Angelo. Illustrated by the Comments of our great modern Critics.   Price Sixpence."

Copies of *Goody Two Shoes* are seldom seen for sale to-day, and many copies are expurgated.   The following quaint chapter is the one chosen for excision, because our children must never hear the word ghost.

" HOW THE WHOLE PARISH WAS FRIGHTENED

"Who does not know Lady Ducklington, or who does not know that she was buried at this parish church?

" Well, I never saw so grand a funeral in all my life; but the money they squandered away would have been better laid out in little books for children, or in meat, drink, and clothes for the poor.   This is a fine hearse indeed, and the nodding plumes on the horses look very grand; but what end does that answer, otherwise than to display the pride of the living, or the vanity of the dead.   Fie upon such folly, say I, and heaven grant that those who want more sense may have it.

" But all the country round came to see the burying, and it was late before the corpse was interred.   After which, in the night, or rather about four o'clock in the morning, the bells were heard to jingle in the steeple, which frightened the people prodigiously, who all thought it was Lady Ducklington's ghost dancing among the bell ropes.   The

people

people flocked to Will Dobbins, the Clerk, and wanted him to go and see what it was; but William said he was sure it was a ghost, and that he would not offer to open the door. At length Mr. Long, the rector, hearing such an uproar in the village, went to the clerk to know why he did not go into the church and see who was there. I go, says William, why the ghost would frighten me out of my wits. Mrs. Dobbins, too, cried, and laying hold on her husband said he should not be eat up by the ghost. A ghost, you blockheads, says Mr. Long in a pet, did either of you ever see a ghost, or know anybody that did? Yes, says the clerk, my father did once in the shape of a windmill, and it walked all round the church in a white sheet, with jack boots on, and had a gun by its side instead of a sword. A fine picture of a ghost truly, says Mr. Long, give me the key of the church, you monkey; for I tell you there is no such thing now, whatever may have been formerly. Then taking the key he went to the church, all the people following him. As soon as he opened the door what sort of a ghost do you think appeared? Why little Twoshoes, who being weary, had fallen asleep in one of the pews during the funeral service and was shut in all night. She immediately asked Mr. Long's pardon for the trouble she had given him, told him she had been locked into the church, and said she should not have rung the bells, but that she was very cold, and hearing Farmer Boult's man go whistling by with his horses, she was in hopes he would have went to the Clerk for the key to let her out."

It

It would seem that even an advanced pedagogist and child culturist might forgive this delightful ghost — like a windmill with jack-boots and a gun, just as a modern grammarian must forgive the verb "would have went" from little Two Shoes, who, as Mr. Charles Welsh says, "really ought to have known better."

The first Worcester edition of *Goody Two Shoes* was printed in 1787, with some alterations suited to time and place. Margery sings "the Cuzzes Chorus which may be found in the Pretty Little Pocket Book of Mr. Thomas," etc., and when she grows up she is made a teacher in Mrs. Williams' "College," which is described in Nurse Truelove's American books.

It will doubtless be a surprise to many that *Tommy Trip's History of Beasts and Birds*, etc., was written by Goldsmith. This little book opens with an account of Tommy and his dog Jowler, who serves Tommy for a horse.

"When Tommy has a mind to ride, he pulls a little bridle out of his pocket, whips it upon honest Jowler, and away he gallops tantwivy. As he rides through the town he frequently stops at the doors to know how the good children do within, and if they are good and learn their books, he then leaves an apple, an orange or a plumb-cake at the door, and away he gallops again tantwivy tantwivy."

As

As a specimen of Tommy's literary skill he gives the lines beginning : —

> " Three children sliding on the ice
> Upon a summer's day," etc.

The description of animals are such as would be expected from the author of *Animated Nature*, an amusing medley of truth and tradition.

The name Tommy Trip seems to have been deemed a taking one in juvenile literature, and is found in many books for children, both in the titles and as the name of ascribed author. It was used until this century. The title-page of *A New Lottery Book by Tommy Trip* is here shown. The manner of using this little *Lottery Book* is thus explained : —

A NEW
LOTTERY BOOK,
ON
A Plan Entirely New;
Designed to allure *Little Ones* into a
Knowledge of their Letters, &c. by
way of Diversion.

BY TOMMY TRIP,
A Lover of Children.

EDINBURGH
Printed and Sold Wholesale,
BY GAW AND ELDER, HIGH STREET.

1819·

Price Twopence.

Title-page of *A New Lottery Book*

" As soon as the child can speak let him stick a pin through the page by the side of the letter you wish to teach him. Turn the page every time and explain the letter by which

which means the child's mind will be so fixed upon the letter that he will get a perfect idea of it, and will not be liable to mistake it for any other. Then show him the picture opposite the letter and make him read the name of."

The antique mind seems to have found even in Biblical days a vast satisfaction in riddles. Quintilian said the making and study of riddles strengthened the reflective faculties.

Old-time jest-books called *Guess Books* were deemed proper reading for children, such as *Joe Miller's* and *Merry Tales of the Wise Men of Gotham;* very stale and dull were the jests. The *Puzzling Cap* was a popular one; also *The Sphinx or Allegorical Lozenges.* Others were *Guess Again,* and one entitled *Food for the Mind,* which bore these lines on the title-page: —

> " Who Riddles Tells and Many Tales,
> O'er Nutbrown Cakes and Mugs of Ale."
> — HOMER.

Nurse Truelove was a popular character in these books, and a popular story was *Nurse True Love's New Year Gift, designed as a present to every little Boy who would become a great Man, and ride upon a fine Horse, and to every little Girl who would become a fine Woman and ride in a Governour's Coach; But Turn over the Leaf and see More of the Matter.* This was originally an English

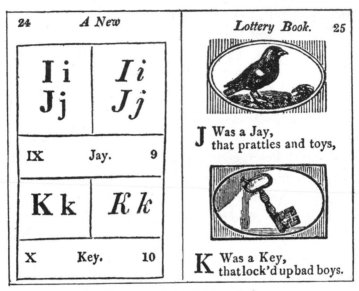

Two Pages of *A New Lottery Book*

lish book, one of Newbery's, as shown by his advertisement already quoted. Thomas Americanized
the Lord Mayor's coach into a Governor's coach,
but he carried out to the fullest extent the English
publishers' mode of advertising. The sub-title of
the book was *History of Mistress Williams, and her
Plumb Cake; With a Word or Two Concerning Precedency and Trade.*

"Mrs. Williams when I first became acquainted with
her was a Widow Gentlewoman who kept a little College
in a Country Town for the Instruction of Young Gentlemen

men and Ladies in the Science of A, B, C. The Books she put into the hands of her Pupils were, 1st, The Christmas Box. 2nd, The Father's Gift. 3rd, Mr. Perry's Excellent Spelling Book. 4th, The Brother's Gift. 5th, The Sister's Gift. 6th, The Infant Tutor. 7th, The Pretty Little Pocket Book. 8th, The Pretty Plaything. 9th, Tommy Trip's History of Birds and Beasts. And when their minds were so enlarged as to be capable of other entertainments she recommended to Them the Lilliputian Magazine and other Books that are sold by Mr. Isaiah Thomas at his Book Store near the Court House in Worcester, &c., &c."

It will be noted that the word college is employed in its old-time meaning of school; but I am not sure that Thomas used it innocently. For in the following pages the text compares Mrs. Williams to "any other old Lady in the European Universities." *The Christmas Box* referred to has a decided American flavor. It was printed in 1789 and is entitled *Nurse True Love's Christmas Box or a Golden Plaything for Children.* It gives the history of one Master Friendly, and is specially forced in style. Here are two sentences : —

" He learned so fast, Dear me ! it did my heart good to hear him talk and read. Why ! he got all the little books by rote that are sold by Mr. Thomas in Worcester, when he was but a very little boy. Then he never missed church. Ah ! he was a charming boy.

" He

" He is chosen Congressman already and yet he is not puffed up.   Well, I saw him seated in a Chair when he was chosen Congressman, and he looked — he looked — I

Frontispiece of *Be Merry and Wise*

do not know what he looked like, but everybody was in love with him."

This latter sentence is accompanied by a cut of Congressman Friendly, imbecile in countenance, seated

seated in a chair fixed on two handles, and borne aloft by four footmen in full livery. This picture had evidently seen service as "a chairing" in some English book. When we think what the Congressmen of that day were, — earnest, simple-hearted patriots, and that Thomas knew them well, — it seems strange that he could have given such stuff to American children. On the inside of the cover are printed these lines : —

> " Come hither, little Lady fair,
> And you shall ride & take the Air.
> But first of all pray let me know
> If you can say your criss-cross row.
> For none should e'er in coaches be,
> Unless they know their A, B, C."

It may interest children to read a short story from one of these little volumes to see the sort of thing children had to amuse them a hundred years ago. This is from a book called *The Father's Gift, or How to be Wise and Happy.*

" There were two little Boys and Girls, the Children of a fine Lady and Gentleman who loved them dearly. They were all so good and loved one another so well that every Body who saw them talked of them with Admiration far and near. They would part with any Thing to each other, loved the Poor, spoke kindly to Servants, did every Thing they were bid to do, were not proud, knew no Strife, but

who

who should learn their Books best, and be the prettiest
Scholar.   The Servants loved them, and would do any
Thing they desired.   They were not proud of fine Clothes,
their Heads never ran on their Playthings when they should
mind their Books.   They said Grace before they ate, and
Prayer before going to bed and as soon as they rose.   They
were always clean and neat, would not tell a Fib for the
World, and were above doing any Thing that required one.
God blessed them more and more, and their Papa, Mama,
Uncles, Aunts and Cousins for their Sakes.   They were a
happy Family, no one idle; all prettily employed, the little
Masters at their Books, the little Misses at their Needles.
At their Play hours they were never noisy, mischievous or
quarrelsome.   No such word was ever heard from their
Mouths as "Why mayn't I have this or that as well as
Betty or Bobby."   Or "Why should Sally have this or
that any more than I;" but it was always "as Mama
pleases, she knows best," with a Bow and a Smile, without
Surliness to be seen on their Brow.   They grew up, the
Masters became fine Scholars and fine Gentlemen and were
honoured; the Misses fine Ladies and fine Housewives.
This Gentleman sought to Marry one of the Misses, and
that Gentleman the Other.   Happy was he that could be
admitted into their Company.   They had nothing to do
but to pick and choose the best Matches in the Country,
while the greatest Ladies for Birth and most remarkable for
Virtue thought themselves honoured by the Addresses of
the two Brothers.   They all married and made good Papas
and Mamas, and so the blessing goes round."

The

The Brother's Gift, or the Naughty Girl Reformed, of which the third Worcester edition was printed in 1791, bore these lines as a motto : —

> " Ye Misses, Shun the Coxcomb of the Mall,
>   The Masquerade, the Rout, the Midnight Ball ;
>   In lieu of these more useful arts pursue,
>   And as you're fair, be wise and virtuous too."

Though useful arts were inculcated by this book, the reward of virtue to the reformed girl was a fine new pair of stays, which are duly pictured.

Another of Newbery's beloved books was *The History of Tommy Careless, or the Misfortunes of a Week.* On Monday Tommy fell in the water, spoiled his coat, and was sent to bed. On Tuesday he lost his kite and ended the day in bed. On Wednesday he fell from the apple tree, and again was put in bed. Thursday the maid gave him two old pewter spoons ; he made some dump-moulds, and in casting his dumps scalded his fingers, and as ever was put in retirement. On Friday he killed the canary bird — and to bed again. On Saturday he managed to incite Dobbin to kick the house dog and kill him ; then he caught his own fingers in a trap, and ended the week in bed as he began it.

When we think of the vast number of these books, it seems strange that so few have survived. The penny books were too valueless to be saved. Sometimes

times we find one among abandoned or discarded piles or bundles of books. It has been the fate, however, of most children's books to be destroyed

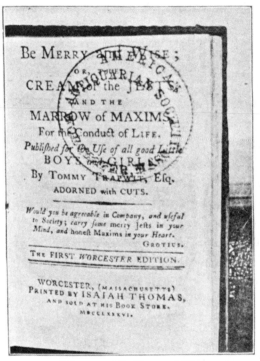

Title-page of *Be Merry and Wise*

by children. With coarse, time-browned paper, poor type, and torn, worn leaves, they are not very attractive. Open one at random. Ten to one you have before you the page upon which centres the
interest

interest of the book, its climax, its adventure, or its high wit. That page was a favorite. Many times you will find crude attempts at amateur coloring of the prints.

In these books is found an entirely different code from that inculcated by modern books or taught by earlier books. The first books for children simply exhorted goodness, giving no reasons, but commanding obedience and virtue. The books of the Puritan epoch taught children to be good for fear of hell. This succeeding school instructed them to be good because it was profitable. All the advice is frankly politic; much is of mercenary mould. Children are instructed to do aright, not because they should, but because they will benefit thereby — and profit is given the most worldly guise, such as riding in a coach, having a purse full of gold, wearing silks and satins, becoming Lord Mayor, or most exalted station of all, "a proud Sheriff." As chief officer of the Crown, the old-time sheriff of each English county was superior in rank to every nobleman in the county. The diarist Evelyn tells that his father when sheriff had a hundred and fifty servants in livery, and many gentleman attendants. Punishment, the abhorrence of parents, and evil results fall upon children not so fiercely for lying, stealing, treachery, or cruelty as they do for soil-

ing

ing their clothes, falling into the water, tumbling off walls, breaking windows or china, and a score of other actions which are the result of carelessness, clumsiness, or indifference, rather than of viciousness. These books would educate (had they been forcible enough to be of profound influence) generations of trucklers, time servers, and money lovers. The natural inclination and the diversity of inclination of children made them rise above these instructions.

COBWEBS TO CATCH FLIES   52

In another part of the fair the boys faw fome children toffed about thus.

They were finging merrily the old nurfe's dit.y.

"Now we go up, up, up,
"Now we go down, down, down;
"Now we go backward and forward,
"Now we go round, round, round."

Page from *Cobwebs to Catch Flies*

It was the constant effort of the artists, authors, and teachers of olden times to imbue youth with the notion that no harm could possibly come to the good

good — unless early death could be counted an evil.
Children were taught that virtue and each good
action was ever, immediately, and conspicuously
rewarded. The pictures repeated and emphasized
the didactic teachings; and morality, industry, and
good intentions were made to triumph over things
animate and inanimate. That the old illustrations
were a delight to children cannot be doubted; they
were so easily comprehended. The bad boys of
the story always bore a miserable countenance and
figure, and the good boys were smugly prosperous.
The prim girls are shown the beloved of all, and
the tomboys equally the misery and embarrassment.
All this is lacking in modern picture books, which
so truly represent real life and things that the
naughty boy is not blazoned at first glance as a
different being from the pious delight.

I am inclined to believe that the old-time gro-
tesqueness was more amusing and impressive to
children than modern realism; that there was a
stronger association of ideas with the emphasis of
disproportion; the absurdities and anachronisms of
scenery and costume were unnoted by the juvenile
reader because he knew no better.

In the children's books which I have examined,
the colored illustrations are all of dates later than
1800 (when dated at all). Mr. Andrew W. Tuer,

in

in the preface to his most interesting collection entitled *Pages and Pictures from Forgotten Children's Books*, says that the coloring was done by children in their teens who worked with great celerity. Each child had a single pan of water-color, a

"William and Amelia," from *The Looking Glass for the Mind*

brush, a properly colored guide, and a pile of printed sheets. One child painted in all the red required by the copy, another the green, another the blue, and so on till the coloring was finished.

There was one book which children loved, that every little child loves to-day — *Mother Goose's Melodies*. Attempts have been made to show that the

the name and collection were both American; that the former referred to one Mrs. Goose or Vergoose, a Boston goodwife. The name Mother Goose is believed by most folk to be of French, not of English or American origin. A collection of nursery rhymes was printed for John Newbery about 1760, under the popular name *Mother Goose's Melodies*; about 1785 Isaiah Thomas issued at Worcester, Massachusetts, an edition of *Mother Goose's Melodies* with the songs from Shakespeare, and certainly this must have been an oasis in the desert of dull books for New England children.

There is no pretence in this edition of Thomas' that the book had any American origin; it is said to be a collection of rhymes by " old British nurses"; and such it really was. Halliwell says many of these nursery rhymes are fragments of old ballads. Mr. Whitmore deems the great popularity of " Mother Goose" due to the Boston editions issued in large numbers from 1824 to 1860.

The preface to the Worcester edition of 1785 *circa* is said to be written by a very great writer of very little books. Could this have been Oliver Goldsmith? Irving, in his *Life of Goldsmith*, refers to the poet's love of catches and simple melodies, and tells of his singing " his favorite song

song about An old woman tossed in a blanket seventeen times as high as the moon." A Miss Hawkins boasted late in life that Goldsmith taught her to play Jack and Jill with bits of paper on his fingers just as we show the trick to children to-day. Included in these melodies are the verses "Three children sliding on the ice," which we know were written by Goldsmith. Here is an example of one of the melodies and its note: —

> " Trip upon Trenchers
>   Dance upon Dishes
> My mother sent me for some Barm, some Barm.
>   She bade me tread Lightly
>   And leave again Quickly,
> For fear the Young Men should do me some Harm.
>   Yet ! don't you see ?
>   What naughty tricks they put upon me !
> They broke my Pitcher
> And spilt my Water
> And huffed my Mother
> And chid her Daughter,
> And kiss'd my Sister instead of me.

" What a Succession of Misfortunes befell this poor Girl ? But the last Circumstance was the most affecting and might have proved fatal."

— Winslow's *View of Britain.*

According to the notion of humor of the day, the notion of Goldsmith, or some other book-hack-

wag

wag, these notes were all ascribed as quotations from some profound author, just as the cuts in *Goody Two Shoes* were said to be by Michael Angelo, and the text from the Vatican. Thus after the rhymes,

"Caroline, or a Lesson to Cure Vanity," from *The Looking Glass for the Mind*

"See-saw, Margery Daw," etc., is the sober comment, "It is a mean and Scandalous Practice in an author to put Notes to a Thing that deserves no Notice. Grotius." After the "Three Wise Men of Gotham," which ends with the lines—

> "If the bowl had been stronger
> My tale had been longer,"

u   is

is the sententious note " It's long enough. Never lament the Loss of what is not worth having. Boyle." Puffendorf, Coke on Littleton, Pliny, Bentley on the *Sublime and Beautiful*, Mapes' *Geography of the Mind*, are other authors and books that are soberly cited.

A very priggish little book was entitled *Cobwebs to Catch Flies*. The tone of its text may be shown in the dialogue about "The Toss About." The brothers who attended a country fair had been forbidden by their mother to ride in the Merry-go-round. Dear Ned wished to try the fun. Dear James said with propriety, " Dear Ned, I am sure our mamma would object to our riding in this Toss-about." Ned answered, " Dear James, did you ever hear her name the Toss-about ? " " No, dear Ned, but I am certain that if she had known of it she would have given us the same caution as she did about the Merry-go-round." Ned paused a moment, then said, " How happy am I to have an elder brother who is so prudent." Whereupon James replied, " I am no less happy that you are so willing to be advised," etc.

A distinctly American book for children was printed in Philadelphia in 1793, a *History of the Revolution*. It was in Biblical phraseology. This sort of writing had been made popular by Franklin
in

in his famous *Parable against Persecution* which he wrote, committed to memory, and pretended to read as the last chapter in Genesis.

Exceeding plainness and even coarseness of speech

"Sir John Denham and his Worthy Tenant," from *The Looking Glass for the Mind*

was presented in the pages of these old-time story-books. It was simply the speech of the times shown in the plays, tales, and essays of the day, and reflected to some degree even in the literature for children. As an example of what was deemed wit may be given a portion of the prologue to " Who Killed

Killed Cock Robin." The book is entitled *Death and Burial of Cock Robin*.

" We were all enjoying ourselves very agreeably after dinner, when on a sudden, Sir Peter's Lady gave so loud a sneeze as threw the whole company into disorder. Master Danvers instead of cracking a nut gave his fingers a tolerable squeeze in the nut-crackers. Miss Friendly who had carried with intent to put a fine cherry in her mouth missed the mark and bit her finger. Sir Peter himself, who was filling a glass of wine, spilled the bottle on the table. Miss Comely and Miss Danvers who were talking with each other with their heads very close to each other very politely knocked them together to see which was the hardest. I myself had twelve of my ten toes handsomely trod on by one of the young ladies jumping off a chair in a fright. But this is not all, no nor half what I was an eye witness of; for just at the time her Ladyship sneezed, I was busy contemplating the beauty and song of Miss Prudence's Cock Robin that was singing and as noisy as a grig when my Lady sneezed which so frightened him he fell to the bottom of the Cage as dead as a Stone."

A widely read little book was somewhat pompously entitled *The Looking Glass for the Mind*. It was chiefly translated from that much-admired work, *L'Ami des Enfans*. Those terse and entertaining tales of Berquin had perennial youth in their English form and were reprinted till our own day.

day.   The illustrations of Bewick have a distinct
value as showing the dress of children.   A few are
here shown.   The first is from *William and Amelia*;
both children are not eight years old.   The long
trained gowns, bare necks, elbow sleeves, and tall
feathered hats are precisely the dress of grown
women of that day, as William's coat and knee-
breeches are the garb of a man.   The two " ladies "
were " walking arm in arm humming a pretty song
then fashionable in the villiage collection of Ballads."
When they glanced at the apples in the tree William, " the politest and prettiest little fellow in the
village," dropped his shepherd's pipe, climbed the
tree, and threw down apples in the ladies' aprons.
As Charlotte got more and bigger apples Amelia
abandoned her " usual pleasing prattle," sulked and
at last ordered William to fall down " on his knees
on this instant " to apologize.   As he refused Amelia
pouted at dinner, would not touch her wine nor
say " Your good health, William," and at last was
ordered by her mother from the table.   William,
after many attempts, sneaked out with some peaches
for her, and thus an affectionate and generous friendship was restored.

Another illustration is for the tale, *Caroline, or
a Lesson to Cure Vanity*.   Caroline's dress is further
described in the text as of pea-green taffety with
fine

fine pink trimmings, elegantly worked shoes, hair
a clod of powder and pomatum. Her " fine silk
slip was nicely soused in the rain " ; her hoop
and flounces and train caught in the furzes, her
gauze hat blew in a pond of filthy water, etc. ; all

" C.arissa, or the Grateful Orphan," from *The Looking Glass for the Mind*

these made her glad to return to a more modest
dress. The illustration for the *Worthy Tenant*
shows Farmer Harris speaking to polite Sophia,
while " Robert was so shamefully impertinent as
to walk round the farmer, holding his nose, and
asking his brother if he did not perceive something
of

of the smell of a dung heap. He then lighted some paper at the fire, and carried it around the room in order to disperse, as he said, the unpleasant smell," etc. *Clarissa, or the Grateful Orphan*, who was so good that the king relinquished a large fortune to her, complete the quartette of illustrations.

A group of books was published just after the end of the colonial period, which had a vast influence on the children of our young Republic. These books were English; the most important of them were: *The History of the Fairchild Family*, 1788 circa, by Mrs. Sherwood; *Sanford and Merton*, 1783, by Thomas Day; *The Parents' Assistant*, 1796, by Maria Edgeworth; *Evenings at Home*, 1792, by Dr. Aikin and Mrs. Barbauld.

The painfully religious tales of James Janeway were not the only ones to familiarize death to the reading child. *The Fairchild Family* was once deemed a most charming, as it was certainly a most earnest book, and it has ever had popularity, for within a few years it has been reprinted in a large edition. I wonder how many death-bed scenes and references there are in that book! Nor are ordinary death-beds the saddest or most grewsome scenes. The little Fairchilds having lost their little tempers and pommelled each other somewhat,
their

their father takes them as a shocking object-lesson
to see the body of a man hung in chains on a

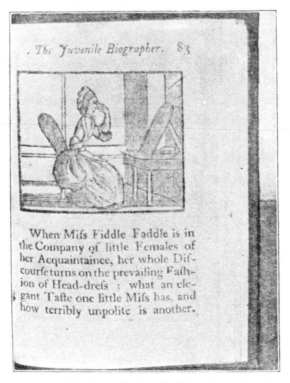

The Juvenile Biographer. 83

When Mifs Fiddle Faddle is in
the Company of little Females of
her Acquaintaince, her whole Dif-
courfe turns on the prevailing Fafh-
ion of Head-drefs ; what an elegant Tafte one little Mifs has, and
how terribly unpolite is another.

Page from *The Juvenile Biographer*

gibbet. The horror of the progress through the
gloomy wood to this revolting sight, the father's
unsparing comments, the hideous account of the
thing, rattling, swinging, turning its horrible countenance

tenance while Mr. Fairchild described and explained
and gloated over it, and finally kneeled and prayed,
— all this through several pages no carefully reared
child to-day would be permitted to read.   Mr.
Fairchild's reason for taking them to this gibbeted
corpse should not be omitted from this account; it
was "to show them something which I think they
will remember as long as they live, that they may
love each other with perfect and heavenly love."

A painful and ever present lesson found on every
page is the sinfulness of the world.   The children
recite verses and quote Bible texts to prove that
all mankind have bad hearts, and Lucy commits
to memory a prayer, a portion of which runs
thus : —

"My heart is so exceedingly wicked, so vile, so full of
sin, that even when I appear to be tolerably good, even
then I am sinning.   When I am praying, or reading the
Bible, or hearing other people read the Bible, even then I
sin.   When I speak, I sin; when I am silent, I sin."

Sandford and Merton is most insincerely recommended by many folk to children to-day.   I
cannot believe any one who has recently read the
book would ever expect a modern child to care for
it.   It is haloed in the memory of people who read
it in their youth and fancy they still like it, but
won't

won't take the trouble to read it and see that they don't.

Jane and Ann Taylor should be added to this class of authors. The poem, *My Mother*, by Ann Taylor, was published in book form, and had many imitations. *My Father*, *My Sister*, *My Brother*, *My Grandmother*, *My Playmate*, *My Pony*, *My Fido*, and lastly, *My Governess*, — all, says the advertisement, " in the same stile," — a style so easily imitated as to seem almost like parody : —

> " Who learnt me how to read and Spell,
> And with my Needle work as well,
> And called me her good little Girl ?
> 　　　My Governess.

> " Who made the Scholar proud to show
> The Sampler work'd to friend and foe,
> And with Instruction fonder grow ?
> 　　　My Governess."

We have the contemporary opinion of Charles Lamb of this new school of juvenile literature. In 1802 he wrote thus to Coleridge : —

" Goody Two Shoes is almost out of print. Mrs. Barbauld's stuff has banished all the old classics of the nursery, and the shopman at Newbery's hardly deigned to reach them off an old exploded corner of a shelf, when Mary asked for them. Mrs. Barbauld's and Mrs. Trimmer's nonsense lay in piles about. Knowledge as insignificant and vapid,

One Day, some one of Miſs Polly's little Acquaintances, coming along the Road near Miſs Charity's Houſe, found her ſtanding and crying over a little Beggar, who ſat by the Side of the Road. This is a juſt Repreſentation of this pitiful Scene.

Her Acquaintance aſked her what ſhe

was crying for. "My dear, (ſaid Polly) this poor little Creature is ſtarving, and I have not a Penny to give her; but if you will lend me Two-pence, if you have ſo much about you, I will certainly pay you again very ſoon. What a terrible Thing it is to think, that while we live upon Dainties, this poor little Girl ſhall be ſtarving!"

"My dear, (ſaid Miſs Polly's Acquaintance) I am happy that I have Two-pence about me, which is all I am worth in the World, and thoſe were juſt now given me by a Gentleman, for my pretty Behaviour to him. Here they are, and you ſhall be indebted to me only One Penny, for I will give her the other myſelf." They eagerly embraced each other.

vapid, as Mrs. Barbauld's books convey, it seems must come to a child in the shape of knowledge; his empty noddle must be turned with the conceit of his own powers when he has learned that a horse is an animal, and Billy is better than a horse, and such-like, instead of the beautiful interest in mild tales which made the child a man, while all the time he suspected himself to be no bigger than a child . . . Hang them! — I mean the cursed Barbauld crew, those blights and blasts of all that is human in man and child."

In the *Boston Gazette and Country Journal,* January 20, 1772, the Boston booksellers, Cox and Berry, have this notice of their wares : —

"The following Little Books for the Instruction and Amusement of all good Boys and Girls : —

The Brother Gift or the Naughty Girl Reformed.
The Sister Gift or the Naughty Boy Reformed.
Hobby Horse or Christian Companion.
Robin Good-Fellow, a Fairy Tale.
Puzzling Cap, a Collection of Riddles.
The Cries of London as exhibited in the Streets.
Royal Guide or Early Instruction in Reading English.
Mr. Winlove's Collection of Moral Tales.
History of Tom Jones, abridg'd.
   "   "   Joseph Andrews "
   "   "   Pamela   "
   "   "   Grandison   "
   "   "   Clarissa   " "

It

It may be seen by the last-named books on this list that another series of books for children were abridgments of *Tom Jones, Joseph Andrews, Pamela,* and other great novels of the day. Rabelais said no abridgment of a book could be a good abridgment ; these are worse than none. The childish reader is notified that if he likes the little books, his good friend, Mr. Thomas, has the larger books for sale.

The engraving of the great Mr. Richardson sitting in his grotto, in 1751, in turban, banyan, and slippers, reading *Sir Charles Grandison* to a group of friends, chiefly admiring young ladies in great hats and padusoy sacques, is typical of his life. He lived in a flower garden of girls, one intimate circle around his feet, and swelling circles extending even to America, — all facing inward and worshipping him and his works. They wept and smiled in a vast chorus at the dull pages of *Pamela,* at the surprising ones of *Clarissa,* and the thousands of interesting ones of *Sir Charles Grandison.* These seven volumes of letters exchanged between sixteen women, twenty men, all lovers, and fourteen Italians who are enumerated as of another sex, and are likewise chiefly lovers, are too prolix to be read to-day, but were a record of love-making which touched every girl's heart a century and more ago.

Little Anna Green Winslow speaks occasionally
in

14 *The* FATHER's GIFT.

Father. Now my Dear, as I find you have learned to spell and read easy words, let me advise you to purchase the Ladder to Learning, which is printed in three Parts, or Steps; the first Part is a Collection of pretty Fables, consisting of Words of only one Syllable; the second Part, of Words not exceeding two Syllables; and the third Part of few Words more than three Syllables. When you have reached the third Step, Attention and Application will soon enable you to read with Pleasure to yourself, and Satisfaction to your Friends, all the little Books published for good Masters and Misses, by your Friend in WORCESTER, near the COURT-HOUSE; a View of whose Shop I here give you.

By

The FATHER's GIFT. 15

By an attentive Perusal of those little Publications, you will attain the esteem of all who know you; you will learn to be dutiful to your Papa and Mama, obedient to your Superiours, loving and kind to your Equals and Inferiours; and, above all, you will learn to fear God, and to call upon him often, that you may, through his Grace, become wise and happy.

I shall

Two Pages of *The Father's Gift*

in her diary of story-books. She had for a New Year's gift the "History of Joseph Andrews abbreviated in guilt and flowered covers." She read the *Pilgrim's Progress*, the *Mother's Gift*, *Gulliver's Travels*, *The Puzzling Cap*, *The French Orators*, and *Gaffer Two Shoes* — this may have been our own Goody, not Gaffer.

The "flowery and gilt" binding of these books, so often spoken of in the notices, is wholly a thing of the past. It was made in Holland and Germany; but recent inquiry about it discovered that the stamps and presses used in its manufacture had all been destroyed. An enthusiastic lover of these little books wrote : —

> "Talk of your vellum, gold embossed morocco, roan, and calf,
> The blue and yellow wraps of old were prettier by half."

They were cheap enough, but a penny apiece, some of them, others sixpence. It is doubtful whether they were ever sold in America in vast numbers. Children lent them to each other. Anna Green Winslow borrowed them, and letters of her day show other children doing likewise. It was a day of book-lending; for circulating libraries were slow of formation. The minister's library was often the largest one in each town, and he lent his precious books to his flock. In the sparse advertisements

advertisements of colonial newspapers are many advertisements of book owners who have lent books, forgotten to whom, and wish them returned.   The

Page of *Vice in its proper Shape*

only way country children had of reading many books was by borrowing.

American boys and girls felt till our own day both bewilderment and impatience at forever reading

ing stories whose local color was wholly strange
to them. Dr. Holmes thus expresses this condition of things : —

"Books where James was called Jem not Jim as we
heard it ; where naughty schoolboys got through a gap in
the hedge to steal Farmer Giles's red-streaks, instead of
shinning over the fence to hook old Daddy Jones's bald-
wins; where Hodge used to go to the ale-house for his
mug of beer, while we used to see old Joe steering for the
grocery to get his glass of rum ; where there were larks
and nightingales instead of yellow-birds and bobolinks ;
where the robin was a little domestic bird that fed at table
instead of a great, fidgety, jerky, whooping thrush."

The debt of amusement which American children
owed to Newbery was paid in this century by the
supply to English children of a vast number of little
books of profit and pleasure, all written by a single
author, "Peter Parley," or Samuel G. Goodrich.
In the middle of the century this gentleman stated
that he had written one hundred and twenty books
that were professedly juvenile. Of these and his
books for older minds about seven million copies
had been sold, and about three hundred thousand
were still sold annually. They were sent to England in vast numbers, and were reprinted there
both with and without the author's permission.
And when the original books were not pirated, the
                                                        name

name Peter Parley was calmly attached to the compositions of English authors, as a vastly salable trade-mark.

Scores of American authors, by the middle of this century, were writing little books for children. These were a class by themselves — Sunday-school books. They do not come within the very elastic time limit set for this chapter. They are not old enough in years, though they are rapidly becoming as obsolete as any children's books of the last century. Books written avowedly for Sunday-schools are in decreasing demand. Those with sectarian teachings, especially, find fewer and fewer purchasers.

CHAPTER XV

CHILDREN'S DILIGENCE

For Satan finds some mischief still
For idle hands to do.
— *Divine Songs for Children. Isaac Watts, 1720.*

COLONIAL children did not spend much time in play. "The old deluder Sathan" was not permitted to find many idle hands ready for his mischievous work. It was ordered by the magistrates that children tending sheep or cattle in the field should be "set to some other employment withal, such as spinning upon the rock, knitting, weaving tape," etc. These were all simple industries requiring slight paraphernalia. The rock was the hand distaff. It was simple of manipulation, but required a certain knack of dexterity to produce even well-twisted thread. Good spinners could spin on the rock as they walked. Tape-weaving was done on a simple appliance, the heddle-frame of primitive weavers, known as a tape-loom, garter-loom, belt-loom, or "gallus-frame." On these small looms girls wove scores of braids and tapes for use as glove-ties, shoe-strings, hair-laces, stay-laces, garters, hatbands, belts, etc., and boys wove garters and breeches-suspenders.

There was plenty of work on a farm even for little children; they sowed various seeds in early spring; they weeded flax fields, walking barefoot among the tender plants; they hetchelled flax and combed wool.

All the work on the flax after the breaking was done in olden times by women and children. It is said there are in all twenty different occupations in flax manufacture, of which half can be easily done by children. Much of the work in domestic wool spinning and weaving was done by little girls. They could spin on "the great wheel" when they were so small that they had to stand on a foot-stool to reach up. They skeined the yarn on a clock-reel. They easily filled the "quills" with the woollen yarn used in weaving bedspreads and set the quills in the middle of the great pointed wooden shuttles. They wound the white warp on the spools, and set the spools on the scarne. They might, if very deft and attentive, help "set the piece," that is, wind the warp threads on the great yarn-beam, pass them through the eyes of the heddles or harness, and the spans of the reed. Girls of six could spin flax. Anna Green Winslow, when twelve years old, speaks often in her diary of spinning;

ning; and when disabled from sewing by a painful whitlow on her finger, wrote that "it is a nice opportunity if I do but improve it, to perfect myself in learning to spin flax."

The Good Girl and her Wheel

In the *Memoirs* of the missionaries, David and John Brainerd, a boy's busy life on a Connecticut farm is thus described : —

"The boy was taught that laziness was the worst form of original sin.   Hence he must rise early and make himself useful before he went to school, must be diligent there in study, and promptly home to do "chores" at evening. His whole time out of school must be filled up with some

service,

service, such as bringing in fuel for the day, cutting pota-
toes for the sheep, feeding the swine, watering the horses,
picking the berries, gathering the vegetables, spooling the
yarn. He was expected never to be reluctant and not
often tired."

This constant employment of a farm boy's time
lasted till our own day; but now conditions have
changed in Eastern farm life. The work still is
hard and incessant, but not so varied as of yore.
Many crops are obsolete; no flax is raised, and
but little wool, and that sold as soon as sheared.
Little grain is raised and no threshing is done by
the flail. Vast itinerant threshing machines go from
farm to farm. Few farmers make cider, which gave
so much work to the boys in autumn. There is no
potash or soap boiling. One of the most delightful
chronicles of obsolete farm industry is written by
Hon. George Sheldon and entitled *The Passing of
the Stall-Fed Ox and the Farmer's Boy.*

The sawing and chopping of wood was a never
diminishing incubus; this outdoor work on wood
was continued within doors in the series of articles
fashioned for farm and domestic use by the boy's
jack-knife and the few heavy carpenter's tools at his
command; some gave to the farm boy the rare
pennies of his spending money. The making of
birch splinter brooms was the best paying work.
For

For these the boy got six cents apiece. The splitting of shoe-pegs was another. Setting card-teeth was for many years the universal income furnisher

Illustration from *Plain Things for Little Folks*

for New England children. Gathering nuts was a scantily paid-for harvest; tying onions a less pleasing one, and chiefly followed in the Connecticut Valley. The crop of wild cherries known as choke-cherries was one of the most lucrative of the boy's resources.

resources. They were much desired for making cherry-rum or cherry-bounce, and would fetch readily a dollar a bushel. A good-sized tree would yield about six bushels. J. T. Buckingham tells of his first spending money being ninepence received from a brush-maker for hog-bristles saved from slaughtered swine.

The story of various silk fevers which raged in America cannot be given here, romantic as they are. From the first venture the care of silkworms was held to be a specially suitable work for children. It was said two boys, " if their hands be not sleeping in their pockets," could care for six ounces of seed from hatching till within fourteen days of spinning, when " three or four more helps, women and children being as proper as men," had to assist in feeding, cleansing, airing, drying, and perfuming them.

The *Reformed Virginia Silk Worm* asserted : —

> " For the Labour of a man and boy
> They gain you Sixty pounds which is no toy."

Mulberry trees were planted everywhere and kept low like a hedge, so children could pick the leaves. All the books of instruction of the day reiterate that a child ten years of age could easily gather seventy-five pounds of mulberry leaves a day, and make great wages. But an old lady, now eighty years

years old, who made much sewing silk in Connecticut in her youth, writes thus to me: "Girls picked most of the leaves. It was very hard work and very small pay. They had ten cents a bushel for picking. Some could pick three bushels a day."

The first thought of spring brought to the men of the New England household a hard work — maple-sugar making — which meant vast labor in preparation and in execution — all of which was cheerfully hailed, for it gave men and boys a chance to be as Charles Kingsley said, "a savage for a while." It meant several nights spent in the sugar-camp in the woods, a-gypsying. Think of the delight of that scene: the air clear but mild enough to make the sap run; patches of snow still shining pure in the moonlight and starlight; all the mystery of the voices of the night, when a startled rabbit or squirrel made a crackling sound in its stealthy retreat; the distant hoot of a wakeful owl; the snapping of pendent icicles and crackling of blazing brush, yet over all a great stillness, "all silence and all glisten." An exaltation of the spirit and senses came to the country boy which was transformed at midnight into keen thrills of imaginative fright at recollection of the stories told by his elders with rude acting and vivid wording during the early evening round the fire; of

hunting

hunting and trapping, of Indians and bears, and those delights of country story-tellers in New England, catamounts, wolverines, and cats — this latter ever meaning in hunter's phrasing wild-cats. Think of " a wolverine with eyes like blazing coals, and every hair whistling like a bell," as he sprung with outspread claws from a high tree on the passing hunter — do you think the boy sat by the fire throughout the night without looking a score of times for the blazing eyeballs, and listening for the whistling fur, and hearing steps like that of the lion in *Pilgrim's Progress*, " a great soft padding paw."

What forest lore the boys learned, too: that more and sweeter sap came from a maple which stood alone than from any in a grove; that the shallow gouge flowed more freely, but the deep gouge was richest in sweet; and that many other forest trees besides the maple ran a sweet sap.

I believe that in earliest colonial days boys also took part in a joyful outing, a public custom known as perambulating or beating the bounds. The memory of boundaries and division lines, of commons, public highways, etc., was kept fresh in the minds of the inhabitants by an old-time Aryan custom, — the walking around them once a year, noting lines of boundary, and impressing these on the notice and memory of young people. To

To induce English boys to accompany these per-ambulations, it was customary to distribute some little gratuity; this was usually a willow wand, tied at the end with a bunch of points, which were bits of string about eight inches long, consisting of strands of cotton or woollen yarn braided or twisted together, ended by a tag of a bit of metal or wood. These points were used to tie the hose to the knees of the breeches; the waistband of the breeches to the jacket, etc. Long after points were abandoned as a portion of dress the wands with their little knot of points were given. Pepys wrote in 1661 that he heard that at certain boundaries the boys were smartly whipped to impress the bounds upon their memories.

Anne Lennod's Sampler

" Beating

"Beating the bounds" was a specially important duty in the colonies where land surveys were imperfect, land grants irregular, and the boundaries of each man's farm or plantation at first very uncertain. In Virginia this beating the bounds was called "processioning." Landmarks were renewed that were becoming obliterated; blazes on a tree would be somewhat grown over — they were deeply recut; piles of great stones containing a certain number for designation were sometimes scattered — the original number would be restored. Special trees would be found fallen or cut down ; new marking trees would be planted, usually pear trees, as they were long-lived. Disputed boundaries were decided upon and announced to all the persons present, some of whom at the next "processioning" would be living and be able to testify as to the correct line. This processioning took place between Easter and Whitsuntide, that lovely season of the year in Virginia ; and must have proved a pleasant reunion of neighbors, a May-party. In New England this was called "perambulating the bounds," and the surveyors who took charge were called "perambulators" or "boundsgoers."

To either man or boy of to-day or any day it would seem an absurdity to name hunting and fishing in a chapter dealing with boys' diligence; for

in

in the sports of the woods and waters colonial boys doubtless found one of their greatest amusements. But these sports were also hard work and were engaged in for profit as well as for pleasure. The scattered sheepfolds and grazing pastures at first had to be zealously guarded from wild animals ; wolves were everywhere the most hated and most destructive beasts. They were caught in many ways ; in wolf-pits, in log-pens, in log-traps. Heavy mackerel hooks were tied together, dipped in melted tallow which hardened in a bunch and concealed the hooks, and tied to a strong chain. If the wolf swallowed the hooks without any chain attached, it would kill him ; but he might die in the depths of the forest and his head could not be brought in to secure the bounty. In old town lists are the names of many boys with " wolf-money set to their credit." A wolf-rout or wolf-drive, which was like the old English " drift of the forest," was a ring of men and boys armed with guns surrounding a large tract of forest. The wary wolves scented their enemies afar and retreated before them to the centre of a circle, and many were killed. Squirrels and hares were hunted in the same way. Once a year in many places they had shooting matches in which every living wild creature was prey, and a prize was given to the one bringing in the most birds' heads and
animals'

animals' tails.   This cruel wholesale destruction of
singing birds as well as game birds was carried on
almost till our own day.

Foxes were destructive in the hen yards.   On a
bright moonlight night the hunters placed a load of
codfish heads on the bright side of a stone wall.
The fish could be smelt afar, and when the keen
foxes approached they were shot by the hunters,
hiding in the shadow.   Bears lingered long even in
the vicinity of cities and were hunted with dogs.
The *History of Roxbury* states that in the year 1725,
in one week in September, twenty bears were killed
within two miles of Boston.

In Virginia deer-hunting was a constant sport.
They were "burnt out," and in imitation of the
Indian way of hunting under the blind of a "stalk-
ing head," the English taught their horses to walk
slowly by the huntsman's side, hiding him as he
approached the deer, who were not afraid of horses.
A diverting sport was what was called "vermin-
hunting."   It was done on foot with small dogs, by
moon or starlight.   Raccoons, foxes, and opossums
were the chief animals sought.   Bounties were paid
for the destruction of squirrels and rattlesnakes.   It
is appalling to see the bounty lists of some New
England towns for snake rattles.   Yet the loss of
life was small from snake bites.   The boys profited
by

Colonel Wadsworth and his Son

by all these bounties, and worked eagerly to secure them.

Wild turkeys were caught in turkey pens, enclosures made of poles about twenty feet long, laid one above another, forming a solid wall ten feet high. This was covered with a close pole and brush roof. A ditch was dug beginning about fifteen feet away from the pen, sloping down and carried under one side of the pen and opening up into it through a board in which a hole was cut just large enough for a turkey to pass through. Corn was strewn the whole length of the ditch. The turkeys followed the ditch and the corn up through the hole into the pen; and held their heads too high ever to find their way out again. Often fifty captives would be found in the morning.

Boys learned "to prate" for pigeons, that is, to imitate their call. This was useful in luring them within gun-shot. A successful method of pigeon-shooting was learned from the Indians. A covert was made of green branches with an opening in the back by which the hunter could enter. In front of this covert, at firing distance, a long pole was raised up on two crotched sticks eight or ten feet from the ground, set so that a shot from the booth would rake the entire length of the pole; hence the crotch nearest the booth was a trifle lower than the other,

at

at the same angle that the gun barrel would take. To lure pigeons from a flock to settle on this pole live pigeons were used as decoys. They were temporarily blinded in a cruel manner. A hole was pierced in the lower eyelid, a thread inserted, and the eyelid drawn up and tied over the eye. A soft kid boot or loop was put over one leg and a fine cord tied to it. The pigeon called the long flyer had a long cord, and by his fluttering attracted pigeons from a flock. The short flyer with shorter cord lured pigeons flying low. The hoverer was tied close to the end of a small pole set on an upright post. This pole was worked by a string, and by moving the pigeon up and down it appeared to be hovering as if to alight. The hunter, loudly prating, sat hidden behind his three blind, fluttering, terrified decoys. Then came a beautiful flash and gleam of color and life and graceful motion, as with a swish of reversed wings a row of gentle creatures lighted on the fatal pole. In a second came the report of the gun, and the ground was covered with the fluttering, maimed, and dead bodies. Fifty-two at one shot, a Lexington man named William Locke killed. Other methods of pigeon-killing were by snaring them in "twitch-ups"; also in a pigeon-bed, baited, over which a net was thrown on the feeding birds.

By

By the seashore whole communities turned to the teeming ocean for the means of life. Every fishing vessel that left the towns of Cape Ann and Cape Cod carried, with its crew of grown men, a boy of ten or twelve to learn "the art and mystery" of fishing. He had a name — a "cut-tail." He cut a wedge-shaped bit from the tail of every fish he caught, and in the sorting-out and counting-up at the close of the trip his share of the profits was thus plainly indicated. Long before these fishing industries were thoroughly organized the early chroniclers told of the share of boys in fishing. Even John Smith stirred up English stay-at-homes, saying: —

"Young boyes, girles, salvages or any others, bee they never such idlers, may turne, carry, and returne fish without shame, or either greate paine: hee is very idle that is past twelve years of age and cannot doe so much; and shee is very old that cannot spin a thread to catch them."

It was natural that boys born in seashore towns should turn to the sea. They found in the incoming ships their sole connecting link with the outside world. Romance, sentiment, mystery, deviltry, haloed the sailor. He was ever welcome to the public, and ever a source of interest whether in tarry working garb, or gay shore togs of flapping trousers, crimson sash, eelskin and cutlasses, or

perhaps

perhaps garbed like Captain Creedon, who appeared in Boston in the year 1662 dressed, so says the letter of a Boston minister, "in a strange habitt with a 4 Cornered Capp instead of a hatt and his Breeches hung with Ribbons from the Wast downward a great depth one over the other like the Shingles of a house." Naturally enough "the boys made an outcry and wondered."

Can it be wondered that two centuries of New England boys, stirred in their quiet round of life by similar gay comets and tales of adventure, have had a passionate ichor in their veins of longing for "the magic and the mystery of the sea," that they have eagerly gone before the mast, and rounded the Horn, and come home master seamen when in their teens. I know a New England family of dignity and wealth in which six successive generations of sons have gone to sea in their boyhood, some of later years running away from home to do so. In Portsmouth, New Hampshire, in 1787, — so tells a newspaper of that date, — were living a man and wife who had been married about twenty years, and had eighteen sons, of whom ten were then at sea.

CHAPTER XVI

NEEDLECRAFT AND DECORATIVE ARTS

She wrought all Needleworks that Women exercise,
With Pin Frame or Stoole all Pictures Artificiall,
Curious Knots or Traits that Fancy could devise,
Beasts, Birds, or Flowers even as things Naturall.

> — *Epitaph of Elizabeth Lucar. Church St. Michael, Crooked Lane, London, 1537.*

HUMAN nature was the same in the seventeenth and eighteenth centuries as to-day; waves of devotion to some special form of ornamentation either for the household or the wardrobe swept over families, neighborhoods, communities; when we reach the days of newspapers we find in their columns some evidence of the names and character of these decorations. In 1716 Mr. Brownell, the Boston schoolmaster, advertised that at his school young women and children could be taught "all sorts of fine works as Featherworks, Filigree, and Painting on Glass, Embroidering a new way, Turkeywork for Handkerchiefs two new Ways, fine new fashion Purses, flourishing

ishing

ishing and Plain work." The perishable nature of the material would prevent the preservation of many specimens of feather-work; but very pretty flowers for head-dresses and bonnets were made of minute feathers or portions of feathers pasted on a firm foundation in many collected shapes. This work may have been suggested by the beautiful feather flowers made in many of the South Sea Islands; perhaps an old sea captain brought some home to his wife or sweetheart as a gift. The sober colors of many of our home birds would not make so brilliant a bouquet as the songless birds of the tropics, especially the millions of the various parrot tribes; still an everyday New England rooster has a wealth of splendid glistening color, while blue jays, red-headed woodpeckers, yellow birds, and an occasional oriole or scarlet tanager could furnish beautiful feathers enough to waken the ire of an Audubon Society.

Painting on glass was an amusement of more scope. In England it was all the mode, and some very quaint specimens survive; simpering beauties, flowers, and fruit were the favorite subjects. Coats of arms, too, were painted on glass, and handsome they were. It is not possible to state exactly the position which the study of armorial bearings and significations had for two or three centuries. It seemed

seemed to bear relatively the same place that a profound study of literature has to-day — the pastime and delight of cultured people. We have been amused for a few years past at the domination of color in literature; every book title had a color word, as *The Red Robe, Under the Red Lamp, A Study in Scarlet, The Red Badge of Courage,* etc. This idiasm — as Mr. Ingleby would call it — has extended to music, and even into scientific suggestion and medicine; but this attributing unusual qualities to colors is nothing new. In the Cotton Manuscripts, a series of essays on music six hundred years old, the relation between music and color, especially in coat armor, is given; for instance, " fire-red " was the most malignant color in arms, and only third in benignity in music. All gentlefolk were profoundly wise as to the meaning of colors in coats of arms, etc., and their influence on the character and life of the persons bearing the arms.

This interest in the study of heraldry wavered in intensity but did not die till the days of a new nation; and we find from the middle of the seventeenth to the middle of the eighteenth century that young girls in the families of gentlefolk paid much attention to the making of coats of arms. Those painted on glass were the richest in color and the most satisfactory, but embroidered ones were more common.

common. The choicest materials were used, the drawing was carefully executed, and the stitches minute. It is interesting to note that the laws of the herald were strictly regarded in the setting of the

Jerusha Pitkin's Embroidery and Frame

stitches. In *azure* the stitches were laid parallel across the escutcheon; in *gules*, perpendicular; in *purpure*, diagonally from right to left, and so on.

Here is shown an unfinished coat of arms of the Pitkin family which belonged to Jerusha Pitkin, who

who was born in 1736. The frame upon which
the work is stretched, the manner in which it is
mounted, the hand-made nails that fasten it, the way
the work is outlined, are all of interest. The needle
still is thrust in the black satin background where
it was left by girlish hands a century and a half ago.
Colored silks, gold bullion and thread to complete
this work have been preserved with it. The embroidery is on black satin, and is lozenge-shaped,
as was the proper shape of a hatchment or mourning emblem; and it is possible that this work was
begun as a funeral piece, commemorative of some
Pitkin ancestor.

Such funeral pieces were deemed a very dignified
observance of respect and mark of affection. They
had as successors what were definitely termed
"mourning pieces," bearing stiff presentments of
funeral urns, monuments, drooping willows, and
sometimes a bowed and weeping figure.

After the death of Washington, mourning designs
deploring our national loss and significant of our
affection and respect for that honored name appeared
in vast numbers. Framed prints of these designs
hung on every wall, table china in large numbers and
variety bore these funereal emblems, and laudatory
and sad mottoes. As other Revolutionary heroes
passed away, similar designs appeared in more limited

ited numbers, and the reign of embroidered "mourning pieces" may be said to begin at this time.
Washington — so to speak — set the fashion. Fa-
miliarized with the hideous Apotheosis pitcher, or
the gloomy Washington's Tomb teacups as set on a
festal board, special mourning embroideries did not
seem oversad for decorative purposes, and soon
no properly ambitious household was without one.
They were even embroidered when the family circle
was unbroken, and an empty space was left yawning
like an open grave for some one to die. Religious
designs were also eagerly sought for. The Tree
of Life was a favorite. A conventional tree was
hung at wide intervals with apples, bearing the
names of various virtues and estimable traits of
humanity, such as Honor, Modesty, Silence, Patience, etc. The sparse harvest of these emblematic
fruits seemed to indicate a cynical belief in scant
nobility of nature; but there was hope of improve-
ment, for a white-winged angel assiduously watered
the roots of the tree with a realistic watering-pot.
The devil, never absent in that day from art, science, or literature, also loomed in blackness beneath
the branches, but sadly handicapped from activity
by being forced to carry a colossal pitchfork and
an absolutely unsurmountable tail of gigantic proportions.

These

These mourning pieces were but decadent successors of the significant heraldic embroideries of earlier days. We passed through trying days in art, architecture, and costume in the first half of this century ; and it was not until we revived the older forms of embroidery, and the ancient stitches, that we rallied from the blight of commonplaceness and sentimentality which seemed to spread over everything.

The most universal and best-preserved piece of embroidery done by our foremothers was the sampler. These were known as sampleths, sam-cloths, saumplers, and sampleres ; the titles were all derived by apheresis from *esampler, exampleir*. The

Lora Standish's Sampler

The sampler "contrived a double debt to pay"
of teaching letters and stitches; it was, in fact, a
needlework hornbook, containing the alphabet, a
verse indicative of good morals or industry, or a sentence from the Bible, the name and date, and some
crude representations of impossible birds, beasts,
flowers, trees, or human beings. Though the sampler's reign in every American household was in the
eighteenth century and the earlier years of the nineteenth, it was the direct successor of the glories of
needlework of English women of earlier years, which
was known and admired on the Continent as *Opus
Anglicanum*. The chief excellency of English needlework has even been closely associated with a high
state of social morals.   In Elizabeth's day Englishwomen still loved needlecraft. Shakespeare, Sid-
ney, Milton, Herrick, all refer to women's samplers.
In a collection of old ballads printed in 1725 is a
"A Short and Sweet Sonnet made by one of the
Maids of Honour upon the death of Q. Elizabeth, which she sewed upon a Sampler of Red
Silk " : —

> " Gone is *Elizabeth* whom we have loved so dear,
>   She our kind Mistress was full four and Forty Year,
>   *England* she govern'd well not to be blamed.
>   *Flanders* she govern'd well, and *Ireland* famed.
>   France she befriended, Spain she had toiled,
>   *Papists* rejected, and the *Pope* spoiled.

To

To *Princes* powerful, to the *World* vertuous,
To her *Foes* merciful, to subjects gracious.
Her Soul is in Heaven, the World keeps her glory,
Subjects her good deeds, so ends my Story."

In the licentious days of King James and King Charles there is little record of women's needlework in court or country, but the Puritan women, the virtuous home makers, revived and encouraged all household arts.

There is no doubt that as a rule the long and narrow samplers are older than those more nearly square. These ancient samplers, especially the few bearing dates of the seventeenth century, are much finer in design, more closely worked, and better in execution than those of later date. The linen background is much more closely covered. They have more curious and varied stitches. Occasionally they are of minute size, but four or five inches long, with exquisitely fine stitches.

Two ancient samplers are here depicted. One shown on page 327 was made by Lora Standish, the daughter of a Pilgrim Father, and it is now at Pilgrim Hall, Plymouth. The interesting and beautiful sampler known as the Fleetwood-Quincy Sampler has such perfect stitches that both sides are alike. It bears the names Miles and Abigail Fleetwood, and the date 1654. It has been in the possession

Fleetwood-Quincy Sampler

session of Mrs. Henry Quincy and her descendants since 1750. There is little doubt that the Miles Fleetwood of the sampler was the brother or nephew of Charles Fleetwood who married Anne Ireton, eldest daughter of great Cromwell. A splendid piece of Anne Fleetwood's embroidery was recently exhibited in the Kensington Museum. It was scarcely a sampler for it bore a curious design in applique work of a lozenge formed by four right-angled triangles, each of a different bit of rich brocade of gold and silver figures on amber or pink ground; all worked together with curious vines and stitches. Miles Fleetwood clung to the royal cause, and thus

thus fell into the obscurity hinted at in the sampler
verses : —

> "In prosperity friends will be plenty,
> But in adversity not one in twenty."

In the older samplers little attention is paid to
the representation of things in their real colors ; a
green horse may balance a blue tree.   And as flat
tints were used there were few effects of light and
shade, and no perspective.   Distance is indicated by
a different color of worsted ; thus the green horse
will have his off legs worked in red.   This is
precisely the method used in the Bayeux Tapestry
and other antique embroideries.

Sampler verses had their times and seasons, and
ran through families.   They were eagerly copied
for young friends, and, in a few cases, were "natural composures " — or, as we should say to-day,
"original compositions."   Ruth Gray of Salem embroidered on her sampler a century ago : —

> "Next unto God, dear Parents, I address
> Myself to you in humble Thankfulness.
> For all your Care and Charge on me bestow'd,
> The means of learning unto me allowed.
> Go on ! I pray, and let me still Pursue
> Such Golden Arts the Vulgar never knew."

To show the extent to which those lines could be
transmitted let me state that they are found on a
                                        sampler

sampler in Dorchester, Massachusetts, worked in 1802, one in Waltham, Massachusetts, one worked in 1813 in a seminary in Boston, one in Medford, one worked in 1790 in Salem by a young girl of ten, another in Lynn, on an English sampler in the Kensington Museum, and in the diary of that Boston schoolgirl, Anna Green Winslow, dated 1771.

There were certain variants of a popular sampler verse that ran thus : —

> " This is my Sampler,
> Here you see
> What care my Mother
> Took of me."

Another rhyme was : —

> " Mary Jackson is my name,
> America my nation,
> Boston is my dwelling place,
> And Christ is my salvation."

The doxology, " From all that dwell below the skies," etc., appears on samplers ; and these lines: —

> " Though life is fair
> And pleasure young,
> And Love on ev'ry
> Shepherd's Tongue,
> I turn my thoughts
> To serious things,
> Life is ever on the wing."

Another

Another rhyme is found with varying words in some of the lines : —

> " Young Ladyes fair when youthful minds incline
> To all that's curious, Innocent, and fine
> With Admiration let your worke be made
> The various textures and the twining thread
> Then let your fingers with unrivalled skill
> Exalt the Needle, Grace the noble Quill."

Some of the verses are as short as the scant but sweet English words on the sampler of Katherine, the wife of Charles II. : —

> " 21st of Maye
> Was our Wedding Daye."

A sampler in the Old South Church in Boston has this inscription : —

> " Dorothy Lynde is my Name
> And this Work is mine
> My Friends may have
> When I am Dead and laid in Grave
> This Needlework of mine can tell
> That in my youth I learned well
> And by my elders also taught
> Not to spend my time for naught."

In the sixteenth and seventeenth centuries it was high fashion to have mottoes and texts carved or painted on many articles where they would frequently catch

catch the eye. Printed books were then rare possessions, and these mottoes, whether of vanity or

Polly Coggeshall's Sampler

piety, took their place. Perhaps inscriptions on various pieces of tableware and drinking utensils were the most common. Specially beautiful and interesting

teresting early examples are the sets of "beechen roundels" known to collectors; that is, sets of wooden plates or trenchers carved with mottoes. Women dexterous of the needle embroidered mottoes and words on articles of clothing. Whole texts of the Bible are said to have been inscribed on the edges of gowns and petticoats.

> "She is a Puritan at her needle too
> She works religious petticoats."

Elaborate vines of flowers and other scroll designs were worked on petticoats, often in colored crewels. There still exists the linen petticoat of Rebecca Taylor Orne, a Salem dame who lived to be one hundred and twenty years old. It is deeply embroidered with trees, vines, flowers, and fruits, on homespun linen. Silk petticoats were also embroidered and painted by young girls, and are beautiful pieces of work.

In New York newspapers we find proof that New York girls were taught decorative accomplishments similar to those which were so fashionable in Boston: —

"Martha Gazley, late from Great Britain, now in the city of New York Makes and Teacheth the following curious Works, viz: Artificial Fruit and Flowers and other Wax-works,

Flowered Apron

Wax-Works, Nuns-work, Philligree and Pencil Work upon
Muslin, all sorts of Needle-Work, and Raising of Paste,
as also to Paint upon Glass, and Transparant for Sconces,
with other Works.   If any young Gentlewomen, or others
are inclined to learn any or all of the above-mentioned
curious Works, they may be carefully instructed in the
same by said Martha Gazley."

The waxwork of Martha Gazley was more fully
detailed in a school advertisement of Mrs. Sarah Wil-
son of Philadelphia.   She taught "waxworks in all its
branches"; flowers, fruit, and pin-baskets, also " how
to take profiles in wax."   This latter was distinctly
art work ; and portraits of Washington and other
Revolutionary heroes still exist in wax — a material
that could be worked with facility ; but was very
perishable.

A

A very full list of old-time stitches has come
down to us, and curiously enough not from any

Mary Richards' Sampler

woman who worked these stitches but from the pen
of a man, John Taylor, " the Water-Poet," in his
Praise of the Needle, 1640.

z   " For

" For *Tent-worke*, Rais'd-work, Laid-worke, Frost-worke, Net-
worke,
Most curious Purles, or rare Italian Cut-worke,
Fine Ferne-stitch, Finny-stitch, New-stitch and Chain-stitch
Brave Bred-stitch, Fisher-stitch, Irish-stitch and Queen-stitch
The Spanish-stitch, Rosemary-stitch and Mouse-stitch
The smarting Whip-stitch, Back-stitch and the Cross-stitch
All these are good, and these we must allow,
And these are everywhere in practise now."

They were doubtless "everywhere in practice,"
in America as well, but nearly all are now but empty
names.

While Dutch women must be awarded the palm
of comfortable and attractive housekeeping, they did
not excel Englishwomen in needlework; though
the first gold thimble was made for Madam
Van Rensselaer, the foremother of our American
patroons; and many beautiful specimens of Dutch
embroidery exist. A sample is here shown which
was worked by Mary Richards, a granddaughter of
the famous Anneke Jans. Mrs. Van Cortlandt
wrote in her delightful account of home life in old
New York : —

" Crewel-work and silk-embroidery were fashionable, and
surprisingly pretty effects were produced. Every little
maiden had her sampler which she begun with the alphabet
and numerals, following them with a Scriptural text or verse
of a psalm. Then fancy was let loose on birds, beasts and
trees.

trees. Most of the old families possessed framed pieces of embroidery, the handiwork of female ancestors."

Pride in needlework, and a longing for household decoration, found expression in quilt-piecing. Bits of calico "chiney" or chintz were carefully shaped by older hands, and sewed by diligent little fingers into many fanciful designs. A Job's Trouble, made of hexagon pieces, could be neatly done by little children, but more complicated designs required more "judgement," and the age of a little daughter might be accurately guessed by her patchwork. The quilt-making was the work of older folk. It required long arms, larger hands, greater strength.

Knitting was taught to little girls as soon as they could hold the needles. Girls four years of age could knit stockings and mittens. In country households young damsels knit mittens to sell and coarse socks. Many fine and beautiful stitches were taught, and a beautiful pair of long silk stockings of open-work design has initials knit on the instep. They were the wedding hose of a bride of the year 1760; and the silk for them was raised, wound, and spun by the bride's sister, a girl of fourteen, who also did the exquisite knitting.

Lace-making was never an industry in the colonies; it was an elegant accomplishment. Pillow lace was made, and the stitches were taught in families

lies of wealth ; a guinea a stitch was charged by some teachers.   Old lace pillows have been preserved to this day, with strips of unfinished lace and hanging

Old Lace Pillow, Reels and Pockets

bobbins, to show the kind of lace which was the mode — a thread lace much like the fine Swiss hand-made laces.

Tambour

Tambour work on muslin or lace, and a lace made of certain designs darned on net, took the place of pillow lace. Nothing could be more beautiful in execution and design than the rich veils, collars, and caps of this worked net, which remained the mode during the early years of this century. Girls spent years working on a single collar or tucker. Sometimes medallions of this net lace were embroidered down upon fine linen lawn.

I have infants' caps of this beautiful work, finer than any needlework of to-day.

CHAPTER XVII

GAMES AND PASTIMES

The plays of children are nonsense — but very educative nonsense.
— *Essay on Experience. Ralph Waldo Emerson, 1860.*

THERE are no more striking survivals of antiquity than the games and pastimes of children. We have no historians of old-time child life to tell us of these games, but we can get side glimpses of that life which reveal to us, as Ruskin says, more light than a broad stare. Many of these games were originally religious observances ; but there are scores that in their present purpose of simple amusement date from mediæval days.

The chronicler Froissart, in *L'Espinette Amoureuse*, tells of the sports of his early life, over five centuries ago : —

> " In that early childish day
> I was never tired to play
> Games that children everyone
> Love until twelve years are done.
> To dam up a rivulet
> With a tile, or else to let

A

A small saucer for a boat
Down the purling gutter float :
Over two bricks at a will
To erect a water mill.

" In those days for dice and chess
Cared we busy children less
Than mud-pies and buns to make,
And heedfully in oven bake.
Of four bricks ; and when came Lent
Out was brought a complement
Of river shells from secret hold,
Estimated above gold,
To play away as I thought meet
With the children of our street."

" The children of our street " has a delightfully
familiar ring. He also names many familiar games,
such as playing ball, ring, prisoner's base, riddles,
and blowing soap-bubbles. Top-spinning was an
ancient game, even in Froissart's day, having been
played in old Rome and the Orient since time im-
memorial.

It is interesting to note the persistent survival of
games which are seldom learned from printed rules,
but are simply told from child to child from year
to year. On the sidewalk, in front of my house, is
now marked out with chalk the lines for a game of
hop-scotch and a group of children are playing it,
precisely

precisely as I played it in my New England home
in my childhood, and as my grandfathers and grandmothers played " Scotch-hoppers " in their day.

In a little century-old picture book, called *Youthful Recreations*, Scotch-hoppers is named and vaguely
explained, and a note says : —

"This exercise was frequently practiced by the Greeks
and Spartan women.   Might it not be useful in the present
day to prevent children having chilblains ? "

Now isn't that stupid?   Every one knows hop-
scotch time is not in the winter when the ground is
rough and frozen or wet with snow and when chilblains are rife.   It is a game for the hard, solid
earth, or a sunny pavement.

The variants of tag have descended to us and
are played to-day, just as they were played when
Boston and New York streets were lanes and cow-
paths.   The pretty game, " I catch you without
green," mentioned by Rabelais, is well known in
the Carolinas, whither it was carried by French
Huguenot immigrants, who retained many of their
home customs as well as their language for so long
a time.   Stone-tag and wood-tag took the place
in America of the tag on iron of Elizabeth's day.
Squat-tag and cross-tag have their times and seasons, and in Philadelphia tell-tag is also played.
                                                    Pickadill

Pickadill is a winter sport, a tag played in the snow. Another tag game known as poison, or stone-poison, is where the player is tagged if he steps off stones. The little books on etiquette so frequently read in the seventeenth century, and quoted in other pages of this book, have this severe injunction, "Tread not pomposely on pebblestones for it

"Scotch Hoppers," from *Juvenile Games for the Four Seasons*

is the art of a fool." A man who was not a fool, one Dr. Samuel Johnson, was swayed in his walk by similar notions.

Honey pots still is played by American children. Halliwell says the "honey pot" was a boy rolled up in a certain stiff position. I have seen it played by two girls carrying a third in a "chair" made by crossing hands. In a popular little book

of

of the last century called *Juvenile Pastimes, or Sports for Four Seasons*, the illustration shows girls playing it.   The explanatory verse reads : —

> " Carry your Honey pot safe and sound
> Or it will fall upon the Ground."

A truly historic game taught by children to each other, is what is called cats-cradle or cratch-cradle. One player stretches a length of looped cords over the extended fingers of both hands in a symmetrical form.   The second player inserts the fingers and removes the cord without dropping the loops in a way to produce another figure. These various figures had childish titles.   If Hone's derivation of the game and its meaning is true, cratch-cradle is the correct name.   A cratch was a grated crib or manger. The adjustment of threads purported to represent the manger or cradle wherein the infant Saviour was laid by his Virgin Mother.   As little girls "take off" the cradle they say, "criss-cross, criss-cross." This like the criss-cross row in the hornbook was originally Christ's cross.

In a quaint little book called *The Pretty Little Pocket Book*, published in America at Revolutionary times, is a list of boys' games with dingy pictures showing how the games were played ; the names given were chuck-farthing ; kite-flying ; dancing

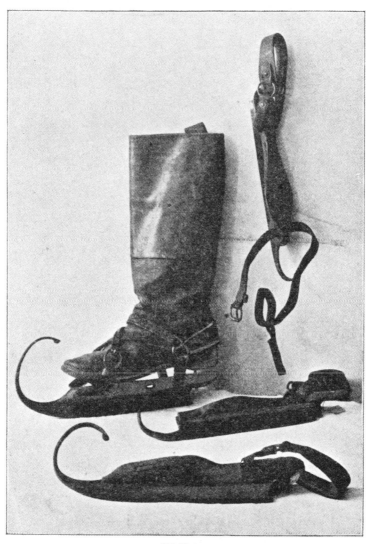

Old Skates

dancing round May-pole; marbles; hoop and hide; thread the needle; fishing; blindman's buff; shuttlecock; king am I; peg-farthing; knock out and span; hop, skip, and jump; boys and girls come out to play; I sent a letter to my love; cricket; stool-ball; base-ball; trap-ball; swimming; tip-cat; train-banding; fives; leap-frog; bird-nesting; hop-hat; shooting; hop-scotch; squares; riding; rosemary tree. The descriptions of the games are given in rhyme, and to each attached a moral lesson in verse. Some of the verses read thus: —

"CHUCK-FARTHING

" As you value your Pence
At the Hole take your Aim.
Chuck all safely in,
And You'll win the Game.

MORAL.

" Chuck-Farthing like Trade,
Requires great Care.
The more you observe
The better you'll fare."

A few of the games are to-day unknown, or little known; for instance, the game called in the book " Pitch and Hussel."

" Poise your hand fairly,
Pitch plumb your Slat.
Then shake for all Heads
Turn down the Hat."

The

The game called " All the birds of the air,"
reads : —

> " Here various boys stand round and soon
> Does each some favorite bird assume ;
> And if the Slave once hits his name,
> He's then made free and crowns the game."

Mr. Newell has given a list and description of
many of the historic singing games and rounds of
American children.   These were known to me in my
childhood: " Here we go round the mulberry bush ; "
" Here come three Lords out of Spain ; " " On the
green carpet here we stand ; " " I've come to see Miss
'Ginia Jones ; " " Little Sally Waters, sitting in the
sun ; " " Green gravel, green gravel, the grass is so
green ; " " Old Uncle John is very sick, what shall
we send him ? " " Oats, pease, beans and barley
grows ; " " When I was a shoemaker ; " " Here I
brew, Here I bake, Here I make my Wedding
Cake ; " " The needle's eye that doth supply ; "
" Soldier Brown will you marry, marry me ? " " O
dear Doctor don't you cry ; " " There's a rose in
the garden for you, young man ; " " Ring around
a rosy ; " " Go round and round the valley ; "
" Quaker, Quaker, How art thee ? " " I put my
right foot in ; " " My master sent me to you, sir ; "
" London Bridge is falling down."

Some

Some of these rhymes were founded on certain
lines of ballads; but without any printed words
or music we all knew them well, and the music
was the same that our mothers used — though our
mothers had not taught us. To-day children all
over the country are singing and playing these
games to the same music. I heard verse after

Skating, from Old Picture Book

verse of London Bridge sung in a high key in the
shrill voices of the children of a New Hampshire
country school this winter. Such a survival in
such an environment is not strange; but it is surprising and pathetic, too, to hear in a public primary
or a parochial school the children of German, Italian,
or Irish parentage chanting "Green gravel, green
gravel, the grass is so green," within the damp and
dingy

dingy yard walls or in the basement playrooms of our greatest city.

The Dutch settlers had many games. They were very fond of bowling on the grass; a well-known street in New York, Bowling Green, shows the popularity of the game and where it was played. They played "tick-tack," a complicated sort of backgammon; and trock, on a table somewhat like a billiard table; in it an ivory ball was struck under wire-wickets with a cue. Coasting down hill became a most popular sport. Many attempts were made to control and stop the coasters. At one time the Albany constables were ordered to take the "small or great slees" in which "boys and girls ryde down the hills," and break them in pieces. At another time the boy had to forfeit his hat if he were caught coasting on Sunday. The sleds were low, with a rope in front, and were started and guided by a sharp stick.

There is a Massachusetts law of the year 1633 against "common coasters, unprofitable fowlers and tobacco-takers," — three classes of detrimentals. Mr. Ernst says coasting meant loafing along the shore, then idling in general, then sliding down hill for fun. In Canada they slid down the long hills on toboggans. In New England they used a double runner, a long narrow board platform on two sleds or or two sets of runners. Judge Sewall speaks of his little daughter going out on sleds, but there is nothing to indicate precisely what he meant thereby.

"Sports of the Innyards" languished in New England. Innkeepers were ordered not to permit the playing of "Dice, Cards, Tables, Quoits, Loggats, Bowls, Ninepins, or any other Unlawful Game in house, yard, Garden or backside." Slide-groat was also forbidden. Mr. Henry Cabot Lodge says the shovel-board of Shakespeare's day was almost the only game that was tolerated. This game was perhaps the most popular of old-time domestic pastimes, and was akin to slide-groat.

I found nothing to indicate that the cruel sport known as cock-throwing, cock-steling, or cock-squoiling ever prevailed in America. In this sport the cock was tied by a short cord to a stake, and boys at a distance of twenty yards took turns at throwing sticks at him till he was killed. This sport was as old as Chaucer's time, and universal among the English.

Judge Sewall wrote of Shrove Tuesday in Boston in 1685 that there was great disorder in Boston by reason of "cock-skailing." Another year he tells of a young lad going through Boston streets "carrying a cock on his back and a bell in his hand." Several friends followed him, loosely blindfolded and

carrying

carrying cart whips ; and under pretence of striking at him managed to distribute their blows with stinging force on the gaping crowd around.   This was an old English custom.   At a later date the sport of shying at leaden cocks prevailed.   The " dumps " which were thrown, and the crude little images of lead and pewter shaped like a cock, were often made and sold by apprentices as part of their perquisites.

Cock-fighting was popular in the Southern colonies and New York.   There are prohibitions against it in the rules of William and Mary College.   Certainly it was not encouraged or permitted here as in English schools, where boys had cock-fights in the schoolroom ; and where that great teacher, Roger Ascham, impoverished himself with dicing and cock-fighting.   Cock-fights were often held on Shrove Tuesday.   The picture of Colonel Richard Wynkoop, shown on the opposite page, was painted when he was twelve years old; the dim figures of two fighting cocks can be seen by his side.   They are obscured by the sword which the colonel carried during the Revolution, and which is thrust in front of the picture.   The cruel Dutch sport of riding for the goose, was riding at full speed to catch a swinging greased goose.   Young lads sometimes took part in this, but no small boys.

In *The Schole of Vertue*, 1557, we read : —

"O,

Cornelius D. Wynkoop, Eight Years Old, 1742

"O, Lytle childe, eschew thou ever game
For that hath brought many one to shame.
As dysing, and cardynge, and such other playes
Which many undoeth, as we see nowe-a-dayes."

Playing cards were fiercely hated, and their sale prohibited in Puritan communities, but games of cards could not be " beaten down." Grown folk had a love of card-playing and gaming which seemed almost hereditary. But I do not believe young children indulged much in card-playing in any of the colonies.

William Bradford, then governor of the colony at Plymouth, thus grimly records in his now famous Log-book, the first Christmas Day in that settlement : —

" The day called Christmas Day ye Govr cal'd them out to worke (as was used) but ye moste of this new company excused themselves, and saide y^t went against their consciences to work on y^t Day. So ye Govr tould them that if they made it mater of conscience, he would spare them till they were better informed. So he led away ye rest and left them ; but when they came home at noon from their work he found them in ye street at play openly, some pitching ye bar, and some at stoolball and such like sports. So he went to them and took away their implements and tould them it was against his conscience that they should play and others work."

2 A   The

The exact description of this game I do not know.
Dr. Johnson says it is a play where balls are driven
from stool to stool, which may be a good definition,
but is a very poor explanation.

The *Pretty Little Pocket Book* says vaguely : —

> " The ball once struck with Art and Care
> And drove impetuous through the Air,
> Swift round his Course the Gamester flies
> Or his Stools are taken by surprise."

At the end of the seventeenth century a French
traveller, named Misson, wrote a very vivacious
account of his travels in England. He sagely noted
English customs, fashions, attributes, and manners ;
and airily discoursed on the English game of foot-
ball : —

> " In winter football is a useful and charming exercise.
> It is a leather ball about as big as one's head, fill'd with
> wind. This is kick'd about from one to tother in the
> streets, by him that can get it, and that is all the art of it."

That is all the art of it ! I can imagine the sentiments of the general reader of that day (if any
general reader existed in England at that time),
when he read and noted the debonair simplicity of
this brief account of what was even then a game of
so much importance in England. The proof that
Misson was truly ignorant of this subject is shown
in

in the fact that he could by any stretch of an author's privileged imagination call the English game of foot-ball of that day "a useful and charming exercise." Nothing could be further from the Englishman's intent than to make it either profitable or pleasing.

Page from *Youthful Sports*

In the year 1583 a Puritan, named Phillip Stubbes, horror-stricken and sore afraid at the many crying evils and wickednesses which were rife in England, published a book which he called *The Anatomie of Abuses*. It was "made dialogue-wise," and is one of the most distinct contributions to our knowledge of Shakespeare's England. Written in racy, spirited English, it is unsparing in denunciations of the public and

and private evils of the day. His characterization of the game of foot-ball is one of the strongest and most fearless of his accusations : —

" Now who is so grosly blinde that seeth not that these aforesaid exercises not only withdraw us from godliness and virtue, but also haile and allure us to wickednesse and sin ? For as concerning football playing I protest unto you that it may rather be called a friendlie kinde of fyghte than a play or recreation — a bloody and murthering practice than a fclowly sport or pastime. For dooth not everyone lye in waight for his adversarie, seeking to overthrowe him and picke him on his nose, though it be uppon hard stones, in ditch or dale, in valley or hill, or whatever place soever it be hee careth not, so hee have him downe ; and he that can serve the most of this fashion he is counted the only fellow, and who but he ? . . . So that by this means sometimes their necks are broken, sometimes their backs, sometimes their legs, sometimes their armes, sometimes their noses gush out with blood, sometimes their eyes start out, and sometimes hurte in one place, sometimes in another. But whosoever scapeth away the best goeth not scot free, but is either forewounded, craised, or bruised, so as he dyeth of it or else scapeth very hardlie ; and no mervaile, for they have the sleights to meet one betwixt two, to dash him against the hart with their elbowes, to hit him under the short ribs with their griped fists and with their knees to catch him on the hip and pick him on his neck, with a hundred such murthering devices."

This

William Rowe Bradley, 1800, *circa*

This was written three hundred years ago, and these are not the words of a modern reporter, "They have sleights to meet one betwixt two, to dash him against the heart with their elbows, to hit him under the short ribs with their griped fists, and with their knees to catch him on the hip and pick him on the neck."

Stubbes may be set down by many as a sour-visaged, sour-voiced Puritan; but a very gracious courtier of his day, an intelligent and thoughtful man, Sir Thomas Elyot, was equally severe on the game.   He wrote, in 1537, *The Boke named the Gouvernour*, full of sensible advice and instruction.   In it he says : —

"Foot-ball wherein is nothynge but beastlye furie and exstreme violence, whereof proceedeth hurte; and consequently malice and rancour do remayne with them that be wounded; whereof it is to be putt in perpetuall silence."

The "perpetuall silence" which he put on the game has not fallen even by the end of three centuries and a half.

Some indirect testimony as to the character of the English game comes from travellers in the American colonies, where the American Indians were found playing a game of foot-ball like that of their white brothers.   John Dunton, travelling in New England
                                                            when

when Boston was half a century old, tells of the Indians' game : —

"There was that day a great game of Foot-ball to be played. There was another Town played against 'em as is sometimes common in England; but they played with their bare feet, which I thought very odd; but it was upon a broad sandy Shoar free from Stones which made it the more easie. Neither were they so apt to trip up one another's heels and quarrel as I have seen 'em in England."

At the same time English boys were kicking the foot-ball around Boston streets, and were getting themselves complained of by game-hating Puritan neighbors, and enjoined by pragmatical magistrates, just as they were in English towns.

Fewer games are played now by both boys and girls than in former times, in England as well as America. In a manuscript list of games played at Eton in 1765 are these titles: cricket, fives, shirking walls, scrambling walls, bally cally, battledore, pegtop, peg in the ring, goals, hop-scotch, heading, conquering cobs, hoops, marbles, trap ball, steal baggage, puss in the corner, cat gallows, kites, cloyster and hyer gigs, tops, humming tops, hunt the hare, hunt the dark lanthorn, chuck, sinks, starecaps, hurtlecap. No games are now recognized at Eton save cricket, foot-ball, and fives. Racquet and hockey flourished for a time. The playing of of marbles was abandoned about 1820, and top-spinning about 1840. Top-time had always opened ten days after the return to school after the summer holidays. Hoops were made of stout ash laths with the bark on, and the hoop-rolling season ended

Doll's Furniture, One Hundred Years Old

with a class fray with hoopsticks for weapons. At one time marble-playing was prohibited in the English universities. It is not probable that those undergraduates habitually played marble any more than do our Princeton University men, who have a day of marble-playing and one of top-spinning each spring.

A

A record of old-time sports would be incomplete without reference to the laws of sport times. These are as firmly established as the seasons, and as regular as the blooming of flowers. Children cannot explain them, nor is there any leader who establishes them. It is not a matter of reason; it is instinct. A Swiss writer says that boys' games there belong chiefly to the first third of the year, always return in the same order, and "without the individual child being able to say who had given the sign, and made the beginning." From Maine to Georgia the first time is, has been (and we may almost add "ever shall be world without end"), marble time. Then come tops. The saying is, "Top time's gone, kite time's come, April Fool's Day will soon be here." Ball-playing in Boston had as its time the first Thursday in April. Whistle-making would naturally come at a time when whistle wood was in good condition. All the boys in all the towns perch on stilts as closely in unison as the reports of a Gatling gun. There is much sentiment in the thought that for years, almost for centuries, thousands of boys in every com-munity have had the same games at the same time, and the recital almost reaches the dignity of history.

CHAPTER XVIII

CHILDREN'S TOYS

Behold the child, by nature's kindly law
Pleased with a rattle, tickled with a straw.
Some livelier plaything gives his youth delight,
A little louder but as empty quite.

— *Essay on Man. Alexander Pope, 1732.*

IN the year 1695 Mr. Higginson wrote from Massachusetts to his brother in England, that if toys were imported in small quantity to America they would sell. In very small quantity, we fancy, though the influence of crown and court began to be felt in New England, and many articles of luxury were exported to that colony as they were to Virginia.

According to our present ideas, playthings for children in colonial time were few in number, save the various ones they manufactured for themselves. They played more games, and had fewer toys than modern children. In 1712, on the list of rich goods brought into Boston by a privateersman and sold there, were " Boxes of Toys." In 1743 the

Boston

Boston News Letter advertised " Dutch and English Toys for Children," and Mr. Ernst says Boston had a flourishing toy shop at that date.   Other towns did

An Old Doll

not, as we know from many shipping orders.

The Toy Shop or Sentimental Preceptor, one of Newbery's books, gives a list of toys which the young English scholar sought; they are a looking-glass, a "spying glass," a " fluffed dog," a pocket-book, a mask, a drum, a doll, a watch, a pair of scales.   Few of these articles named would really be termed toys.   Some of the games already alluded to, such as top-spin-

ning, hoop-rolling, and the various games of ball, required toys to carry them on; but they seemed to fall into classification more naturally in the chapter on games than in this one..

I have often been asked whether the first childish girl

girl emigrants to this solemn new world had the comfort of dolls. They certainly had something in the semblance of a doll, though far removed from the

An Old Doll

radiant doll creatures of this day; little puppets, crude and shapeless, yet ever beloved symbols of maternity, have been known to children in all countries and all ages; dolls are as old as the world and human life. In the tombs of Attica are found

found classic dolls, of ivory and terra-cotta, with

French Doll

jointed legs and arms. Sad little toys are these; for their human guardians are scattered dust. Dolls were called puppets in olden times, and babies. In the *Gentleman's Magazine*, London, September, 1751, is an early use of the word doll, "Several dolls with different dresses made in St. James Street have been sent to the Czarina to show the manner of dressing at present in fashion among English ladies." This circulation of dressed dolls as fashion transmitters was a universal custom. Fashionplates are scarce more than

than a century old in use. Dolls were sent from house to house, from town to town, from country to country, and even to a new continent.

These babies for fashion models came to be made in large numbers for the use of milliners; and as the finest ones came from the Netherlands, they were called " Flanders babies." To the busy fingers of Dutch children, English and American children owed many toys besides these dolls. It was a rhymed reproach to the latter that—

> " What the children of Holland take pleasure in making,
> The children of England take pleasure in breaking."

Fashions changed, and the modish raiment grew antiquated and despised; but still the " Flanders babies" had a cherished old age. They were graduated from milliners' boxes and mantua-makers' show rooms to nurseries and play-rooms where they reigned as queens of juvenile hearts. There are old ladies still living who recall the dolls of their youth as having been the battered fashion dolls sent to their mammas.

The best dolls in England were originally sold at Bartholomew Fair and were known as " Bartholomew babies." The English poet, Ward, wrote : —

> " Ladies d'y want fine Toys
> For Misses or for Boys

Of

Of all sorts I have Choice
    And pretty things to tease ye.
I want a little Babye
As pretty a one as may be
    With head-dress made of Feather."

In *Poor Robin's Almanack*, 1695, is a reference to a " Bartholomew baby trickt up with ribbons and knots " ; and they were known at the time of the landing of the Pilgrims.   Therefore it is not impossible that some Winslow or Winthrop maid, some little miss of Bradford or Brewster birth, brought across seas a Bartholomew baby and was comforted by it.

A pathetic interest is attached to the shapeless similitude of a doll named Bangwell Putt, shown facing page 370.   It is in the collection at Deerfield Memorial Hall.   It was cherished for eighty years by Clarissa Field of Northfield, Massachusetts, who was born blind, and whose halting but trusting rhymes of longing for the clear vision of another world are fastened to the plaything she loved in youth and in old age.

Nothing more absurd could be fancied than the nomenclature " French " attached to the two shapeless, inelegant creatures, a century old, shown on pages 364 and 367.   Yet gawky as they are, they show signs of hard usage, which proves them to have

had

had a more beloved life than the case of elegant Spanish dolls, on page 389, which were evidently too fine ever to be touched. The "White House Doll" spent the days of her youth in the White House at Washington, with the children of the President, John Quincy Adams, and is still cherished by his descendants.

French Doll

Skilful jack-knives could manufacture home-made dolls' furniture. Birch bark was especially adaptable to such uses. The wicker cradles and "chaises" of babies were copied in miniature for dolls. Tin toys were scarce, for tin was not much used for domestic utensils. A

tin

tin horse and chaise over a hundred years old is shown on page 373, and a quaint plaything it is. The eternal desire of a child for something suggestive of a horse found satisfaction in home-made hobby-horses; and, when American ships wandered

Dolls and Furniture

over the world in the India trade, they brought home to American children strange coaches and chariots of gay colors and strange woods; these were often comical copies of European shapes, sometimes astonishingly crude, but ample for the ever active imagination of a child to clothe with beautiful outlines. An old coach is shown on page 369, with the box in which it was originally packed.

packed. It is marked Leghorn, but is doubtless Chinese.

The word "jack" as a common noun and in compound words has been held to be a general term applied to any contrivance which does the work of a boy or servant, or a simple appliance which is subjected to common usage. In French the name

Chinese Coach and Horses

Jacques was a term for a young man of menial condition. The term "country jake" is of kindred sense. Jack lord, jack meddler, jackanapes, Jack Tar, smoke-jack, jack-o'-lantern, black-jack, jack-rabbit, the term jack applied to the knave in playing cards, and the expressions jack-at-a-pinch, jack in office, jack in bedlam, jack in a box, jack of all trades, and many others show the derivative meaning.

ing.   Hence jack-knife may mean a boy's knife.
In English dialect the word was jack-lag-knife,
also jack-a-legs, in Scotch, jock-te-leg — these by a
somewhat fanciful derivation said to be from Jacques
de Liege, the celebrated cutler.

Old Jack-knives

A good jack-knife was the most highly desired
possession of a boy.   Days of weary work and
hours of persistent pleading were gone through with
in hundreds of cases before the prize was secured.
Barlow knives had a century of popularity.   Some
now in Deerfield Memorial Hall are here shown.
Note the curved end, a shape now obsolete, but in
truth an excellent one for safe pocket carriage.
                                                    Knives

Bangwell Putt

Knives of similar shape have been found that are known to be a century and a half old. I have never seen in America any of the old knives used as lovers' tokens, with mottoes engraved on them, referred to by Shakespeare. The boy's stock of toys was largely supplied by his own jack-knife: elder pop-guns, chestnut and willow whistles, windmills, water-wheels, box-traps, figure 4 traps. Toy weapons have varied little from the Christian era till to-day. Clubs, slings, bows and arrows, airguns, are as old as the year One. Ere these were used as toys, they had been formidable weapons. They were weapons still, for some years of colonial life. In 1645 the court of Massachusetts ordered that all boys from ten to sixteen years old should be exercised with bows and arrows.

Skating is an ancient pastime. As early as the thirteenth century Fitzstephen tells of young Londoners fastening the leg bones of animals to the soles of the feet, and then pushing themselves on the ice by means of poles shod with sharp iron points.

Pepys thought skating "a very pretty art" when he saw it in 1662, but it was then a novelty to him, and he was characteristically a little afraid of it; justly disturbed, too, that the Duke of York would go "though the ice was broken and dangerous, yet he he would go slide upon his scates which I did not like — but he slides very well."

Wooden skates shod with iron runners were invented in the Low Countries. Dutch children in New Netherlands all skated, just as their grandfathers had in old Batavia. The first skates that William Livingstone had on the frozen Hudson were made of beef bones, as were those of mediæval children. In Massachusetts and Connecticut, skating was among the many Dutch ways and doings practised by English folk in the new

White House Doll

world. The Plymouth Pilgrims brought these Dutch customs to the new world through their long and intimate sojourn in Holland; the New Haven and Connecticut Valley settlers learned them through their constant trade and intercourse with their

their neighbors, the Dutch of Manhattan ; but the Massachusetts Bay settlers of Boston and Salem had known these Dutch ways longer, — they brought them from England across seas, from the counties of Essex and Suffolk, where the Dutch

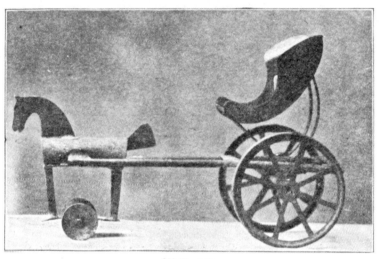

Old Tin Toy

had gone years before and married with the English.

New England boys in those early days went skating on thin ice and broke through and were drowned, just as New England boys and girls are to-day, alas! Judge Sewall wrote in his diary on the last day in November, in 1696, that many scholars went

went to "scate" on Fresh Pond, and that two boys, named Maxwell and Eyre, fell in and were drowned.

Advertisements of men's and boys' skates and of "Best Holland Scates of Different Sizes," show a

Doll's Wicker Coach

constant demand and use. In an invoice of "sundry merchandise" to Weathersfield, Connecticut, in the year 1763, are twelve pair "small brass scates, @ 3/ — £3, 16/." I do not know the age of the skates shown opposite page 346. No date less than a hundred years ago is ever willingly assigned

to

to such relics. They are similar in shape to the ones shown on page 349, in the illustration taken from a book for children entitled *Children's Sports*, published a century ago, which ends its dissertation on skating with this sensible advice : —

" 'Tis true it looks exceeding nice
To see boys gliding on the ice,
And to behold so many feats
Perform'd upon the sliding skates,
But before you venture there
Wait until the ice will bear,
For want of this both young and old
Have tumbled in, — got wet and cold."

It was not until October, 1771, that a pleasure-filled item appeared, " Boys' Marbles." In *The Pretty Little Pocket Book* are these lines : —

" MARBLES

" Knuckle down to your Taw.
Aim well, shoot away.
Keep out of the Ring,
You'll soon learn to Play.

MORAL

" Time rolls like a Marble,
And drives every State.
Then improve each Moment,
Before its too late."

Boys

Boys played with them precisely as boys do now. The poet Cowper in his *Tirocinium* says of the games of his school life : —

> " The little ones unbutton'd, glowing hot
> Playing our games and on the very spot
> As happy as we once, to kneel and draw
> The chalky ring, and knuckle down at taw."

The terms used were the same as those heard to-day in school yards : taws, vent, back-licks, rounces, dubs, alleys, and alley-taws, agates, bull's-eyes, and commoneys. Jackstones was an old English game known in Locke's day as dibstones. Other names for the game were chuckstones, chuckie-stones, and clinches. The game is precisely the same as was played two centuries ago ; it was a girl's game then — it is a girl's game now.

Battledores and Shuttles were advertised for sale in Boston in 1761 ; but they are far older than that. Many portraits of children show battledores, as that of Thomas Aston Coffin. All books of children's games speak of them. It was, in fact, a popular game, and deemed a properly elegant exercise for decorous young misses to indulge in.

CHAPTER XIX

FLOWER LORE OF CHILDREN

In childhood when with eager eyes
The season-measured years I view'd
All, garb'd in fairy guise
Pledg'd constancy of good.

Spring sang of heaven ; the summer flowers
Bade me gaze on, and did not fade ;
Even suns o'er autumn's bowers
Heard my strong wish, and stay'd.

They came and went, the short-lived four,
Yet, as their varying dance they wove,
To my young heart each bore
Its own sure claim of love.
—J. H. Card. Newman, 1874.

THE records of childish flower lore contained in this chapter are those of my own childhood ; but they are equally the records of the customs of colonial children, for these games and rhymes and plays about flowers have been preserved from generation to generation of New England children. The transmission of this nature lore

has

has been as direct and unaltered in the new world as in Great Britain. Some of these customs, such as the eating of hollyhock cheeses and the blowing of dandelion clocks, came originally, as have other play usages, from England ; many were varied in early years by different conditions in the new world, by local fitness and suggestion.

One chapter in Mr. Newell's book upon the *Games of American Children* dwells upon the conservatism of children. The unquestioning reception of play formulas, which he proves, extended to the flower rhymes and lore which I have recollected and herein set down. These inherited customs are far dearer to children than modern inventions. There is a quaintness of expression, a sentiment of tradition, that the child feels without power of formulating.

If the paradise of the Orientals is a garden, so was a garden of old-fashioned flowers the earthly paradise for a child : the long sunny days brought into life so many delightful playthings to be made through the exercise of that keen instinct of all children, destructiveness. Each year saw the fresh retelling and teaching of child to child of happy flower customs almost intuitively, or through the " knowledge never learned at schools," that curious subtle system of transmission which everywhere exists among

Stella (Bradley) Belluas, 1800, *circa*

among children who are blessed enough to spend
their summer days in the woods or in a garden.
The sober teachings of science in later years can
never make up the loss to those who have lived
their youth in great cities, and have grown up de-
barred from this inheritance, knowing not when

"The summer comes with flower and bee."

The dandelion was the earliest flower to stir the
children's memories ; in New England it is "the
firstling of the year." In the days of my childhood
we did not wait for the buttercup to open to learn
whether we "loved butter"; the soft dimpled chin
of each child was held up, as had been those of other
children for past decades, to catch the yellow reflection of the first dandelion on the pinky throat.

The dandelion had other charms for the child.
When the blooms had grown long-stemmed through
seeking the sun from under the dense box borders,
what pale green, opal-tinted curls could be made by
splitting the translucent stems and immersing them
in water, or by placing them in the mouth! I taste
still their bitterness! What grace these curls con-
ferred when fastened to our round combs, or hung
over our straight braids! — far better than locks of
corn silk. And what adorning necklaces and chains
like Indian wampum could be made by stringing
"dandelion

"dandelion beads," formed by cutting the stems
into sections! This is an ancient usage; one
German name of the flower is chain-flower. The
making of dandelion curls is also an old-time
childish custom in Germany. When the dandelion had lost her golden locks, and had grown
old and gray, the children still plucked the downy
heads, the "clocks" or blowballs, and holding aloft
these airy seed vessels, and fortifying the strong
young lungs with a deep breath, they blew upon
the head "to see whether my mother wants me,"
or to learn the time o' day.

> " Dandelion, the globe of down,
>   The schoolboy's clock in every town,
>   Which the truant puffs amain
>   To conjure back long hours again."

The ox-eye daisy, the farmer's whiteweed, was
brought to New England, so tradition tells, as a
garden flower. Now, as Dr. Holmes says, it whitens
our fields to the great disgust of our liberal shep-
herds. It soon followed the dandelion in bloom,
and a fresh necklace could be strung from the starry
blossoms, a daisy chain, just as English children
string their true pink and white daisies. This daisy
was also used as a medium of amatory divination,
by pulling from the floret the white ray flowers,
saying, "He loves me, he loves me not," or
                                                    by

by repeating the old "apple-
seed rhyme " : —

> " One I love,
> Two I love,
> Three I love, I say,
> Four I love with all my heart,
> Five I cast away," etc.

Flower oracles are mediæval,
and divination by leaves of grass.
Children to-day, as of old, draw
grass stalks in the field and match
them to see who will be " It."
Walther von der Vogelweide
(1170–1230) did likewise : —

> " A spire of grass hath made me gay —
> I measured in the self-same way
> I have seen practised by a child.
> Come, look, and listen if she really does,
> She does, does not, she does, does not,
> she does."

The

The yellow disk, or "button," of the ox-eye daisy, which was formed by stripping off the white rays, made a pretty pumpkin pie for the dolls' table. A very effective and bilious old lady, or "daisy grandmother," was made by clipping off the rays to shape the border or ruffle of a cap, leaving two long rays for strings, and marking in a grotesque old face with pen and ink. A dusky face, called with childish plainness of speech a "nigger head," could be made in like fashion from the "black-eyed Susan" or "yellow daisy," which now rivals the ox-eye daisy as a pest of New England fields.

Though the spring violets were dearly loved, we slaughtered them ruthlessly by "fighting roosters" with them. The projecting spur under the curved stem at the base of the flower was a hook, and when the violets "clinched" we pulled till the stronger was conqueror, and the weaker head was off.

What braided "cat-ladders," and quaint, antique-shaped boats with swelling lateen sail and pennant of striped grass could be made from the flat, sword-like leaves of the "flower-de-luce!" Filled with flowers, these leafy boats could be set gayly adrift down a tiny brook in the meadow, or, with equal sentiment, in that delight of children since Frois-sart's day, the purling gutter of a hillside street after a heavy midsummer shower. The flowers chosen

chosen to sail in these tiny crafts were those most human of all flowers, pansies, or their smaller garden sisters, the "ladies'-delights" that turned their laughing, happy faces to us from every nook and corner of our garden.   The folk names of this flower, such as "three-faces-under-a-hood," "johnny-jump-up," "jump-up-and-kiss-me," "come-tickle-me," show the universal sense of its kinship to humanity.   I knew a child who insisted for years that pansies spoke to her.   Another child, who had stolen a rose, and hidden it under her apron, called out pettishly (throwing the rose in a pansy bed), "Here! take your old flower" — as the pansy faces blinked and nodded knowingly to her.

The " dielytra " (bleeding-heart, or lady's-eardrops we called it) had long, gracefully drooping racemes of bright red-pink flowers, which when pulled apart and straightened out made fairy gondolas, or which might be twisted into a harp and bottle.   How many scores have I carefully dissected, trying to preserve intact in skeleton shape the little heart-shaped "frame" of the delicate flower!   The bleeding-heart is a flower of inexplicable charm to children ; it has something of that mystery which in human nature we term fascination.   Little children beg to pick it, and babies stretch out their tiny hands to it when showier blossoms are unheeded.

What

What black-headed puppets or dolls could be made from the great poppies, whose reflexed petals formed gay scarlet petticoats ; and also from the blossoms of vari-colored double balsams, with their frills and flounces ! The hollyhock, ever ready to render to the child a new pleasure, could be tied into tiny dolls with shining satin gowns, true fairies. Families — nay, tribes of patriarchal size had the little garden-mother. Mertensia, or lungwort, we termed " pink and blue ladies." The lovely blossoms, which so delighted the English naturalist Wallace, and which he called " drooping porcelain-blue bells," are shaped something like a child's straight-waisted, full-skirted frock. If pins are stuck upright in a piece of wood, the little blue silken frocks can be hung over them, and the green calyx looks like a tiny hat. A child friend forbidden to play with dolls on the solemn New England Sabbath was permitted to gather the mertensia bells on that holy day, and also to use the cherished income of a prosperous pin store. It was discovered with maternal horror that she had carefully arranged her pink and blue ladies in quadrilles and contra-dances, and was very cheerfully playing dancing party, to beguile the hours of a weary summer Sunday afternoon.

Mr. Tylor, the author of *Primitive Culture*, calls
our

our attention to the fact that many of the beloved plays of children are only sportive imitations of the serious business of life. In some cases the game has outlived the serious practice of which it is a copy — such as the use of bows and arrows. Chil-

Playing Marbles

dren love to produce these imitations themselves with what materials they can obtain, not to have them provided in finished perfection. Thus the elaborately fitted-up doll's house and imitation grocery store cannot keep the child contented for days and weeks as can the doll's room or shop counter furnished by the makeshifts of the garden. The child makes her cups and saucers and furniture herself.

self.   She prepares her own powders and distillations
and is satisfied.

A harvest of acorn cups furnished table garni-
ture, but not a cherished one; they were too
substantial; we preferred more fragile, more perishable wares.   Rose-hips were fashioned into tiny
tea-sets, and would not be thought to be of great
durability.   A few years ago I was present at the
opening of an ancient chest which had not been
thoroughly searched for many years.   In a tiny
box within it was found some cherished belong-
ings of a little child who had died in the year
1794.   Among them was one of these tea-sets made
of rose-hips, with handles of bent pins.   Though
shrunken and withered, the rose-hips still possessed
some life color, but they soon fell into dust.   There
was something most tender in the thought of that
loving mother, who had herself been dead over
half a century, who had thus preserved the childish
work of her beloved daughter.

Poppy pericarps made famous pepper-boxes, from
which the seed could be shaken as pepper; dishes
and cups, too, for dolls' tea-tables, and tiny handles
of strong grass stems could be attached to the cups.
For the child's larder, hollyhocks furnished food in
their mucilaginous cheeses, and the insipid akenes
of the sunflower and seeds of pumpkins swelled the
feast.

feast. A daintier morsel, a drop of honey, the "clear bee-wine" of Keats, could be sucked from the curved spur of the columbine, and the scarlet-and-yellow trumpet of the beautiful coral honeysuckle, mellifluous of the name, as well as from the tubes of the heads of clover. We ate rose-leaves, also, and grass roots, and smarting peppergrass. The sorrel and oxalis (which we called "ladies' sorrel") and the curling tendrils of grape-vines gave an acid zest to our childish nibblings and browsings.

The gnarled plum trees at the end of the garden exuded beautiful crystals of gum, of which we could say proudly, like Cornelia, " These are my jewels." Translucent topaz and amber were never more beautiful, and, void of settings, these pellucid gems could be stuck directly on the fingers or on the tip of the ear. And when our vanity was sated with the bravery, or we could no longer resist our appetite, there still remained another charm: with childish opulence, like Cleopatra, we swallowed our jewels.

A low-growing mallow, wherever it chanced to run, shared with its cousin hollyhock the duty of providing cheeses. These mallow cheeses were also eaten by English children. In allusion to this the poet Clare wrote : —

> " The sitting down when school was o'er
> Upon the threshold of the door,

Picking from mallows, sport to please,
The crumpled seed we call a cheese."

These flower customs never came to us through
reading. All our English story-books told of making cowslip balls, of breaking the shepherd's purse,
of playing lords and ladies with the arum — what
we call jack-in-the-pulpit; yet we never thought of
making any kindred attempts with these or similar
flowers. We did gather eagerly the jack-in-the-
pulpit, whose singularity of aspect seems always to
attract the attention of children, and by pinching it at
the base of the flower made it squeak, " made Jack
preach." But like true republicans we never called
our jacks lords and ladies.

The only liking we had for the portulaca was in
gathering the seeds which grew in little boxes with
a lid opening in a line around the middle. Oh,
dear! It doesn't seem like the same thing to hear
these beloved little seed-boxes described as " a pyxis,
or a capsule with a circumscissile dehiscence."

From the live-for-ever, or orpine (once tenderly
cherished as a garden favorite, now in many localities
a hated and persistent weed), we made frogs, or
purses, by gently pinching the fleshy leaves between thumb and forefinger, thus loosening the
epidermis on the lower side of the leaf and making
a bladder which, when blown up, would burst with

a delightful pop. The New England folk-names by which this plant is called, such as frog-plant, blow-leaf, pudding-bag plant, show the wide-spread prevalence of this custom. A rival in sound could be made by popping the foxglove's fingers. English countrywomen call the foxglove a pop.

Spanish Dolls

The morning-glory could also be blown up and popped, and the canterbury-bell. We placed rose petals and certain tender leaves over our lips, and drew in the centres for explosion.

Noisy boys found scores of other ways to make various resounding notes in the gardens. A louder pop could be made by placing broad leaves on the extended thumb and forefinger of one hand and striking

striking them with the other.   The boys also made squawks out of birch bark and fiddles of corn-stalks and trombones from the striped prickly leaf-stalks of pumpkins and squashes.

The New England chronicler in rhyme of boy-hood days, Rev. John Pierpont, called this sound evoked from the last-named instrument " the deeper tone that murmurs from the pumpkin leaf trom-bone."   It is, instead, a harsh trumpeting.   These trombones were made in Germany as early as the thirteenth century.

An ear-piercing whistle could be constructed from a willow branch, and a particularly disagreeable sound could be evoked by every boy, and (I must acknowledge it) by every girl, too, by placing broad leaves of grass — preferably the pretty striped ribbon-grass, or gardener's garters — between the thumbs and blowing thereon.   Other skilful and girl-envied accomplishments of the boys I will simply name : making baskets and brooches by cutting or filing the furrowed butternut or the stone of a peach ; also fairy baskets, Japanesque in workmanship, of cherry stones ; manufacturing old-women dolls of hickory nuts ; squirt-guns and pop-guns of elder-berry stems ; pipes of horse-chestnuts, corn-cobs, or acorns, in which dried sweet-fern could be smoked ; sweet-fern or grape-stem or corn-silk cigars.

Some

Some child customs successfully defy the law of the survival of the useful, and ignore the lesson of reason; they simply exist. A marked example of these, of bootless toil, is the laborious hoarding of horse-chestnuts each autumn. With what eagerness and hard work do boys gather these pretty nuts; how they quarrel with one another over the possession of every one; how stingily they dole out a few to the girls who cannot climb the trees, and are not permitted to belabor the branches with clubs and stones for dislodgment of the treasures, as do their lordly brothers! How carefully the gathered store is laid away for winter, and not one thing ever done with one horse-chestnut, until all feed a grand blaze in the open fireplace! At the time of their gathering they are converted to certain uses, are made into certain toys. They are tied to the ends of strings, and two boys, holding the stringed chestnuts, play cob-nut. Two nuts are also tied together by a yard of cord, and, by a catching knack, circled in opposite directions. But these games have a very emphatic time and season, — the weeks when the horse-chestnuts ripen. The winter's store is always untouched.

From a stray burdock plant which had escaped destruction in our kitchen garden, or from a group of these pestilent weeds in a neighboring by-path, could

could be gathered materials for many days of
pleasure. The small, tenacious burs could be easily
wrought into interesting shapes. There was a
romance in our neighborhood about a bur-basket.
A young man conveyed a written proposal of marriage to his sweetheart reposing in one of the spiny
vehicles. Like the Ahkoond of Swat, I don't know
"why or which or when or what" he chose such an
extraordinary medium, but the bur-basket was forever after haloed with sentiment. We made from
burs more prosaic but admirable furniture for the
dolls' house, — tables, chairs, and cradles. Traces
of the upholstery clung long and disfiguringly to
our clothing, but never deterred us from the fascinating occupation. To throw these burs upon
each other's clothing was held to be the commission
of the unpardonable sin in childish morals; still it
was done "in holiday foolery," as in Shakespeare's
day.

The milkweed, one of our few native weeds, and
a determined settler on its native soil, furnished
abundant playthings. The empty pods became
fairy cradles, and tiny pillows could be made of the
beautiful silk. The milkweed and thistle both furnish pretty, silvery balls when treated with deft
fingers; and their manufacture is no modern fashion. Manasseh Cutler, writing in 1786, says: —

"I

"I was pleased with a number of perfectly white silken balls, as they appeared to be, suspended by small threads along the frame of the looking-glass. They were made by taking off the calyx of the thistle at an early stage of blooming."

Ingenious toys of amusing shapes could be formed of the pith of the milkweed, and when weighted with a tack would always fall tack downward, as did the grotesque corn-stalk witches.

Pressed flowers were devoted to special uses. I cannot recall pressing any flower save larkspur,— the "lark-heels" of Shakespeare. Why this flower was chosen I do not know, unless for the reason that its colors were so enduring. We used to make charming wreaths of the stemless flowers by placing the spur of one in the centre of another flower, and thus forming a tiny circle. A favorite arrangement was alternating the colors pink and blue. These stiff little pressed wreaths were gummed on a sheet of paper, to be used at the proper time as a valentine,— were made for that definite purpose; yet I cannot now recall that, when February came, I ever sent one of these valentines, or indeed had any to send.

I have found these larkspur wreaths in a Pike's Arithmetic, used a century ago, and also in old Bibles, sometimes fastened in festoons on the title-

page,

page, around the name of a past owner. Did Dr. Holmes refer to one when he wrote his graceful line, " light as a loop of larkspur "?   A similar wreath could be made of the columbine spurs. A friend tells me she made scores in her youth; but we never pressed any flowers but larkspur.

Many pretty wreaths were made of freshly gathered flowers. The daintiest were of lilac or phlox petals, which clung firmly together without being threaded, and the alternation of color in these wreaths — one white and two purple lilac petals, or two white phlox petals and two crimson — could easily prove the ingenuity and originality of the child who produced them. In default of better-loved flowers, the four-o'clock, or marvel-of-Peru, was made into a similar garland.

In the beautiful and cleanly needles of the pine the children had an unlimited supply for the manufacture of toys. Pretty necklaces could be made for personal adornment, resembling in miniature the fringed bark garments of the South Sea Islanders, and tiny brooms for dolls' houses. A thickly growing cluster of needles was called " a lady." When her petticoats were carefully trimmed, she could be placed upright on a sheet of paper, and by softly blowing upon it could be made to dance. A winter's amusement was furnished by gathering and storing

the

the pitch-pine cones and hearing them snap open
in the house. The cones could also be planted
with grass-seeds, and form a cheerful green growing ornament.

Leaf Boats made from Flower-de-luce

From birch bark gathered in long wood walks
could be made cornucopias and drinking-cups, and
letters could be cut thereon and thereof. There
wandered through the town, harmless and happy,
one of "God's fools," whose like is seen in every
country

country community. He found his pleasure in
early autumn in strolling through the country, and
marking with his jack-knife, in cabalistic designs,
the surface of all the unripe pumpkins and squashes.
He was driven by the farmers from this annoying
trespass in the daytime, but " by brave moonshine "
could still make his mysterious mark on the harvest
of the year. The boys of the town, impressed by
the sight of a garden or field of squashes thus curiously marked, fell into a habit of similar inscription,
which in them became wanton vandalism, and had
none of the sense of baffled mystery which always
hung around and illumined poor Elmer's letters. A
favorite manner of using the autumn store of pumpkins was in the manufacture of Jack-o'-lanterns,
which were most effective and hideous when lighted
from within.

"The umbrellas are out!" call country children
in spring, when the peltate leaves of the May apple
spread their umbrella-shaped lobes, and the little
girls gather them, and the leaves of the wild sarsa-
parilla, for dolls' parasols. The spreading head of
what we called snake grass could also be tied into
a very effective miniature parasol. There is no
sense of caste among children when in a field or
garden — all are equally well dressed when " bedi-
zened and brocaded " with garden finery. Green
leaves

leaves can be pinned with their stems into fantastic
caps and bonnets ; foxglove fingers can be used as
gloves ; the blossoms of the jewelweed make pretty
earrings ; and the dandelion and daisy chains are not
the only necklaces, — the lilac and larkspur chains
and pretty little circlets of phlox are proudly worn ;
and strings of rose-hips end the summer.   The old
English herbalist says "children with delight make
chains and pretty gewgaws of the fruit of roses."
Truly, the garden-bred child walks in gay attire
from May to October.

The "satten" found by the traveller Josselyn, in
seventeenth-century New England gardens, formed
throughout New England a universal plaything, and
a frequent winter posy, in country parlors, on mantel
or table.   The broad white oval partition, of satiny
lustre, remaining after the side valves had fallen,
made juvenile money, and the plant went by the
appropriate name of money-in-both-pockets.

Other seeds were gathered as the children's spoils :
those of the garden balsam, to see them burst, or to
feel them curl up in the hand like living creatures ;
those of the balsam's cousin, the jewelweed, to watch
them snap violently open — hence its country
name of touch-me-not and snapweed.   When the
leaves were hung with dew it deserved its title
of jewelweed, and when they were immersed in
                                                                    water

water its other pretty descriptive folk name of silver-leaf.

A grotesquery could be formed from the seed-pods in the centre of the peony, when opened, in such a way that the tiny pink and white seeds resembled two sets of teeth in an open mouth. Imaginary miniature likenesses were found in the various parts of many flowers: the naked pistil and stamens of one were a pair of tongs; another had a seed ovary which was a lady, a very stout lady with extending hoops. The heart's-ease had in its centre an old lady washing her feet; the monk's-hood, a devil in his chariot. A single petal of the columbine, with attached sepals, was a hovering dove, and the whole flower — Izaak Walton's "culverkeys" — formed a little dish with a ring of pigeon-heads bending within.

There were many primitive inks and staining juices that could be expressed, and milks and gums that exuded, from various plants. We painted pictures in our books with the sap from the petals of the red peonies, and blue juice from the blossom of the spiderwort, or tradescantia, now a neglected flower. We dyed dolls' clothes with the juice of elderberries. The country child could also dye a vivid red with the juice of the pokeberry, the " red-ink " plant, or with the stems of the blood-root;

root; and the sap crushed from soft, pulpy leaves, such as those of the live-for-ever, furnished a green stain.

There was a certain garden lore connected with insects, not so extensive, probably, as a child would have upon a farm.   We said to the snail : —

> "Snail, snail, come out of your hole,
> Or else I will beat you as black as a coal."

We sang to the lady-bug : —

> "Lady-bug, lady-bug, fly away home ;
> Your house is on fire, your children will burn."

We caught the grasshoppers, and thus exhorted them : —

> "Grandfather, grandfather gray,
> Give me molasses, or I'll throw you away."

We believed that earwigs lived for the sole purpose of penetrating our ears, that dragon-flies flew with the sole thought of sewing up our lips — devil's darning-needles we called them.   To this day I instinctively cover my mouth at their approach. We used to entrap bumble-bees in the bells of monopetalous flowers such as canterbury-bells, or in the ample folds of the hollyhock, and listen to their indignant scolding and buzzing, and watch them gnaw and push out to freedom.   I cannot recall ever being stung in the process.

We

We had the artistic diversion of " pin-a-sights."
These were one of the shop-furnishings of pin
stores, whose curious lore, and the oddly shaped
and named articles made for them, should be recorded ere they are forgotten.   A " pin-a-sight "
was made of a piece of glass, on which were stuck
flowers in various designs.   Over these flowers was
pasted a covering of paper, in which a movable flap
could be lifted, to display, on payment of a pin, the
concealed treasures.   We used to chant, to entice
sight-seers, " A pin, a pin, a poppy-show."   This
being our rendering of the word " puppet-show."
I recall as our " sights " chiefly the tiny larkspur
wreaths before named, and miniature trees carefully manufactured of grass-spires.   A noted "pin-
a-sight," glorious still in childish history and tradition, was made for my pin-store by a grown-up girl of
fourteen.   She cut in twain tiny baskets, which she
pasted on glass, and filled with wonderful artificial
flowers manufactured out of the petals of real blossoms.   I well remember her " gilding refined gold "
by making a gorgeous blue rose out of the petals of
a flower-de-luce.

I cannot recall playing much with roses ; we fashioned a bird out of the buds.   The old English
rhyme describing the variation of the sepals was
unknown to us : —

"On

" On a summer's day in sultry weather
Five brethren were born together :
Two had beards, and two had none,
And the other had but half a one.''

Still, with the rose is connected one of my most
tender child memories, — somewhat of a gastronomic
cast, yet suffused with an element of grace, — the
making of " rosy-cakes." These dainty fairy cakes
were made of layers of rose-leaves sprinkled with
powdered sugar and cinnamon, and then carefully
enfolded in slips of white paper. Sometimes they
were placed in the garden over night, pressed between two flat stones. As a morsel for the epicure
they were not altogether alluring, although inoffen-
sive, but decidedly preferable to pumpkin or sunflower seeds, and they were englamoured with
sentiment; for these rosy-cakes were not destined
to be greedily eaten by the concocter, but were to
be given with much secrecy as a mark of affection,
a true love token, to another child or some beloved
older person, and were to be eaten also in secret.
I recall to this day the thrill of happiness which the
gift of one of these little paper-inclosed rosy-cakes
brought to me, in the days of my childhood, when
it was slipped into my hand by a beautiful and gentle
child, who died the following evening, during a
thunder-storm, of fright. The tragedy of her death,

2 D   the

the memory of the startling glimpses given by the vivid lightning, of agitated running to and fro in the heavy rain and lowering darkness, and the terrified summons of kindly neighbors, — all have fixed more firmly in my mind the happy recollection of her last gift.

Another custom of my youth was watching at dusk the opening of the twisted buds of the garden primrose into wan, yellow stars, " pallid flowers, by dew and moonlight fed," which filled the early evening with a faint, ineffable fragrance that drew a host of encircling night moths. Keats said they " leaped from buds into ripe flowers," a habit thus told by Margaret Deland : —

> " Here, in warm darkness of a night in June,
> *   *   *   *   *   children came
> To watch the primrose blow.
>   Silent they stood,
> Hand clasped in hand, in breathless hush around,
> And saw her shyly doff her soft green hood
> And blossom — with a silken burst of sound ! "

In our home garden stood a clump of tall primroses, whose beautiful flowers, when opened, were four inches in diameter. When riding, one summer evening, along a seaside road on Cape Ann, we first saw one of these queens of the night in an humble dooryard. In the dark its seeds were gathered

ered and given by an unknown hand and a flower-
loving heart to my mother, to form under her " fair
tendance " the luminous evening glory of her garden.
And on summer nights this stately primrose still
blooms in moonlight and starlight, though the gentle
hand that planted it is no longer there : —

> " Yon rising Moon that looks for us again
> How oft hereafter will she wax and wane
> How oft hereafter look for us
> Through this same Garden — and for *one* in vain."

To every garden-bred child the sudden blossoming
and pale shining in the gloaming have ever given
the evening primrose a special tender interest, — a
faintly mystic charm through the chill of falling dew
and the dim light, and through a half-sad atmosphere
which has always encircled the flower, and has been
felt by many of the poets, making them seldom sing
the evening primrose as a flower of happiness.
With the good night of children
to the flowers, I close this
record of old-time
child life.

Index

Ye labor and ye patience, ye judgment and ye penetration which are required to make a good index is only known to those who have gone through with this most necessary and painful but least praised part of a publication.

— *William Oldys, 1687.*

Bathing,